My darling,
I know how
you love a good
war yarn and
this one if is
by Hermione's
daddy so bound
to be a goodie!!
enjoy
Love Ton
LH
x.

PAID TO PREDICT

Books by

Ewen Southby-Tailyour

Military Histories and Biographies

Falkland Islands Shores
Reasons in Writing: A Commando's View of the Falklands War
Amphibious Assault Falklands: The Battle for San Carlos (with Michael Clapp)
Blondie: A Life of Lieutenant-Colonel HG Hasler, DSO, OBE, Royal Marines
The Next Moon. A Special Operations Executive Agent in France (with Andre Hue)
HMS Fearless. The Mighty Lion
3 Commando Brigade, Helmand
Commando Assault, Helmand
Nothing Impossible. A Portrait of the Royal Marines 1664–2010 (Editor)
Exocet Falklands. The Untold Story of Special Forces Operations

Fiction
Skeletons for Sadness
Death's Sting

Reference
Jane's Amphibious Warfare Capabilities (Editor)
Jane's Amphibious and Special Forces (Editor)
Jane's Special Forces Equipment Recognition Guide (Editor)

PAID TO PREDICT

Duplicity,
Deceit and
Dishonesty
among 'Allies'

The un-redacted diaries of a British
monitor with the European Community
Monitoring Mission (and the SIS) in
the Former Republic of Yugoslavia.
Autumn 1993-Spring 1994

EWEN SOUTHBY-TAILYOUR

FONTHILL

All views and comments expressed in these diaries and this account are those of the author and, unless specifically stated otherwise, are neither those of the British Foreign and Commonwealth Office or of the now-defunct European Community Monitoring Mission

Ewen Southby-Tailyour

Fonthill Media Language Policy

Fonthill Media publishes in the international English language market. One language edition is published worldwide. As there are minor differences in spelling and presentation, especially with regard to American English and British English, a policy is necessary to define which form of English to use. The Fonthill Policy is to use the form of English native to the author. Ewen Southby-Tailyour was born in Scotland and educated in England and France, and now lives at Ermington, South Devon, therefore British English has been adopted in this publication.

www.fonthillmedia.com
office@fonthillmedia.com

First published in the United Kingdom
and the United States of America 2020

British Library Cataloguing in Publication Data:

A catalogue record for this book is available from the British Library

ISBN 978-1-78155-768-6

Typeset in 10.5pt on 13pt Minion Pro
Printed and bound in England

Contents

The Author

Ewen Southby-Tailyour was educated at Stubbington House, the Nautical College Pangbourne and Grenoble University before being commissioned into the Royal Marines in 1960 and specialising as a Landing Craft officer. In 1963 he served with the French *Commando Hubert* in the Mediterranean and, later, with the United States Marine Corps in Turkey. In 1968, while on a two-year secondment he was awarded the Sultan of Oman's Bravery Medal during the Dhofar War. In 1978 he commanded the Royal Marines detachment in the Falkland Islands during which time he charted many of the beaches and inshore passages; consequently, in 1982, he led the initial seaborne assault into San Carlos Waters at the start of the land battles for the liberation of the Falkland Islands. Following this campaign he was appointed an OBE and elected the British *Yachtsman of the Year*. On retirement in 1992 as a lieutenant-colonel he established an amphibious consultancy before being employed by the Foreign and Commonwealth Office for duties in the Former Republic of Yugoslavia in 1993. He resigned the following year as he refused to falsify his daily reports covering the alleged breaking of UN Arms Embargo 713 by, *inter alia*, Germany and the United States.

In 2019 he was elected a Younger Brother of Trinity House.

He lives with his wife Patricia in south Devon and the French Pyrenees and enjoys water-colour painting, skiing and single-handed, offshore sailing although, more often now, he prefers to be picking blackberries during gales at sea.

From 1999 to 2015 he was the editor of *Janes Amphibious and Special Forces*. This is his sixteenth book; an earlier book, *Death's Sting* (Westlake Books and available on Amazon) is a fictional version of *Paid to Predict* that describes many of the events that the author did not witness at first hand.

Author's Notes

I do not like much of what I have written between these covers for I did not like much of what I was often required to do or witness in the Former Republic of Yugoslavia in the early 1990s. Nevertheless, every word is a direct quote from my diaries, letters, signals and reports that passed through my hands. In the text that follows I have indented these quotations but, unless specifically stated otherwise, they will be from my diaries.

I should make it clear at the start that this account does not concern itself with the convoluted machinations and toing and froing of affairs, military, political and diplomatic as Yugoslavia split up during the so-called Bosnian War from 1992 to 1995. These collusions, coupled with the actions and decisions of the United Nations and United States (the latter, towards the end, hinging on the re-election campaign of President Clinton) were complicated enough for those 'in theatre' let alone for those witnessing events from afar. I can only tell my miniscule part of the larger story by simply describing the life of a junior monitor during the period that led up to Croatia's Operation Storm against the Republic of Serbian Krajina in August 1995. At the end I offer a very potted history of events during this time but within the main text there will be no mention of such as the tribulations of the Muslim enclaves of Srebrenica, Zepa and Gorazde, nor of the siege of Sarajevo, the plight of the Muslim refugees in Tuzla nor the murder of those 7,079 who failed to make this 'safe' haven. My sole concern is, and was, the build up to the worst case of ethnic cleansing (among many other equally horrific examples) throughout the whole sorry business. For background reading I can recommend no better book than Misha Glenny's *The Fall of Yugoslavia. The Third Balkan War.*

I can only describe actions as I saw them then and not how I might wish to see them now. The inevitable result will be that the current Croat and Serb regimes will, I am certain, take no time in denouncing everything I write—vigorously!

In 1993 I travelled to the Former Republic of Yugoslavia as a monitor with the European Community Monitoring Mission in the naïve hope that I could help make a small difference to a few individuals. I did not. Once in theatre the Foreign and Commonwealth Office invited me to report on Croatia's anticipated preparations for war against the 'so-called' Republic of Serbian Krajina. I was, in effect, being 'paid to help predict' the future; a future that became more and more obvious as time went by. Most of us knew that the ethnic cleansing of 200,000 Krajina Serbs by Croatia would take place sometime and that this would be the result of the illegal breaking of United Nations Arms Embargo 713 … but although I, and a few other monitors, reported the truth of the situation no one, further up the European Community command chain, appeared to do anything for fear of United States recriminations.

At the same time I was tasked, informally and unpaid, by the Secret Intelligence Service to keep an eye on one or two individuals. I managed to observe just one gentleman in detail, a Serb who for war crimes I did not believe he committed, at least, not in my short time, was sentenced to fifteen years in a Croatian jail (later reduced to thirteen and a half) and who was freed on 20 March 2020.

This is not a tale full of fun and humour and, in retrospect, it is one that I wish I had not experienced for I never expected to be personally involved in such overt duplicity, deceit and dishonesty among, so-called, European 'allies'.

Ewen Southby-Tailyour
South Devon
Summer 2020

Introduction

On my fiftieth birthday—18 January 1992—and after thirty-two extremely happy and professionally satisfying 'gap years' as a Royal Marines officer I was suddenly, but not unexpectedly, unemployed: according to my more honest friends I had also the distinct disadvantage of being unemployable. There were, though, two unfinished books hovering, spectre-like, over my all-too-often-silent typewriter while the muse remained her usual unhelpful self, leaving me to ponder a future away from the Corps and the keyboard.

Towards the end of 1991 and in my last months of military service I had established a consultancy that, with the help of specific experts, offered expertise in a number of amphibious-related subjects. By early 1993 the design and procurement of the new generation of the Royal Navy's replacement amphibious ships, with which I had been involved through the final four years of my service, was entering an expected slack period between Invitations to Tender being issued to various designers and ship builders and before the eventual receipt and assessments of those tenders by the MOD. Once received I, and others involved in the evaluating process, would be back in business. This gap in the convoluted Defence Procurement procedure had been an ideal moment actively to seek temporary employment.

As well as forming my own 'amphibious' consultancy on retirement I had also registered with a marvellous organisation called the *Officers' Association* which, fortnightly, sends out a list of jobs likely to appeal to retired military officers. Few of these 'advertisements' concern themselves with 'matters amphibious' yet with more hope than expectation, I stuck with the *Officers' Association*. More accurately, they stuck with me despite my never applying to run a golf club, London livery company or the bursar's department of a preparatory school. 'Situations vacant' such as these were outside my capability and would, anyway, have required a higher 'interest-retention threshold' than I possessed ... until, quite suddenly, I was staring at the following in mid-September 1993:

VACANCY No 12/118C. VERY URGENT. COMPANY REPRESENTATIVE. (Seagoing short term contract). WORLDWIDE AND CONFIDENTIAL. Age 32 to 50 (ideally 35–40). SALARY: Negotiable. CLOSING DATE: ASAP. THROUGH CLIENT'S CONSULTANT. The client wishes to employ a recently retired naval officer (probably Lt Cdr/Cdr rank) who has recent seagoing experience, preferably in command but second in command of a frigate or destroyer, having passed all ship command exams might do or possibly a qualified deep sea navigator. The Company Representative's task is to be the company's seagoing representative for anything from one to six months in a 1,500 ton, 80 metre vessel in which very sensitive meetings will take place. There are security implications.

The job will not entail commanding the vessel but the candidate, ideally, should have the capability in the event of an emergency. The candidate must have great charm and tact as he will also have the task of facilitating the meetings on board. A good knowledge of radio operating and procedures is required. Contact Colonel … at the Officers' Association by telephone asap.

I read it quickly then, realising that I did not meet any of the requirements, dismissed the idea. I was over 50—just—and had never commanded a naval ship, although I had commanded Royal Marines landing craft squadrons. On the plus side I had held a Royal Navy 'bridge watch-keeping ticket',[1] was a civilian 'Ocean' Yachtmaster and qualified Commercial Sailing Skipper and 'examiner'. Tact would be a missing ingredient at any interview while my radio operating ability was limited to the handheld, short-range VHF equipment in my yacht. However, on reflection it sounded intriguing so I read it twice more in slow time. Out of curiosity rather than any personal or financial *force majeure* I telephoned the *Officers' Association*.

.   .   .   .   .

Over the next two years I wished, often, that I had not set this ball rolling but now that the whole chain of events has run its course I can view much of what happened, if not with amusement then at least as a warning to myself to be more careful in the future before trying, in effect, to regain a lost youth of action and excitement. But this is 2020 and far removed from that day in 1993 when I read *Vacancy Number 12/118C.*

Following retirement, excitement of a non-military nature was supplied by continuing to explore under sail in the higher latitudes and, in the summer of '93 by entering my new, 12 ton, gaff cutter *Black Velvet* in the two-handed round Britain and Ireland race with my, then 19 year-old son, Hamish, as co-skipper. In truth the race was an excuse to visit Barra in the Outer Hebrides and Lerwick in the Shetlands rather than Cork and Lowestoft—also two of the four, compulsory, 48-hour stops. We came last of the finishers in the race but probably had the most fun. Eventually the boat was delivered back to her builders to have outstanding work finished and I was at a loose end. The two books were still 'under way' but, with no prospect of any money from them until their completion and as the expected six months lull in the lengthy procurement process for the Royal Navy's new amphibious shipping was starting, I remained 'available' and so took the bait.

On telephoning the *Officers' Association* I learned that they knew no more other than that I was the only applicant so far to come through that organisation and that I should telephone a certain London number. Without hesitation I did so on Thursday 23 September. The owner of the voice at the other end turned out to be involved in what might loosely be termed 'international personal protection' and was acting for yet another organisation—no names, personal or commercial, at this stage—who were equally loosely described as 'ship brokers'.

Still with no clue what any duties would be other than that the successful candidate, providing he was 'positively vetted', would be working for an 'international body' and then only if 'certain events occur'.

'Was I still interested?' I did not know.

'Fascinated?' Perhaps.

'Curious?' Certainly.

With a level of optimism that could only have been matched by my youngest dog I faxed my CV through to the 'ship brokers' and returned to the typewriter. That Sunday evening I was summoned by telephone for a meeting at 1300 the next day in London.

The initiating company, Candy Logistics,[2] was acting for the 'ship-brokers' who, not by coincidence I suspected, occupied the larger part of the second floor of the same imposing building close to Liverpool Street station. Candy Logistics's 'personal protection' director knew nothing other than what he had placed with the *Officers' Association* but he had known enough to forward only my name out of three applicants to the 'ship broker' who was, by now, already *au fait* with my CV. In due course the 'broker' and his wife were escorted down the corridor to meet me with, I hoped, more details. After a conversation on this and that—oddly, I thought at the time, mostly 'that'—I was asked if I minded if my CV was forwarded to the United Nations. If not, and I pretended not to be taken aback, I was to return home and listen to every BBC news bulletin until I heard that General Aidid of Somalia had been captured. Charming though everyone was, they gave nothing more away. The 'broker'—if indeed that was what he was—and his wife left and I returned to south Devon only marginally less puzzled.

1993 witnessed the height of the UN involvement in the internal affairs of Somalia but the first inkling I had of this 'area of interest', but not yet of the specific task, was an unidentified voice on the telephone a day later telling me that if General Aidid was arrested I was to, 'Drop everything, pack an overnight bag,' long pause, 'on reflection,' the voice eventually continued, 'seven nights might be more sensible—and a longer-term suitcase that should contain tropical, sea-going clothes for up to six months.' I was then to telephone for travel instructions; but there was still no clue to the task or the eventual destination.

'You need not commit yourself yet,' the voice declared, 'All we ask, at this stage, is for you to be prepared merely for the initial, seven-day briefing at a destination that will be disclosed in due course.'
There was no clue what the expression 'there are security implications' meant and no idea what financial rewards there would be other than the vaguest of suggestions that $125 per day might be the 'going rate; but I was 'on' and said so—at least as far forward as the 'seven-day briefing in the undisclosed destination'.

A further message for me to telephone the 'broker' was received in south Devon. My name had by now been cleared by the UN's vetting system and passed to a Deputy Secretary General.[3] If Aidid was captured I would be flown to New York for an interview and then direct to Naples for a detailed briefing. Only then would I be allowed to know what the task involved and only then would I be required to accept or refuse the work. On the chance that it would be the latter 'they' did have one other name up their sleeve but they were keen not to use him.

However there was a downside for it was expected that, once it knew that it had been duped (the United States' aim was to indict the general for a number of crimes) the US would track him down ... and, rather ominously, 'dispose of him.' I was beginning to put two and two together: the watch-keeping ticket and the possibility of 'ship command' being helpful clues as were the 'tropical, sea-going clothes for six months'.

Despite the international press corps interviewing Aidid in his various hideaways, American forces in Somalia were unable to catch up with their quarry and so, while an impatient UN waited, I was initiated more and more into the proposal and the details. It was also a good time for the UN to perfect its plans and while that was taking place I was increasingly up-dated with specifics. It was, I thought with intensifying concern, just as well that the elusive general had not yet been apprehended for there was much in the UN's scheme—in concept and in fact—that needed perfecting if American suspicion was to be avoided until too late.

By now I was privy to the Deputy Secretary General's detailed preparations which were simple but far from watertight. Once Aidid had been arrested by the military he would be handed over to the UN's jurisdiction supposedly, as far as the United States was concerned, while Somalia then quietened down. He would not be seen again until a permanent peace had been in place long enough for his return to be insignificant: much in the manner that the British had spirited Archbishop Makarios away to the Seychelles until it was 'safe' for him to return to Cyprus in March 1956. The UN decided that a similar ploy might work with Aidid and Somalia.

As this would be beyond the American mind-set to comprehend it was necessary for Aidid to be somewhere where he could not be found for as long as six months. The Americans certainly wished to 'interview' the general but, equally certainly, they also intended his 'unintentional' demise. This would exacerbate the problem in Somalia: again the result of such a death was beyond American understanding. Thus the UN's 'private' proposal was developed to keep Aidid at sea, out of sight of land and the Americans, for up to half a year. Although before ships' Automatic Identification System (AIS, which can, of course be switched off) became a legal requirement in 2002 for vessels over 300 gross tons I could not help thinking that the UN's belief that a US nuclear submarine would be unable to track down a 2,500 ton vessel was a touch naive! Nevertheless I was still 'on'!

The original idea had been to use a Greek ship-owner's luxury yacht 'on charter' but we all agreed that that could be destroyed very quickly, and without trace, by an American warship. The Deputy Secretary General was certain that if the Americans knew that they had been hoodwinked, they would not hesitate to sink any vessel with all hands. The US military would clearly feel that retaliation would be necessary against a man they considered to be 'a simple black warrior who, with little more than native cunning, had been able, much to many people's hidden admiration, to outwit the greatest military power on Earth'.[4]

By coincidence, at that precise moment, there was a civilian-owned, heavy-lift, 2,500 ton, military landing ship loading Pakistani tanks in the Gulf area and bound for Mogadishu. The port of registry of the ship and the nationality of her officers and crew were not mentioned and I did not, then, feel the need to ask. After convoluted discussions in which I was closely involved it was decided that, as a tank landing ship (or LST in NATO parlance) built to military standards of damage control, would be marginally less easy to sink outright, she should be earmarked then commandeered when necessary. Plans were drawn up to fit the LST with pre-fabricated cabins in the tank deck for Aidid and his guards; some of whom we agreed, for bargaining purposes, could be American. Who, how, and under what guise they would be brought on board, was the UN's problem and thankfully not mine. Methods of calling for help should the ship be attacked were also considered.

Having become involved, in increasing stages, with the details there was now no reason for me to stage through Naples although I would still be given the opportunity to 'opt out' during my formal acceptance and briefing in New York by a Deputy Secretary General. The Secretary General himself, Boutros Boutros-Ghali, knew he was taking a great risk with UN/USA relations but feelings then rang strongly over the USA's contempt for the finer points of the United Nation's work; a contempt obviously endorsed through the UN's distrust of America's motives and methods.

A 'very senior' United Nations official in London admitted to me that the UN had become increasingly tired of unsuccessful, unilateral US military actions that only proved the then current view that, in his precise and rather alarming words, 'America regards the UN as a gigantic condom which it can use, for its own selfish ends, to fuck the rest of the world with apparent impunity … and without paying for the privilege.'

In the end General Aidid was never caught and so, with some relief but rather more regret that an unusual adventure did not take place, I returned to gazing at the silent typewriter… yet, unknown to me at the time, and why this introduction is relevant, my name as a possible volunteer for 'unusual tasks' with 'security implications' was finding its way from the UN to the Foreign and Commonwealth Office and the Secret Intelligence Service, then, in due course—damn it!—it came to the attention of the European Community Monitoring Mission in the 'Former Republic of Yugoslavia'. The 'damn it' is because the failing Somali job had set me, unwittingly and unknowingly, on the slippery slope towards temporary employment as a European Community monitor.

1

London for Briefings

Towards the end of September 1993 a Foreign and Commonwealth Office (FCO) official telephoned me with the news that the United Nations Protection Force (UNPROFOR) in the Republic of Former Yugoslavia was seeking volunteers. If I was interested I should contact their recruiting agency. I did, but my experience did not match their requirements. A few days later my still-mute typewriter was temporarily abandoned when the FCO invited me to an interview on 30 September, this time for a monitoring post with the European Community Monitoring Mission (ECMM) in the Balkans. I was no longer interested, life had moved on, slowly, but it had moved. I refused the invitation. In reply an unimpressed Foreign Office official explained that as I had been 'fascinated' by the UN job off Somalia (how did they know?) why was I not interested in what they, the FCO, now had to offer in the Balkans? Out of curiosity—plus the attractions of free travel to London and overnight expenses—I agreed to attend the interview. As my CV at the time was nautically-orientated I suggested that I re-wrote it emphasising the more military aspects of my past. 'No,' they said firmly, 'The information they had would probably cover what they were looking for.'

The interview, conducted by the FCO's Julian Metcalf, took place at 1545 in a suite of grand King Charles Street offices and was an alarming affair. During preparations for civilian life I had attended various courses on how to conduct oneself on these occasions and I had, years before, successfully attended the rather more serious Resistance to Interrogation Course run by the Army's Intelligence Corps at Ashford in Kent (and, less comfortably, on the Yorkshire Moors). I was also well practised in what we called the 'upside down reading course', when standing in front of a senior officer's desk while attempting to check that what he was saying was actually what he had written! ... but no course had quite prepared me for this interview—and it was an interview I was not sure I wanted to pass anyway.

At some stage in King Charles Street I was asked my opinion of what was happening in the former Yugoslavia. With no intention of failing the interview on purpose I replied that I had no views, 'It is all desperately muddling,' I said truthfully, 'and I hope that, if successful, the FCO will tell me what to think.'

'Why,' the senior FCO representative asked, ignoring my comments, 'did you think your nautically-biased CV suits you for the job on offer?'

'Actually, I didn't think it did which is why I offered a more military résumé of my career.' Then I added without trying to appear flippant, 'The Danube runs through the former Yugoslavia and I suppose that it might be possible that I am posted to one of its banks.'

There was a noticeable pause and then, 'Why do you want to serve in Bosnia, Mr Tailyour?'

'Well, since you ask, I'm not sure that I do. It was you that invited me here!'

Quite frankly I did not know what I wanted to do except that, deep down, I needed to see if I could regain some of the operational excitement I had learned to love when with the Royal Marines. Playing guardian angel to an East African warlord, while steaming around the uninhabited corners of the Indian Ocean, seemed to come closer to that ideal than being a European Community monitor.

Increasingly certain that I had failed I caught an early train to south Devon the next morning to find that a letter from the FCO had already arrived thanking me for attending the interview and telling me that I was offered, subject to a medical examination, an appointment with the European Community Monitoring Mission for precisely 364 days starting in two months: on 30 November. Then I surprised myself and began the first steps towards an alien life. I decided to accept the post … but provided I served 'on the coast' and for just six months.

'Oh,' said the wonderful girl at the other end of the telephone, 'the coast is precisely where we most want you to serve but it will be up to you, once you are 'in theatre', to get yourself there. We cannot tell the ECMM where to send its monitors … and six months is fine!'

I was surprised, for the implication that not only was I required for my nautical background but equally surprised that unless the FCO had access to a postal system unknown to the rest of the country, the letter from Cath Baker of the Eastern Adriatic Unit, dated 30 September, must have been written during, or even before, the interview for it to have reached my house, almost at the same time as I did!

I am still, twenty-seven years later, unsure why I signed up to the FCO appointment. Certainly I missed the loyalty, spirit, cheerfulness and camaraderie of the Royal Marines and in a rather perverse way I also missed the adrenaline of operations, or at least training for them which, boringly, apart from four or five occasions, it had mostly been. Nevertheless, I accepted the FCO's terms.

My appointment as a monitor then took an unexpected twist when I was summoned to a series of meetings with the Secret Intelligence Service (the SIS or, more informally, MI6) in, among other out-of-the-way places, a 'private' restaurant in Soho. During these meetings it became clear that, unpaid and thus un-attributable, I was being asked to keep an eye on one or two 'characters' in

Serbia and Croatia. To cover the latter geographical area of interest, was a further reason to, somehow, serve on the Dalmatian coast.

Briefings and a medical assessment—more of a question and answer session than a slap and tickle inspection—followed until, by the end of November, I was ready to monitor although, through no fault of the FCO, utterly unaware of what a monitor actually did. I knew what the FCO and the SIS wanted me to do but these were in-house requirements happily and purposefully divorced from the European Community Monitoring Mission.

The most intriguing fact I learned was that an ECMM monitor's uniform was all white to denote 'purity of purpose' and to stand out among those in other uniforms who, presumably, had less 'purity of purpose'! This was a bizarre status emphasised further by our being unarmed in a very fluid, unstable war zone. As I was to discover, this 'uniform' was fine in the summer but in the winter snows was a rather effective camouflage and thus produced precisely the opposite effect to that intended! There were to be other, although sadly not enough, humorous aspects.

Apart from the personal basics, 'specified clothing' would be issued 'on loan' once I arrived at the ECMM's Headquarters in Zagreb, the capital of Croatia. This list included white T shirts (when would I wear those I wondered?) to be worn above a pair of white trousers. Various items of white, foul-weather clothing and arctic kit such as might be issued to the Royal Marines in North Norway, added to the 'trousseaux'. I knew it might be cold but not, surely, that cold. Additionally, we were expected to buy, against reimbursement, our own white socks (seven pairs apparently) and four, lightweight, white jerseys (I packed two white submariners roll-neck sweaters and a sleeveless, cricketing jumper) … but, specifically emphasised, we would not be reimbursed for the statutory white underpants— which I never bought. The final paragraph of the monitor's briefing, under the subtitle 'special equipment' read, rather ominously:

> Flak jackets can be loaned from the Management Officer in ECMM in Zagreb. However you should be aware that you will be held fully responsible if the flak jacket is lost and you will be charged the full replacement cost of £600. This will be enforced rigorously.

I was also advised to pack, among other more obvious items for a peripatetic existence, a large number of candles, a short wave wireless, a mosquito net and 'dog tags'.[1] I was, too, introduced to the FCO's substantial rates and allowances which, as an ex-serviceman seemed remarkably generous but which also emphasised, in my cynical mind, how the other half live. My pay would be £144.66 per day (taxable) and an allowance of 70 Deutschmarks (Dm) per day for daily subsistence plus 30 Dm per day for laundering my white uniforms and telephone calls home 'to reassure families that we were safe and well after sorties'. As we were also to operate in both Serbian and Croat currency (and, more than often, in American dollars) the chances for accounting confusions were high.

A staggering £4.95 per day (non-taxable) was added for what the FCO was pleased to call Special Difficult Post Allowance. I was never quite sure what was meant by that for life in Serbia and Croatia was never as cut off as, for instance, being totally incommunicado at sea in one of HM's ships or at the end of lengthy lines of communication in the deserts of south Yemen or the hills of the Falkland Islands: none of which attracted Special Difficult Post Allowance. Indeed this was an allowance unknown to the Armed Forces. In practice I never discovered if the word 'post' referred to the appointment itself or to the mailing system. Nevertheless, the FCO knows how to look after its own and obviously has a more powerful lobby in such matters within the Treasury than does the MOD. I simply smiled indulgently while, with good grace, accepting a total daily rate three times what I had been earning as a substantive Royal Marines major (wearing the rank of a 'local', unpaid lieutenant-colonel) after 32 years' service. With absolutely nothing to spend my pay on, except wine, it was obviously going to be a good time for the Tailyour coffers if not for the Tailyour humour: which was soon to be placed under extreme pressure.

As 30 November loomed it was time to find out precisely what the roles of a European Community monitor in the Former Republic of Yugoslavia were. As far as I was concerned there were three aspects to the forthcoming adventure: firstly I was a member of the ECMM; secondly, I was required to report direct to the Foreign and Commonwealth Office as indeed were all other British monitors, and I have no doubt that other countries had similar arrangements for their own officers in the field while thirdly, I was required to keep in personal touch with an SIS officer (an old and valued acquaintance of mine) and await his instructions. I was not a 'paid-up' member of that august organisation but one that was merely being asked to 'help out' under certain circumstances.

In all previous operational theatres with which I had been involved I had had a pretty good idea of what was expected of me and, where relevant, of my marines and the unit or ship in which I was serving. This time I had not the slightest idea what lay ahead and thus no foreboding of the confusions that were to face me and for which, in many cases, as I was to discover, I was totally unfit to unravel. Nevertheless, with my mind clear of such worries, my final days in England were spent in an idyllic visit to the Isles of Scilly followed by a short period tidying up my affairs at home before Patricia and I drove to London to spend my last night at the Royal Ballet watching Sir Frederick Ashton's Beatrix Potter extravaganza. What a contrast to my new life these carefree days were to be.

Zagreb for Orders

The next morning, waiting at Heathrow for the delayed Croatia Airlines flight to Zagreb, I realised I was, rather unexpectedly, not looking forward to this particular 'unknown' and went in search for an early 'Horses Neck'.[1]

Once the Croatia Airlines flight had at last taken off life was instantly made amusing and unexpectedly instructive by the delightful gentleman sitting next to me in the aisle seat. Eric Elstob, the manager of what his visiting card declared was the Foreign and Colonial Management Limited, introduced himself over pre-lunch drinks and, by the brandy stage, he had briefed me on the plight of Croatia. Although I was not to know it at the time, his exposé was in far more detail, and honest and unbiased detail at that, than I was to glean from the Monitoring Mission itself. Eric's views were unequivocal. 'The Croatians,' he explained, 'like to think of themselves as not being Balkan but rather middle European. German is certainly the second language although many of the young speak good English. The people of the Dalmatian coast feel more in tune with the Germans while the Serbian/Croat hostility is regarded as being similar to that between Ulster and the southern Irish.'

As lunch came to an end he clarified rather mournfully that, 'Rather than a Havel (Czechoslovakia) in charge, Yugoslavia has inherited two very second-rate leaders in Milošević (Serbia) and Tuđman (Croatia).'

'Conflict in the Balkans,' he stated, 'can, as it is so often, be analysed in geographic and economic terms. The Hapsburgs ruled Croatia while Slovenia had always been much richer than the orthodox, Turkish-ruled Serbia. Although the same nation, the prosperous Austro-Hungarian provinces were in effect given to the poorer Serbia as spoils of war at the Peace of Versailles in 1919. Since when there has been a constant and massive transfer of resources from the north to the south with the GNP-split being perhaps as marked as one third to two thirds. The Croats tended to provide the industrialists and the professionals and the Serbs the officials and the administrators but now all the *intelligentsia* and those with money have left both countries leaving behind what might be described as the dregs of an earlier society to fill the vacancies.' He laughed, 'Except in the police and armed forces where the brains never existed anyway!'

With prescience he elucidated, 'The Serbs are right to worry about the dissolution of Yugoslavia for when normality returns they will be left even worse off, economically and socially, than the Slovaks.'

'Currently' Eric finished, pouring two miniatures of brandy as we began the descent into Zagreb, 'the GNP of Croatia in 1990, the last year for which figures are available, was $15,350 million: which has to be significantly below the country's potential. Since the breakup of Yugoslavia the currency has roared into hyperinflation with 9,000 Croat dinars to the British pound. In all aspects Croatia is now a Third World country.'

I was to discover for myself, over the coming six months, that, as Eric Elstob had hinted, there was huge but dormant potential throughout Croatia. 'The Dalmatian coast has all the tourist attractions of the Greek islands while the inland area around Zagreb is a fertile plain. The south bank of the Danube also has the same possibilities as a vibrant agricultural area. They even manufacture rather good chocolate.'

This was by far the best introduction to Croatia—if not the other countries that once formed Yugoslavia—that I was to receive.

We landed into 25° F (-4° C) and poor visibility at Zagreb airport where, with a mix of experienced and novice monitors of many nationalities, I was herded by an administration officer into one of a brace of minibuses for the eight-mile drive to the ECMM's Headquarters housed in Hotel 'I'. Looking around me in the cramped vehicle it was clear that most of my fellow travellers were old hands at the ECMM business as, meeting up after a period of leave, they teased and laughed among themselves; shouting in a mixture of European languages above and around heads. I had not been a 'new boy' since joining the Sultan of Muscat's Armed Forces in 1966 and sat in silence, deep in thought, gazing at the muddy slush beyond the window.

Hotel 'I'—which I soon learned was pronounced Hotel 'I' or, more phonetically, 'É'—was a fine, and very large, example of a 'communist concrete' structure. Set in the middle of a flat and featureless landscape a few miles from Zagreb—now much built upon—it had been completely taken over by the ECMM.[2]

From the wide front doors and reception desk a long corridor, lined with huge potted plants, stretched ahead. At its far end this passage opened into the main bar which traversed the width of the ground floor. Apart from the extensive flora the corridor also contained glass-fronted offices which, in earlier days, would have housed small emporia full of local produce and merchandise. Now these inward facing windows were crudely decorated with some national flag or other proclaiming the individual allegiance of its occupants while each flag also vied with the blue European Union flag that paradoxically seemed to deny that allegiance. 'Not much unity here it would appear,' I thought rather uncharitably with all the experience of two minutes.

Having booked in at the front desk I struggled upstairs with my two large suitcases and hand-luggage before returning to the ground floor for an introductory brief. Here I met the two other new British monitors: Roger Sugden, lately of the Fleet Air Arm and destined to be an airfield monitor, and Mike Haller, a driver, recently with the United Nations.

I wrote in my diary.

We have already been issued with our ID cards in an efficient manner and been given a brief on the hotel's functions.

My first impression is that we seem to be in the country of one of the protagonists which strikes me as being odd as we must, presumably be impartial. Additionally, all the ECMM Headquarters interpreters are Croatians and yet they must be translating all sorts of things that should not be for their eyes I would have thought.

Then, on a more personal note:

Told that I am going to the capital of one of the other protagonists, Knin in the Serbia occupied part of Croatia known as the Republic of Serbian Krajina or RSK. Most emphatically not recognised by Croatia. Everyone says it is a fascinating area and one of the keys to the whole problem. Either way, Knin looks a long way from the sea but clearly an absorbing time stretches ahead.

A beer or two after dinner—eaten beneath one of many large signs ordering that, 'No food is to be taken out of the dining room'. Opinions from all sides are expressed and argued continually. There are as many views about the past and the future as there are people here.

Dinner had been a help-yourself arrangement from huge, semi-spherical urns surrounded by numerous small dishes set around a large central table. On opening the first container I immediately resolved that it would be useful for my stomach to get in early but that would also mean enjoying a form of high tea at 6 o'clock. It was obvious that at any later time there would be nothing left.

I noted, too, that the Belgians [3] were:

Running the ECMM and would appear to be trying very hard for such a small country. Nevertheless, the jokes on notice boards all around the large bar mixed in with the numerous 'do and do not' signs remind me of a school's assembly hall or common room.

I'm not sure whether or not it is the military trying to be civilians or civilians trying to do the job in the manner they perceive the military would do it.

At the end of this long day of travel and opposing emotions I managed to telephone home from my bedroom, a call which, I suspected, was going to cost a bomb on my bill. At that moment telephone bills were at the bottom of my 'worry' list for, just as I was beginning to get off to sleep, I was startled into full conscientiousness by a lengthy burst of machine gun fire outside, or within a hundred yards or so, of my window. We had been told earlier that gunfire was an unlikely feature of Hotel 'I' despite signs everywhere pointing to doors marked SHELTER. I tried one on my way to bed but it was bolted.

> Bed at 0010 and a cup of hot chocolate in the peace and quiet of my room thanks to Patricia's forethought in send me off with a small travelling kettle—at least it would be peaceful but for the near continuous shooting outside.

The next morning heralded a day of briefings by a succession of Belgians that became …

> … more and more repetitive while imparting less and less real information and I wonder when we will actually be told what our duties are. I remember Mike Shuttleworth[4] telling me that when he asked the same question he was told that all he needed to be a monitor was a pair of binoculars and a walking stick!

It all seemed rather muddling not to say puzzling, as no one seemed quite able to say exactly, or even vaguely, what the daily 'mechanics' of our job was. There was much talk of, and many short briefings on, safety in the field—all pretty obvious stuff—but no briefing on how we should or could avoid finding ourselves in the situations they described: such as entering mine fields to recover dead bodies or preventing local hostilities between Croat and Serbs forces as well as actions to circumvent kidnap or ambush. It struck me that these were all an everyday part of our *modus operandi* … or were they actions to be avoided as not being part of our job … but, then, what was our job?

A few briefings were well delivered and contained useful historical information but most were barely-relevant essays read from papers without the presenter looking up, all delivered in, quite understandably but difficult to follow, a foreign-accented monotone. Some of the lecturers lacked knowledge of their subject and just repeated what was written in front of them. Seldom were we invited to ask questions. Overall there was very much a NATO HQ atmosphere throughout Hotel 'I' but without the military professionalism. Newcomers seemed to be unwelcome for we took up too much time being indoctrinated; which was of course odd considering the daily turnover of personnel and the need for well-briefed monitors about to conduct tricky negotiations.

On the domestic side, the hotel food was acceptable under the circumstances—if there was any left!—but I suspect that we ate rather more goat-burgers than ham- or beef-burgers as advertised on the daily-changing menus. Thankfully, I like goat.

Then, a sign of the future as I would know it, appeared on 2 December when about 20 Greeks swaggered into the hotel in preparation for their country taking over the

European Union's presidency by the turn of the year. This advance party equated to two Greeks for every one departing Belgian. While they took stock of their surroundings we three British newcomers attended yet more briefs including, at last, a good one by Roger Vincent, a retired Royal Navy commander whom I had met before. Roger was a round, 'Pooh Bear' style of officer: always smiling he gave us our first sensible, operational brief. Despite his subject not concerning my area I had asked to sit in to get some idea from a British monitor what it was we were required to achieve and how. Although his views were aimed at Zagreb—where I was very glad not to be staying—it was a properly delivered address followed by a useful question period.

When Roger had finished he escorted us outside to a 'chacon'—a large military shipping container—permanently parked in the snow where a chaotic and often hilarious 'issuing of stores' took place. This disorganised vignette was played out with the three of us, sometimes all but naked and sometimes dressed for the deep Antarctic, while being measured up for, and trying on, various items of our white uniform. There had not been a resupply from whoever in King Charles Street was responsible for British diplomatic logistics in Zagreb so many of the more usual sizes of kit had long gone. Consequently, there was little that fitted a smallish person such as myself nor, paradoxically, a largish person such as Roger Sugden. Eventually I choose three pairs of white, light cotton, naval-cooks' trousers that were too tight around the middle—a problem that would be solved by the expected diet in Knin—but they were, as near as made no difference, the right length.

Next, three, long-sleeved, white shirts were offered that were too tight around the collar but about right in sleeve length: the nearest the system could manage and as I was intending to wear my white, silk *shamagh* (a left-over from my days with the Sultan of Oman's Armed Forces) as a winter scarf these were fine. Next, an American style white, plastic belt was handed across which I knew I would not wear as my trousers were never going to fall down although I reckoned that it might come in useful for some as yet, un-designed purpose. I refused the proffered T shirts.

Now looking like the budding monitors we aspired to be we bundled our 'civilian' clothes and spare 'tropical' uniforms under both arms and trudged our way back through the snow to our rooms for a good laugh in front of a full-length looking glass. I was also clutching the regulation ECMM baseball hat: a hideous, blue device with the gold EU stars on the front above the broad peak. I swore to myself that I would never wear it and I remained true to my word. In fact, I am not sure that I ever saw it again!

In my new uniform I made my way to the bar for a pre-lunch glass of wine where two, white-clad backs faced me. I summoned the barman. Oblivious to my presence the bar-side conversation, surprisingly in English, went like this:

'Have you seen the new British monitor?'

'Yes. Why do you ask?'

'Don't you think he is taking it rather too seriously?'

'How come?'

'You must have noticed. He has even had his hair dyed white!

I laughed.

Faces turned around sharply. The nearest one muttered, 'Sorry.'

'Not at all, I smiled, for my hair had been naturally white for some years, 'that's probably the funniest thing I shall hear while I am out here.' The Dane, Lennart Leschly, and I were to become good companions in the Republic of Serbian Krajina and, later, on the Dalmatian coast.

The temporary Head of the United Kingdom Delegation to the ECMM, now Julian Metcalfe who had chaired my initial FCO interview in King Charles Street, was by chance on a visit to 'his men in the field' and invited us to join him for a welcoming lunch. This was followed by a comprehensive and wide-ranging brief during which he explained that as far as the FCO was concerned—and nothing to do with the ECMM—he was, he explained, being 'Paid to Predict' based on the information and intelligence we passed back: rather obviously, not through the European Community. As this was his job in the FCO so it was our job, while in the Former Republic of Yugoslavia, to help him with his 'predictions'. He gave us a history lesson of the Krajina, to whose capital, Knin, he had recently travelled, This allowed me to write in my diary, but without too much genuine conviction:

Knin sounds thought-provoking, despite being far from the sea.

Julian's prognosis on Croatia and Krajina was fascinating from both the political point of view as well as their historical and geographical juxtapositions and I became aware for the first time that there were a number of totally different 'wars' being waged across the Balkans. What was happening and had happened in Bosnia was peripheral to what was happening and had happened in Croatia and the Serb-occupied Krajina—or border regions—between Croatia in the north and west and Bosnia-Herzegovina to the east.

In very simple terms, with the collapse of communism, Germany forced the rest of the world to recognise (some would argue, prematurely) Croatia as a separate sovereign state in 1991. With their fears of domination now coming to fruition the Croatian Serbs of Krajina—the border land between Croatia and Bosnia-Herzegovina—were worried that the old hatred of the fascist-based *Ustaše* towards them would once again come to the fore. They were right to be concerned for Croatia was already re-introducing a number of *Ustaše* symbols such as the red and white chequer board on its new national flag while the old *Ustaše* kuna was replacing the Croat dinar as the national currency. At the same time a number of streets were being renamed after *Ustaše* heroes: even swastikas and giant 'U's began to appear daubed on roads and public buildings; not to be removed. Some soldiers, as I was to see for myself, had begun to sport swastika armbands on their uniforms. This concern forced the Serbs of Krajina, a region within the newly independent Croatia, to declare their own independence as the Republic of Serbian Krajina (RSK) with Knin as its capital. During the Second World War Nazi Germany had supported the Croat *Ustaše* while the Yugoslav National Army (JNA) had supported the Serbian *Četniks* and thus the hatred continued—and continues.

These are the very barest of facts behind the formation of the self-styled RSK from which it might be readily accepted that this breakaway state, illegal in international law, was an inevitable consequence of various insensitive actions by Croatia. People spoke as though the Krajina region of Croatia had recently been occupied unlawfully and yet the population, originally encouraged to settle in the borders as a buffer against the Muslims to the east, had not changed for over 500 years.

It has now been confirmed that I am definitely off to Knin to join Team November Three responsible for the border adjacent to Zadar. This is a much disputed area and one that is still being fought over—even as I write—despite a ceasefire and the presence of the United Nations Protection Force (UNPROFOR): but then everything out here is happening despite ceasefires.

Nevertheless I still hoped to be involved in coastal duties—if there were to be any on offer. However it was also clear that what the FCO might want from me and what the ECMM did with me were, rightly, two different matters. I knew that any future lay with my ingenuity.

Kettle, bath plug, short-wave wireless, Earl Grey tea and Walkman are already invaluable in this strange society where conversations are difficult even though English is the language of the mission—I suppose if you are the only Englishman and try to join a table of Belgians who, somewhat naturally, are all speaking their own language, you should be regarded as a bit of a spoiler for they then have to talk in English for the sake of one among eight at the dinner table.

Apart from Mike Shuttleworth, one of the two ECMM monitors that I already knew as a life-long friend and former Royal Marine helicopter pilot, was Martin Garrod. Known locally as 'Monitor Martin' but more formally as Lieutenant-General Sir Martin Garrod KCB, OBE, he was, later, to be appointed a CMG for his outstanding work. Martin, a past Commandant General Royal Marines, had brought with him, very much to the Mission's advantage, the attributes of a hard-working, thoroughly decent and honest soul. I already knew him to be much admired for his work in the besieged city of Mostar even if his daily reports were regarded by the Belgians as being 'too long by one and a half yards!'

Knowing Martin as I did (he had been the senior lieutenant responsible for the very earliest stages of my training as a young Royal Marines officer, later he had been my brigadier when I had commanded a minor unit in the 3rd Commando Brigade) I knew that his reports would be fascinating, detailed, well thought-out, studious and balanced. Perhaps, and this is the impression I received in those early days, all the Belgians wanted was an easy time so that they could all go home and forget about it.

More shooting outside my window as I was changing for dinner instantly reminding of the Dhofar war in in the Hadramaut region of the Oman when a sniper would try to prevent me from enjoying my daily cold bath in an oil drum on the edge of the wadi before the evening 'stand-to' and partridge, roasted in an ammunition box.

Dinner that evening—not roast partridge!—was especially arranged by the British to say goodbye to Julian who had been in Zagreb temporarily filling in for the last Head of Department, Guy Hart, before a new one could be appointed. Godfrey Garrett, known as a 'diplomat with considerable experience in Eastern Europe', was due to arrive on 31 December.

Julian is described in my diary as 'a good hand whom I admire greatly'. He had recently toured the Krajina and written a most comprehensive account about the future of the area as he perceived it. 'It would be interesting to see if he is right,' I thought. In his final UK Delegation newsletter Julian wrote, in part:

My own short stint in ECMM HQ has been fascinating. Impressions are mixed, possibly muddled. The song 'Nights in White Satin' takes on an altogether new meeting when heard in an eerie bar in Bihać to the echo of distant gunfire. And strange how that same gunfire seems so much closer when the Land Rover breaks down a few minutes later on the way home to the hotel euphemistically known as the 'freezer' … To be used as a propaganda football to be lectured to, or shot at was, I freely admit, a novel and at times frightening experience. 'Good', I hear you all chortle, now that wretched man from the Foreign Office knows what life is really like.

As he left the hotel that evening Julian handed me a single sheet of paper headed *Regional Centre (RC) Knin Priorities of Work* and a copy of a signal from the Brussels headquarters of the European Union to the outgoing Belgium Head of Mission with the words, 'I think you might find these relevant to where you are going.'

Back in my room I read them with interest despite knowing next to nothing of the area nor, in the signal, any of the names mentioned.

The signal was headed:

At the request of the international committee for former Yugoslavia Secretariat the presidency transmits herewith a report on the recent Krajina talks from 23 to 28 of November 1993…

After intensive preparation by shuttle diplomacy a negotiating team composed of ambassadors Ahrens and Vollebaek and UNPROFOR's General Pellnas sponsored secret talks between a Croat government delegation … and a Krajina–Serb delegation led by 'President' Hadzič ….

The talks … were centred on a draft ceasefire agreement. The agreement would provide for a disengagement of at least 2 km and, among others, monitoring by UNPROFOR and ECMM. At the end of the talks … The Croats declared themselves ready to fully accept the agreement and decided immediately but it became clear, however, that none of the Serbs shortly before the Krajina elections on 12 December saw themselves in a position to sign a document that contained important Serbian concessions ….

In practical terms the second sheet of paper was to be more useful.

Regional Centre Knin priorities of work are as follows;
1 Monitor and report the political situation
2 Insure liaison with UNPROFOR HQ, UNPROFOR Units and other international organisations.
3 Participate in confidence building measures such as tripartite meetings and the activities that evolve from them.
4 Monitor and report the humanitarian and the Human Rights situation.
5 Monitor and report the military situation.
6 Arrange/assist with humanitarian operations in coordination with humanitarian organisations.
7 Monitor and report the state of the economy and infrastructure.
8 Assist in accomplishing ceasefires and separation forces by mediation.
9 Develop priorities for the economic infrastructure reconstruction.
10 Coastal priorities as stated by Head of Regional Centre Knin.

Priority number 10 was clearly of the most interest to me but before I succumbed to a welcome sleep on my last night in Zagreb I reflected on what someone had told me during the day. I was not quite sure who it was but I quote here from the narrative I tapped into my computer before turning in:

You'll find that the Dutch *MilitaireInlichtingendienst* operates across the area and, hardly surprisingly, the German *Bundesnachrichtendienst* is also pretty active. The French *Direction générale de la sécurité extérieure* seem to be everywhere and, as always, making a bloody nuisance of themselves; not least of all because they have their own internal radio network. Israel's Mossad try to worm their way into everyone's business, worried no doubt about any Muslim influence. But quite why the Danish *Forsvarets Efterretningstjeneste*, is involved in Croatia beats me … unless, for whatever national reason, they all want to fight over the pieces when it goes tits up. And be aware that the US Military Attaché in Zagreb is a Serb-hater and you can read into that what you like.

I had been forewarned.

Knin for War Crimes and a Covert Beech Recce

It had been decided that I would travel to the ECMM's Regional Centre based in the RSK's self-styled capital at Knin (or RCK) on the 3 December 'shuttle' with, among others, Lennart Leschly the Dane who played the piano rather well and who carried a portable, electronic contraption in his baggage. As with all the other Regional Centres across the former Yugoslavia the Knin Regional Centre was subdivided into Coordinating Centres although in this case there was only one, on the Dalmatian coast and known as Coordinating Centre Zadar (or CCZ). This Coordinating Centre was further subdivided into teams at Zadar and, most notably as far as I was eventually to be concerned, at Split some 75, straight-line miles further down the coast.

Even after so short a visit I could not wait to get away from the ECMM's HQ and knew I would be glad not to see this communist–concrete monstrosity too often. Not only did it house all the clichéd hang-ups of a multi-national headquarters but most of the phobias as well. The British staff in the hotel were ex-armed forces officers or the FCO's professional diplomats doing well a task they understood but a few of the others seemed to take a naïve pride in believing that the headquarters could never be wrong while the front line monitors remained a 'blasted nuisance' with their requests and genuine concerns.

The superb mountain passes were stunning in the half visibility which occurred in patches between banks of fog until we began the descent from the snow-covered uplands towards the Dalmatian coast. Here was a sudden and dramatic change of scenery although not of temperature. Indeed, at one point, the driver had to brake suddenly to prevent being caught in a remarkable display of a katabatic wind as it fell off a hanging valley 900 feet above. From the comparative safety of the mini-bus we watched as dust, leaves, small rocks and large branches poured through the trees like a waterfall roaring down an escarpment, all at an estimated eighty miles an hour. I had never seen anything like that, even in the littoral mountains of North Norway.

As we descended the coastal ridge towards the Adriatic Sea the northern Adriatic islands enthralled me for this was my first sight of the sea for far too long. The islands were beautiful in their very barrenness and I had a sudden longing to be among them. Already November there was not a yacht to be seen, a luxury for those of us used to sailing the south coast of the British Isles; nor were the islands covered in snow which made a change from the previous hours, indeed the previous days since leaving England. By the time the temperature had risen from 28° F to 57° F (-2° C to 14° C) during the three-mile drop to the coastal town of Senj I was already toying with the idea of deserting the Foreign and Commonwealth Office. I would not ask for much; a five-ton, gaff-rigged cutter would do me for a week or two or until my conscience caught up with my actions.

Regrettably, we drove steadily on, south-eastwards down the coast.

Thirty-five miles later at Prizna we stopped at the ferry crossing to the island of Pag where, on the mainland side, we were met by the 'shuttle' up from Zadar. Vehicles, drivers and passengers were exchanged then, once afloat, we were able to stretch our legs with a soft drink and refreshing sea air for the one-and-three-quarter nautical mile crossing. It was good to be at sea if only with a throbbing diesel beneath my feet and yet this brief interlude was spoilt by Lennart, the otherwise civilised, piano-playing Danish monitor. Expressing my surprise when he tossed his empty, plastic drink bottle into the sea, where it was destined to end up on some beautiful stretch of Dalmatian coastline, he merely shrugged his shoulders in reply while muttering to the effect that the Croats deserved it. I was not too sure.

Although we could have remained on the mainland all the way to Zadar, where I hoped we might enjoy a night stop—and briefing—at the Coordinating Centre's hotel, all ECMM vehicles had to use the Pag island ferry to avoid the Maslenica bridge which was under intermittent bombardment by the Serbs in Krajina. The original bridge had been destroyed in November 1991 so now there was a pontoon arrangement but this, too, was under near permanent shelling. There were rumours that the Croatians were digging some form of 'mini-channel tunnel' (as it was popularly described) but yet another rumour suggested that one end was about to come up on the Serbian side of the Confrontation Line!

On the way into Zadar we passed ruined houses that had either been destroyed, Lennart explained, by the daily indiscriminate shell-fire or that had been torched by Croats because they had been owned by Serbs. At long last, for it had been a lengthy and cramped journey in over-laden and far-from-new vehicles, we arrived at the Zadar hotel where we were met by Matt Burnford, late of the Royal Tank Regiment and currently a most effective head of the Coordinating Centre.

Entering this hotel was a strange experience. As I remember it now, 27 years further on, the main door opened not only on to a large lobby backed by a long concierge's desk but this was also a desk that stretched to the right, changing into a bar as it did so. Recent shell damage was obvious as were the rather crudely-amateur attempts to repair it or even hide it. The place was crammed with knots of miserable-looking people who, I was to learn quickly, were a mix of refugees and 'displaced persons'; instantly recognisable by the far-away gaze of desperation on their faces and the tattered remnants of what, in many cases, had been fine and, in notable numbers, expensive clothes. The children, although clean, had a desperate, near-feral look about them as they and their parents, grandparents and next of kin wandered listlessly around and through the foyer. It was a sight that I was to become used to although I never became used to the reasons for it.

I have been told that a refugee has had to cross an international border and gets the full treatment (such as it is) whereas a displaced person has been displaced from within his or her own country by the war or ethnic cleansing. However, as Croatia does not recognise the Republic of Serbian Krajina as being a foreign country all those Croats who have had to leave—or been forced to leave—Krajina are officially classified as displaced persons and therefore are not eligible for any help.

Lennart and I were greeted with the good news that we would not be continuing by minibus to Knin that evening for quite unexpectedly a 'spare' Land Rover—as unlikely an event as a smiling refugee—had been conjured up; seemingly out of nowhere. We would take it, without a driver, to Knin on the morrow.

There is a power cut in the hotel this evening, as apparently there is every evening. There is no hot water, no loo paper and no bath or basin plug. Luckily I am prepared for these last two inconveniences. Equally luckily I am very happy with a cold shower especially after a stuffy, eight-hour drive.

The hotel had been hit recently by artillery shells following which a British monitor had shown remarkably courage in the face of almost certain further bombardment by helping to rescue many refugees from the un-stable upper floors. Unable to cope with the sheer volume of desperate people he had shouted for assistance from a visiting Greek general but this officer refused and simply cowered in the assembly area on the far side of the car park. It was a well-known, but rather sad, incident relayed to me by a member of the hotel staff that, had I been clairvoyant, might have been a pointer of things to come.

The ECMM's suite of offices were on the ground floor using the inner 'bedroom' as a more-secure operations room and the outer 'day room' as the office. The Head of the Coordinating Centre had his own suite on the opposite side of the corridor while other monitors were spread around various ground floor rooms. It struck me as being a rather useful arrangement but as with all the downstairs rooms it was dark because the open verandas that otherwise led direct to the hotel's lawns had been barricaded with walls of 'hollow' bricks. These certainly let fresh air in but equally certainly kept the sun out—along with, presumably, the blast from shells fired from the other side of the Confrontation Line.

Supper was a sirloin steak with *Popeye* wine, known as such after the cartoon character on the label. This was as rough a red wine as Popeye himself was a sailor, but rather pleasant for all that, in a Mediterranean sort of way. After dinner and various briefings on the local situation along this part of the Dalmatian coast I returned to my darkened room and, slightly disturbed by what I had seen, wrote by candlelight.

> Remarkably, the food is really very good—for us—but it is an embarrassing situation as the ECMM has its own table permanently laid in the centre of the dining room and is rather lavishly (by local standards) bulging with wine and T-bone steaks. An ostentatious show. The poor locals, whether displaced persons or refugees, have to pass our table to collect their meagre loaf of bread and pots of thin stew, a form of gruel I would guess. I cannot help feeling that this could be organised in a more sympathetic manner but I am too new here to comment and must keep my council. The Greeks are already *de facto* in charge and I don't suppose they give a damn or would bother to see my point. Clearly the Belgians did not either for it was they that set up this unfeeling arrangement. Not leadership as I know it; on the other hand 'they' would argue that we are not in the leadership business.

Following an undisturbed night's sleep with no gunfire to influence my dreams, I woke to a cool clear, almost tropical dawn which, in Arabia, would have heralded a great heat. After breakfast we loaded the Land Rover for Knin, a cargo that included the Regional Centre's correspondence. Yet I held little hope that mine would be included for I knew that the onward delivery of mail became more of a lottery the further away it travelled from Zagreb.

With the Land Rover overladen not only with our own luggage and various 'ECMM boxes' but also with mail and parcels for Croats still living—indeed, imprisoned—in the RSK, Lennart drove us past ruined houses and the 'largest ammunition dump in Croatia'. The multi-storey car park of Zagreb's marina had been turned into a vast army lorry park with each vehicle stuffed to its gills with munitions. Apparently there were still yachts for hire with evening racing sometimes organised. One or two monitors were known to have taken part but, looking at the state of those yachts still moored, I doubted it. Interestingly, the rows of ammunition lorries were unguarded.

At the border we were halted for about an hour as our papers—expectedly— did not seem to be quite in order. Three scruffy Croat border guards checked, then double checked and, even more labouredly, treble checked to see if our car's registration number and our own identification card numbers tallied. To my untrained eyes and nose I guess they had been 'on the pop' for most of the night while, as they 'inspected' us they were still chewing their breakfast. They were unkempt, dirty, smelly and unsmiling.

While we waited Lennart explained that every smallest element of administration had to be in place for the guards would take great delight in finding some excuse not to let us through. Even the planned timing of our crossing from Croatia into the RSK had to be exactly adhered to, to the minute, or we would be turned back. Now, after much excited talking and checking followed by yet more talking and checking over a radio, they grudgingly let us pass.

These Croat army soldiers were living in a squalid bunker—in truth, little more than a damp and dark dugout—and although they appeared to be in a common uniform there was nothing uniform about their clothes other than that they were disgustingly filthy. Surrounding their mud and scrub-covered shelter notices warned of the presence of mines either side of the road we had just travelled. Shallow shell holes pot-marked the tarmac and immediate country-side. 'Heaven knows', I thought, 'where on earth do they go to the loo with shells arriving indiscriminately and unannounced?' I stopped thinking.

At last, we drove for a mile or so through the mine fields of no-man's-land to a United Nations' checkpoint where, easily recognisable in our white clothes and white but dusty Land Rover, we were waved through with a smile. The countryside now was rocky with thick scrubland as we traversed a form of plateau with no sign of Knin, apparently only two miles ahead; until, quite suddenly, we were looking down the sides of an escarpment with the RSK's capital below at the junction of three valleys. We had arrived on the edge of a vast gash in the surface of the globe with the town sprawling beneath us and, even from this position it looked desolate and filthy, lying beneath its own thick, smog-like atmosphere. Descending the steep incline it became apparent that not only did the town look desolate and dirty, it was. The predominant colour of the buildings, at least those that were left intact, were shades of grey; the dusty trees and bushes were no brighter and nor were the hoardings, the street signs or the people as they trudged their weary way from empty shop to empty shop.

Lennart wiggled the Land Rover past the ubiquitous burnt out or boarded-up garages and small businesses to the back of what appeared to be just another half finished, white walled, red roofed, two-storied building about half a crow-mile or so to the north-east of the town's centre. Here the team that met us were far more pleased to greet a 'new' Land Rover than two more monitors.

The Regional Centre's headquarters were at the top of an unfinished, cement staircase with bare pipes and cables running across and above the steps at awkward heights. Stumbling my way up I was greeted by Patrick Brooke the Deputy Head of Regional Centre Knin and an Arabic-speaking, cavalry officer who had served in the Sultan of Muscat's Armed Forces, although after me. He was also a friend of my sister Veryan and of her then husband David Williams-Wynn. Patrick had given them their first lurcher dog called *Hash bin Bash*! I almost felt at home.

Patrick confirmed immediately that while I learned the ropes I would be attached to Team November Three led by a French *Commando Marine* lieutenant called Jack—'He prefers the English spelling and pronunciation'—and Jeff, a Belgian army warrant officer, 'You will meet them this evening when they return from patrol.' That same evening I would also meet Paul Ortholan the Arabic-speaking, French Head of the Regional Centre who was to become a great ally although all his good work was eventually to be undermined by his successor; another Frenchman.

In the meantime, and as there were no catering facilities in the headquarters, six of us piled into the Land Rover and made for the United Nations barracks on the western outskirts of Knin, known as UN Sector South, for lunch—and another culinary eye-opener.

> The canteen was in a vast hanger that I suspect had once housed the Yugoslav National Army's armoured vehicles. Uniforms of every conceivable western nation queued at a long serving counter where we were doled out our 'ration'. As there was no fresh meat, vegetables or bread available from local sources we were served 'compo'[2] from an unknown country of origin that, I was convinced, was certainly not Britain. Probably African. As it happens I like British compo!

There was at least one friend in that huge dining hall. Johnny Crosland, an ex-Parachute Regiment officer whom I had known during the Falklands campaign, came across and, from behind, thumped me on the back. Turning, it was good to see a welcoming, smiling face. Johnny was working for the United Nations although he did not tell me his precise role and as he had also been in the Special Air Service I did not feel the need to ask.

We felt (at least I felt) very self-conscious in my white uniform among people of every conceivable race and creed wearing a mixture of uniforms or outlandish civilian clothes:

> All are somehow involved in the UN, aid agencies or Non-Government Organisations in this extraordinary part of the world.

Back at the headquarters I briefly met Jack and Jeff, my future team-mates. Their common language was French but both spoke to me in English, as indeed the ECMM regulations required. I gave no hint that I could speak French—of a sort—deciding that that was powder I most definitely wanted to keep dry. The brief introductions completed, the Land Rover delivered me to the RCK's living quarters, further towards the town's eastern outskirts.

The 'motel', of which I had heard much, turned out to be an assortment of two or three 'linked' buildings. Owned and run by Mr Šifko it was probably the only such establishment still operating in Knin; thanks to the ECMM's monitors and the passing, international press corps. Based round a café-cum-bar and with rooms and *en-suite* showers on the upper two floors, it was the town's social hub and always very 'busy'. There was a lift that no one used because of the many, irregularly-timed power cuts throughout each 24 hour period. My room was comfortable but with no electricity and no heat it was, frankly, bloody cold as I unpacked properly for the first time since leaving home.

At 1630 I returned to the headquarters, close to the town's hospital, and the first of a series of briefings at which I met the other members of the Regional Centre, gaining the immediate impression that while most of the other monitors may have been revelling in the routine I thought that it was, surprisingly, far too regimented for original work with many rules and little leeway for initiative. Nevertheless I was to write in my diary that evening that:

> I should not make up my mind on such aspects until I have been more closely involved.

After a beer or two in the half-built but already fairly dilapidated building— with the unfinished entrance where a door frame will one day be fitted, guarded by a friendly Alsatian—I returned to the motel and a brief moment of peace. I even achieved a luke-warm shower before meeting Lennart for dinner.

> Everyone smokes and nothing throughout the building either electrical, plumbing or construction is actually made properly. It is all rather fun!

Dinner was advertised on a black-board as *Wiener Schnitzel* with dry red wine from Kosovo; this latter contained in two-litre plastic Coca-Cola bottles (the white in Pepsi-Cola bottles) and was roughish but pleasant. The menu and its presentation certainly added to the atmosphere of being in a war zone in some strange way. Dry, old bread was the only accompaniment to the veal apart from an imaginative garnish of cloves of garlic; clearly the customary method of embellishing the flavourlessness of it all. The veal was, from the first mouthful onwards, mostly bread crumbs that effectively hid the gristle from view but not from taste! Nevertheless a noble effort with what was available.

We were joined by two other monitors so we diners were an international mix of British, Danish, French, German and Irish monitors—which made discussions interesting. The 'state of the RSK nation' was not easy to take in as there were so many views on how the place had reached the state it had, *vis-á-vis* Croatia, and whether or not it should or could do anything about it. A conundrum known, apparently, within the Regional Centre's teams as the 'view of no horizon'.

Listening to the various monitors and to Lennart who was, I only now discovered, the Operations Officer of Regional Centre Knin, I thought that I might have been beginning to get the gist of the problem but it was not going to be easy.

My first full day in Knin Regional Centre was a Sunday. Following a demonstration on the fitting of snow chains to the Land Rovers and after the daily briefing at 0900, Peter Strauss, a German, offered to show me the local countryside. He was elderly and had served in the last war in, I think, 'transport'. He looked, behaved and talked precisely like the pink-faced German colonel depicted in *Those Magnificent Men and their Flying Machines* but he had a heart of serious, old gold and called everyone 'my dear'. Always ready to help—'Sure, my dear'—Peter was by far the nicest and most balanced 'foreigner' in Knin.

Peter drove the Regional Centre's old Renault P4 car up to 'the Valley of Silence' to visit a platoon of Kenyan soldiers protecting 26 elderly, very elderly indeed in most cases, Croat women. Their lonely village had been 'ethnically cleansed' of males and then all-but destroyed by the RSK. In fact there was one ancient Croat gentleman who, along with 'his' ladies, had for some inexplicable reason been spared death.

As Peter was keen that I should see something verging on 'culture' we returned via Knin Castle. Perched on top of the hill at the bottom of the valley this sprawling fort, begun in the 9th century, is the second largest such structure in Europe and offered excellent views of the town of 15,000 but which now had swelled to 30,000 with refugees and displaced persons despite a marked decrease in food supplies. The afternoon had been an interesting insight into the surrounding area in the company of a most amusing German monitor. I thanked him profusely.

The next morning the 0800 briefing preceded my first patrol with Jack and Jeff; 'apparently' it was a typical day of work in the Knin area with the Frenchman and the Belgian speaking only French between themselves; oblivious to the fact that I could follow much of their conversation.

Our first rendezvous was a rundown pharmacy from where Jack had arranged to collect Hepatitis A vaccines to take to an outlying village. In conversation with the 'shopkeeper', the title chemist would be far too grand, our interpretress explained that Jack had mistakenly asked for Hepatitis B vaccines and there were none. As there were no Hepatitis A vaccines either we came away empty-handed. I gathered that this was typical obfuscation rather than a cock-up on Jack's part. Nevertheless, it was an obfuscation that I did not understand until the interpretress pointed out that the 'pharmacist' knew that the medicines were for Croats and not Serbs.

Driving for an hour we arrived at a town that appeared to have no name and where we checked the vaccine situation with the director of the local 'hospital', in effect a one-man clinic. There were no vaccines here either, at least not for us to deliver to Croatians. On, then, we went, to a Kenyan army camp to give the platoon commander a lift to meet the commanding officer of the local Serbian battalion. Despite this meeting having been confirmed in advance the Serb officer was not available. Again I was told that this was quite normal and part of a Knin-wide attempt to make our working conditions nigh impossible.

Both 'sides' do not apparently understand what we are trying to achieve and seem to put everything in our way to make our lives difficult. The aim, apparently, is to prevent us operating at all in the hope that under those circumstances we will all go away. The ECMM directives, Standard Operating Procedures (SOPs) and concepts are all very well but I wonder if they reflect what is needed and what is workable, let alone achievable? Not one of them actually says what is involved in monitoring and none of the lectures told us either.

Before lunch we visited the local branch of the United Nation's Civilian Police force (UNCIVPOL) although I was not privy to the reason for this unplanned diversion. In practice this was little more than a minor deviation on our way to reach the highlight of Jack's day; lunch in a hotel in Benkovać, a town as close to the Confrontation Line as it was possible to be. This once-smart establishment, with which I was to become familiar whenever Jack was on patrol, was totally empty yet trying very nobly to keep up appearances.

With the French marine 'replete' we moved on to the humanitarian side of our day by visiting a village so that the inhabitants could telephone their relatives in Croatia using our rather cumbersome mobile telephone. The village had never been visited by the ECMM or the UN while most of the hamlets in this part of the RSK were totally deserted having been ethnically cleansed of most Croats by the Serbian army. Those that remained were living in fear of renewed ethnic cleansing to Croatia as displaced persons and not as refugees.

For a newcomer this last visit of the day was a harsh example of the distastefulness of it all for the queue to use the telephone was simply too long. Each user was allowed a strict five minutes in a forlorn attempt to give as many as possible the chance to make contact 'with the other side.' It was a heart-breaking sight watching faces as they spoke to their kin, sometimes for the first time in two years and us then having to exercise rough discipline in order to give the next in line a chance to do the same. All too often the news from Croatia was bad and not alleviated by the other two monitors, hardened to their task, simply grabbing the handset and pressing the 'off' button before offering it to the next family, at the end of the allotted time.

Back to Knin to type out the patrol report which has to be ready by about 1800 so that it can be incorporated in the Regional Centre's consolidated daily reports from across its three monitoring teams, ready for despatch to ECMM HQ in Zagreb. Any relevant snippets in each team's reports are inserted, highlighted and, hopefully acted upon at a higher international level. At least, I am told, that is the theory but there seems a certain cynicism that nothing actually gets further than our own HQ and even less goes beyond to the international bodies who could, if they were aware of a problem, do something with the information.

I am told that today was a very normal day. Both Jack and Jeff are delighted that they have an Englishman to type the report in English. I may be able to write English but my typing has to be the slowest in the Mission. Eventually I walked back in the dark to the motel which may not have been very wise in my white uniform. This took about three quarters of an hour but I must take some exercise somehow; sitting all day in a Land Rover is not good for the fitness.

7 December turned out to be an interesting day. Following the 0800 briefing for the three Knin teams, November Three set off for a number of destinations although I was to write in my diary that evening:

> I have not yet worked out how the patrols are decided upon or indeed organised and who approves or coordinates them but I suppose it must be the Operations Officer despite him not seeming to take any detailed interest in our work. Thus there is no coordination between the teams: at least, not to my still-untrained eye. No TB testing kits, as yet, which appears to be N3's fault because the Serbs claim that Europe does not use them. I think this is an excuse for not giving them to us as they suspect that we are trying to help a 'minority' village of Croatians—which is partially true but I hope we make no favours for either faction this side of the Confrontation Line. A sick civilian or sick child is still a sick civilian or a sick child in my simple mind.

As soon as we had cleared the town and risen out of its claustrophobic, smog-blanketed valley Jack and Jeff began their daily discussion on where best to stop to make their personal telephone calls home. With an 'intended prescience' I had never let on to my fellow monitors that I was, then, a passable French speaker and, although growing stale, was once a 'colloquial' Arabic speaker (which, too, was to become useful). This made listening to Jack and Jeff interesting and especially so that morning for the conversation, in French, went something like this:

Jack: 'I've been told I'm being sent to the coast at Split. I won't go.' This came as no surprise to me for one of his interminable phrases in his limited English was, 'I soldier. I trained to kill. I not monitor.'

Jeff: 'I wouldn't want to go there either as all one does is study the civil service and the economics.'

I pricked up my ears for this could be the chance for which I and my 'contacts' in London were waiting. If Jack did not want to go to the coast then I most certainly did. Of course, I could not at that moment ask what the coastal duties were without revealing that I understood French so I would have to tackle Patrick before he flew home on leave. Jack and Jeff then continued their interminable 'private' conversations revealing, as so often, their disloyal views of the ECMM and, worse still, of their fellow monitors.

One of our planned stops for the day was the small town of Karin Plaza,[2] at the southern end of the inland sea *Karinsko More*, in order to discuss local problems with local dignitaries. As we approached what in happier days would count as a seaside resort, our interpretress described it to me as being Serbia's only outlet to the sea, even calling it the Serbian Sea. 'As such,' she was interested to know, 'could it, therefore, serve any use as a trading harbour? Is it deep enough? Can ships unload here?'

Pricking up my ears once more I was keen to know too as would be, I hoped, my contact in Defence Intelligence 4, one of whose duties included world-wide beach intelligence and for whom I had worked on and off over the years; regardless of what other tasks I was being employed to undertake at the time.[3]

As we approached from the south-west six artillery shells, fired from Croatia in quick succession, exploded in the water a few hundred yards from the town sending up plumes of sunlit spray and reminding us—quite unnecessarily—that Karin Plaza was very much on the front line.

With the mayor's shattered roof open to the sky, courtesy of an earlier Croat bombardment, we met him and the school's head teacher in the latter's temporary accommodation. Karin Plaza had been shelled recently forcing the teacher to move into another house immediately opposite his own, across a narrow, muddy, rubble-and water-filled street. Here the damage was, apparently, easier to live with.

They received 20 artillery shells on Sunday night.

Towards the end of this meeting, at which we had by then been joined by the local chief of police I realised that any chance of an informal beach reconnaissance was about to slip away. Pleading the need to have a 'pee' and on being told, as I had guessed, that there was no running water in the house it was suggested that I walked down to the beach—'But you will have to have a police escort.'

Walking across the sand towards the tideline I tried to estimate the weight-bearing properties of the foreshore and its exits while trying to recall the half-forgotten 'instructions' in a little-known, naval handbook called *Let's Go Beachcombing*.[4] At the water's edge I took off my shoes, rolled up my trousers and walked into the cool Serbian Sea up to thigh height to begin what was probably the longest pee in Serbian medical history. All the while I was digging the sand with my toes while attempting to gauge the underwater gradient and further weight-bearing properties. Finished, eventually, I turned towards the shore, only then I noticed that my escort was an UNCIVPOL Argentinian policeman wearing what I took to be 'Malvinas war' medals. Despite not being given to spontaneous laughter I was suddenly convulsed for here was an Argentinian army veteran guarding me while I conducted a covert beach reconnaissance on someone else's shore. In broken English I was asked what I found so amusing but I did not have the heart to tell him.

In our HQ I included a brief beach reconnaissance statement in our Daily Report to Brussels.

The possibilities of the RSK using the beach at Karin Plaza as a loading/unloading port were investigated.

Due to the lack of permission to visit the neck of the 'Serbian Sea' and the inadvisability of conducting an overt (or even a covert) survey, only an outline impression was obtained: however it is thought that, at a future date, this may be useful as a starting point for a more detailed study. Naturally, it was not possible to go across the front line to ascertain the suitability of the approaches beyond Ribenica.

Currently this 'harbour' would appear to be the only potential outlet to the open sea available to the RSK and although it is never likely to be suitable for heavy traffic it might be considered feasible for landing craft of a substantial size: yet even this assumption must contain strong caveats as, for instance, the dimensions (and particularly the clearance) of the bridge over the Ribenica Kanal are unknown at present.

Next morning, 8 December, as was becoming my daily habit, I walked from the motel to the headquarters after a cold shower—a very cold shower indeed. One has to make some form of effort as all day is spent sitting in either smoke-filled Land Rover or a smoke-and-raquia-filled room.

Raquia (also spelt *rakia*) was to feature often in my life over the next few months. The rather more acceptable, indeed sometimes delicious, *slivovitz* is made from distilling damson plums while its poorer cousin is the result of distilling the skins of plums and grapes to a proof as high as 80 per cent, apparently. I learned very early that those offering it—usually senior military or police officers, those involved in the civil service such as town mayors or executives from the higher echelons of the few remaining businesses—seldom drank it while assuming that we would do so out of politeness. There was one aim and one aim only and that was for our 'hosts' to assume that they had the advantage over us as they remained sober while we did our polite duty … and made the decisions they wanted us to make. By the time I was to reach the coast and in charge of my own team I had developed a technique of appearing to drink my ever-filled glass while actually pouring most if it into a wide-necked glass jar in my top-opening briefcase placed between my feet. This way I could pretend to have taken the bait while actually remaining on a par of sobriety with my hosts. Thus I hoped I was not such the pushover in our always difficult discussions as they might have believed. It helped too if, at the end of the meeting, I remembered to screw the lid back on.

The day also introduced a rare glimmer of happiness into our lives, although our joy was miniscule when compared with that we witnessed on delivering a large cardboard box to a very elderly woman living alone in a part-ruined village, of which she was one of only five inhabitants. We, of course, had no inkling of the importance of this parcel until she opened it when, suddenly, this noble and dignified Croat lady burst into tears and then uncontrollable sobbing. To begin with I was unsure whether these were tears of elation or sorrow so I stared at anything I could except the single inhabitant of that bare, cold room.

Unknowingly we had delivered to this widow presents from her son in Croatia. Until this poignant and dramatic moment, she had not heard of him for three years, assuming, all that time, that he was long dead. I thought it best we left her to her new found relief but Jeff and Jack did not agree. They were right for it was clear that she needed us to help celebrate this wonderful revelation; which we did with copious quantities of *raquia*, freshly brewed coffee and recently baked bread.

It was, though, time for me to begin engineering my move to the coast in order to carry out some of my Foreign Office instructions and so, before he left for leave the next day, and armed with the news that Jack was refusing to go to Split, I invited Patrick Brook to my motel room for a glass of whisky.

During the conversation, held by candle light with both of us sitting on my bed—my room had no chair—I learned that Paul had already agreed with Patrick that I should move to Split with Robert Lekeu, a Belgian air force lieutenant-colonel of logistics, as the new Team Leader. I suppose I should have queried the ability of a monitor to refuse orders but that would not have been useful to my own aspirations. Patrick was deliciously indiscreet, although perhaps understandably so since we were old friends, and gave me good information on the Danish 'frogman' who was, at that time, the Team Leader in Split—and about to be sacked. Clearly he had no time for the Dane and if what he said was only half true (and I suspected that it was all true) then I could only agree with him that the 'frogman' (or, as Patrick called him, '*l'homme de grenouille*') should not be the Team Leader in such an important Dalmatian city.

As I was the duty monitor that night I slept on a sofa in the headquarters operations room until 0600 on 9 December and yet another patrol to Benkovać in order that Jack and Jeff could make their private telephone calls before the Frenchman enjoyed his lunch. We then returned without having achieved very much.

The atmosphere in the motel could become most lively when there were more than three or four of us but by oneself, as I often was, it was intimidating with the place full of armed and drunk Serb soldiers. On those occasions I changed into civilian clothes; not that I needed any excuse to delay shifting out of the all-white uniform.

With so many 'foreign' journalists using the place one might, with luck, be mistaken for one of them. Good God! ... that will never do ... but the RSK welcomes journalists who will, it is hoped, state their case fairly, while not trusting the ECMM at all. As a monitor rather than a journalist I would not like to get into an argument with a drunk soldier and his badly-maintained Kalashnikov AK 47.

On arrival at the headquarters the next day I was astonished to find that our Land Rover had no starter motor. I remonstrated with Jack, and rather less with Jeff who was too ineffectual to get involved in any difficult discussions. We could easily start it, I explained, by stopping on a hill or getting the dozens of people who turn up at telephone meetings to push-start us but Jack, who saw this as an ideal opportunity to have an unscheduled day off, was adamant. I, too, was adamant that we could not wait until a spare part came from Zagreb via Zadar, at the same time pointing out, in straight forward Anglo-Saxon terms, which I knew Jack most definitely did understand, that we should be out doing our job.

'After all,' I explained, 'we can give these people absolutely bugger all but the one thing we can give them is the ability to telephone their relatives and friends on the other side. We should take every opportunity to do so even if it is not convenient for us. I did not think, I finished, 'that being unable to use the self-starter on our Land Rover is too much of a hindrance to the one piece of humanitarian aid we can offer at the moment.'

I had much to learn. We did not patrol that day and I noted in my diary:

One has to have a strong constitution here—socially, morally, physically and emotionally. Changed for dinner and walked back to the HQ with my own gin and wine bought from the motel bar as a precaution against the inevitable lager (supper was promised but there were no further details) as my stomach cannot take the fizzy 'beer' that we will have to drink at a 'party'.

As it happened the 'party' was not as I was expecting, added to which, a monitor was to join that evening who was to be central to much that happened to Team Split—which I had yet to join—from this day onwards; sometimes for good, but often not.

By the time I arrived in the Operations Room the evening was well underway. Having poured myself a gin and water, before stowing the precious bottles of 'Plymouth' and red wine in a 'secure' place, I turned to greet three new faces.

Two monitors had appeared during the afternoon: one Greek, one Swede plus a French driver. I can now not remember either the Frenchman or the Swede for I was to leave Knin within a fortnight and never saw them again. On the other hand the tall, dark-haired Greek naval officer, Vassilis Dertilis, who was shortly to dominate my life, had me at a disadvantage from the start. He had certainly done his homework. Before I had taken my first sip of the much needed spirit he pushed himself in front of me.

'You are Ewen Tailyour!' It was not a question but a statement of fact and while I was still trying not to look too taken aback he continued, 'I was at your Royal Naval Staff College at Greenwich with a mutual friend, Captain Steve Taylor,' and with that short introduction, without a handshake or a word spoken by me, Vassilis walked away and I took the long-awaited, massive gulp. He had caught me off guard, unable to work out, in those brief moments, why I was suddenly wary; although his overbearing self-confidence should have offered me a clue. Unknown to me, perhaps because I was late at the 'office' pre-dinner drinks, Vassilis had made arrangements for us to eat in Knin Castle to where we were driven in an assortment of Land Rovers and minibuses that, from my brief experience, I knew did not all belong to the ECMM.

The castle, 300 feet above Knin and approached via a winding, narrow and steep lane, which I had visited only a few days earlier with Peter Strauss, was not, as far as I was aware, equipped for dinner parties, or any other form of party, but I was still a new boy and made no comment. All I understood was that it was most definitely a bring-your-own-bottle party but who was supplying the food remains a mystery although it appeared that Vassilis, or his embryo Greek delegation in HQ ECMM, was paying.

On arrival—wondering what on earth we were in for at this out-of-the-ordinary event and where any food was likely to have come from—we were ushered into the great and very draughty hall where two long parallel tables were crossed by an equally long 'top table'. Knives, forks, plates and empty plastic mugs had been set in front of wooden benches. It could have been an English boarding school's dining hall.

My Coca-Cola bottles of red wine were, happily, augmented by Peter's Pepsi bottles of white in a combined effort to introduce some taste into the evening, and all the while I was preparing, with some growing concern, to keep Vassilis Dertilis at arm's length.

Dinner in the castle was interesting and a trial as English was not spoken. Everyone spoke in their own tongue to their neighbours while I maintained my apparent inability to understand French and I certainly don't speak Greek which appeared to be the only other major language of the evening. The help-yourself food was fried, salty cold ham plus a mixed grill of unidentifiable meats and sausages, chips—no vegetables. I was glad to get away in the first vehicle to leave and then, almost as a relief, enjoyed a latish night with a 'self-punishing' raquia or two in the motel's bar.

Vassilis sat at the top table and even gave a speech in English from which I gathered that he is one of the advance party for the day Greece takes over the European presidency from Belgium. A take-over that has already, de facto if not de jure, begun. From what little I know at the moment he would appear to be a Greek naval captain with 'a past'. Already I am not sure that I trust him one inch for he has clearly been sent here for a purpose. Soon I hope we shall see what that purpose is but right now he clearly believes himself already to be in charge and is letting everyone know this.

By 15 December I felt I had experienced enough to write twelve pages of A4 paper to my first cousin, Robert Tailyour.[4]

Nothing in 32 years in the Royal Marines can prepare one for this place …

I am in a town called Knin, the so-called capital of the so-called Republic of Serbian Krajina or RSK. When Yugoslavia began breaking up Croatia was formed but this land also contained a much older state of Krajina, which, illegally, but understandably, then declared independence.

In the RSK the ECMM is seen as a spying organisation in the pay of the Germans, largely because Germany supported Croat independence and also because we are all believed to be German! Nor are we liked because the EU does not insist in supporting the arms embargo not just against Croatia but all the others as well. Many Croat arms and much equipment is German in origin and, more worryingly, many Croat soldiers also wear Nazi emblems on their uniforms.

But neither is the ECMM respected in Croatia because we did nothing to prevent the formation of the RSK within what the Croats regard as Croat territory. The fact that the Krajina has existed for 500 years as a race of people is ignored by the Croats.

From my brief involvement so far, the ECMM seems to be doing an excellent and invaluable job. For a start, it was the first international agency to be involved and all the monitors come from Europe, therefore there is no USA involvement and this pleases all sides as far as I can make out. We monitor the political scene at all levels and report back each day, eventually, to Brussels. In theory!

In addition, we monitor military movements in order to help the brokering of local ceasefires. We can cross borders and unlike UNPROFOR are actually seen to be absolutely neutral for we are involved on both sides of the border.

Although the RSK has declared independence from Croatia, it does not yet want to be part of a larger Serbia, Croatia does not like this because the RSK owns the water supply (therefore, the electricity) and has cut the north–south railway line. Croatia on the other hand, has the ports and outlets to international trade. The stupid thing is that both countries need each other for trade. Neither can exist in isolation. One of our other jobs is to repatriate the dead, and prisoners of war across the border.

Political awareness is limited. Serbs with money, experience and an understanding of international politics have left for foreign countries, leaving the RSK with few educated people. This does not help in our daily talks.

I am writing this in the middle of a thunderstorm by candlelight in a half built motel on the outskirts of Knin.

All international bodies are treated with suspicion and are blamed for the situation:

The ECMM for being spies

The UNPROFOR for having no teeth

The International Committee of the Red Cross for being too selective in its work

The United Nations High Commission for Refugees for being too selective in its distribution of aid.

None of this is true, of course, but tell that to a Croat or a Serb. Apart from the British monitors, most of the rest are civilians or serving military personnel and are here for a year. Consequently, not many of them have their heart in the job so the attitude is far too often: It is impossible. I'm used to saying let's give it a try but one French marine officer and one Belgian warrant officer in my team will find every excuse not to go on a patrol. They will be glad when I move away to the coast next week.

Our daily work starts about 0600 with a briefing. Then we are on the road visiting local hamlets with those very few Croats who still live in them, making sure they have not been massacred by the RSK. We carry French tin hats and flak jackets as every day there are cross-border shellings on to civilian villages. For instance, 1000 artillery rounds were fired into Croatia the day before yesterday, then 70 rounds came back during a three pronged attack into the RSK in our area. This includes the RSK shelling of a school deep in Croatia to show just how far they can reach.

There is far too much hatred on all sides, each country proclaiming itself to be whiter than white but they are all as black as black as far as I am concerned. I have personally seen ethnic cleansing on both sides and hear of horrifying atrocities. We are vulnerable and unarmed. Yesterday two of our Land Rovers were shot at, each by about 15 high velocity rounds. Each night there is shooting around our hotel, but usually just drunken immature soldiers.

Next week I will move to the coast where the ECMM has a number of teams. In Split I will be working with a Belgian monitor. One of our jobs will be to negotiate a new border crossing point in the south of the RSK, so that aid and food for ECMM and UNPROFOR can get into the RSK more easily. I don't hold out much for our chances or the route. Both being mined on all sides … Other tasks will be to help the EU decide where money for the regeneration will best be spent.

My other job, I have been told by the FCO (nothing to do with the ECMM) is to keep an eye on the Algerian and Iranian influence in the port of Split. They (along with the US and Germany who are helping Croatia) are believed to be breaking the embargo by supplying logistic support to the Muslims in Bosnia. I shall also be monitoring the political and economic positions in the ports and on the islands.

I have conducted a covert beach reconnaissance on the edge of a 'lake' in the Republic of Serbian Krajina, which is linked to the Med through other lakes held by Croatia. Beach surveys take on a different meaning with armed, United Nations civilian policemen watching my every move—an Argentine would you believe! I had a very long pee off the beach into the lake and so managed a three page special report for DI4. Fascinating stuff!

To sum up, I am seeing things here I hope never to see again and meeting people I sincerely hope never to meet again but that is why we are here and, I believe, doing a most worthwhile job. But thank God for all my Royal Marines training and experience.

12 December was Election Day across the Republic of Serbian Krajina. For Team November Three of the ECMM's Regional Centre, Knin, it was a day of contrasting

monitoring activities beginning with a dawn thunderstorm followed by one high velocity shot immediately outside my window as I was dressing. Elsewhere it was a clear, cold morning with snow on the closer hills. Jack, Jeff and myself were due to visit a Kenyan battalion stationed just our side of the Confrontation Line, responsible for monitoring Serbian military activities and the breaking of ceasefires along their section of the border.

As we drove down Knin's main street towards the road that led up the escarpment we passed a familiar shop, from which Peter would buy his wines. It had been destroyed during the night. Extraordinarily, it was owned by a Serb woman who managed to obtain her rare produce from the Croat coast to sell, rather understandably, at a high price. Now her shop had been gutted out of jealousy by some who could not afford to pay her charges. 'But,' the duty interpretress explained, 'I know her and she will start up again tomorrow ...' and she did.

Due to Jeff's Belgian-style map reading skills—I was never privy to a map in the back of the Land Rover which may have been just as well—finding the Kenyan battalion was not easy and yet the delay was to be worth it despite part of our detour including a disturbing incident. Frustration at the Belgian infantry warrant officer's inability to read a map forced me into the left-hand passenger seat (our Land Rovers were right-hand drive) a few minutes before we were stopped by an impromptu roadblock manned by the RSK army. With soldiers leaning into both the open passenger and driver's windows the smell of second-hand *raquia*, garlic and fish stew was overpowering—and even that word was not strong enough to describe the stench! For some reason they had taken exception to our presence in the area and were pointing their cocked AK 47s across the front of our noses, inside the windscreen. The one on the left, nearest to me, fired a burst that passed about three inches in front of my and Jack's heads to disappear out of the driver's window where it impacted in a cloud of dust in the dried scrubland; sadly just missing his colleague! My only sensible reaction was to show no reaction; then, realising they might just have overstepped the mark, even for a drunk, we were instantly waved on our way with ears ringing. Had I been armed I would almost certainly—and ill-advisedly—have shot the bastard dead!

Despite the surrounding countryside being targeted by, as it turned out, 70 artillery shells that morning we were given a most professional brief by a Kenyan army officer on the recent and current situation. This expert brief was conducted over an equally excellent breakfast of omelettes and bacon. The officers' mess was one of the four corners of a huge gym-like hall with absolutely nothing in it but serving counters, a scattering of trestle tables and collapsible chairs. One of the other three corners contained the senior non-commissioned officers' mess while the other two were 'offices'. The camp had no running water: water for drinking, washing, washing up, laundry and 'flushing' the 'lavatories' was collected in buckets from an oil drum outside but from where that was filled was not obvious, and I did not ask!

It was all rather civilised with the close artillery rounds impacting throughout our visit supplying little more than a stimulating, audible backdrop to the overall military- and business-like atmosphere. It did, though, strike me as odd that the shelling stopped as soon as we left. One aspect that did not strike me as being odd but that certainly struck me as being amusing—yet practical—was the headdress the Kenyan soldiers wore. To keep out the cold, instead of their blue, United Nations helmets most wore fur-lined, blue hats on top of blue, woollen balaclavas. It was difficult not to smile let alone laugh but that would have been to mock unkindly a very practical solution to their 'ethnic' problem of 'climate control'.

The moment we arrived back at our headquarters my life, quite unexpectedly, took a turn upwards when Jack and Jeff were peremptorily dismissed from the front of the Land Rover to be replaced by a French driver and Paul Ortholan our urbane, civilised, French head of the Regional Centre. Mysteriously, he whispered to me to be quiet or to speak only in Arabic. As instructed I remained, puzzled, in the back with the duty interpretress.

Over the preceding days I had heard the name of a Serb army officer mentioned a number of times by other monitors and whenever his name cropped up the interpretresses would, theatrically, pretend to swoon. However the answers to my questions had been vague: nobody had ever actually met him although some had occasionally pointed to a far hill overlooking the coastal plain while explaining that 'over there' is where he has his training camp. 'Training whom and for what?' Nobody knew anything other than that Captain Dragan Vasiljković was a Serb idol, a war hero best left alone: supposedly a shady character who spoke with an Australian accent having served with the Australians in Vietnam.

The head of our Regional Centre must have done his homework for as we drove away from the headquarters he turned and said, in English, 'I hope this will please you. At last we are going to meet Captain Dragan.'

First we had to run the gauntlet of the local Canadian platoon commander. Lieutenant Kevin Brown was a prickly officer in whose domain Captain Dragan lived and my first impression of him was exactly as described. He did not like civilians in any form nor of any nationality and, as I noted at the time, treated us all with disdain; if he bothered to take any notice of us at all. During our initial briefing it was clear that he was talking to us under sufferance, especially as a three-pronged attack was at that moment in progress from Croatia into the RSK, aimed at the Miranje crossing. Indeed, from inside his briefing room we could hear an exchange of distant artillery fire. After his briefing I felt it necessary to take Kevin aside and explain my military background, why I was there and why I was particularly keen to meet Captain Dragan. Quite suddenly, but as I hoped, we became confidantes. Shortly, he was to connive with me in fixing a private visit to 'The Captain', a visit that was to be known only by, and sanctioned only by, himself and Paul.

Now Kevin drove us in his Mercedes 'jeep' through the low mountain passes to Captain Dragan's camp, accompanied by a well-armed Canadian escort while

Paul and I, in our ECMM white uniforms, were equipped only with my camera and a notebook. This was one of the rare occasions that I carried a camera for if stopped by an RSK patrol they were in the habit of destroying them on the spot. As mine was my mother's 1934 Leica I was not keen for this to happen. I also owned a modern Leica but it was rather less reliable.

The entrance to the camp was a surprise. Instantly it was obvious we were entering a well-disciplined military establishment unlike any I saw either in the RSK or later in Croatia. The 'front' gate was robust, smart and well-guarded by uniformed, red-bereted, fit-looking soldiers with clean, modern, Russian weapons. Standing just inside was the thin, almost gaunt, Captain Dragan wearing 'patrol uniform' with a pistol and two grenades clipped to his belt. He shook our hands and greeted us enthusiastically. My immediate perception was that he spoke with a South African rather than an Australian accent while my second impression was that he was too 'macho' to be a good soldier although, I thought at the time, he might actually be a good leader. Later that evening I wrote:

> There was something strangely suspicious about him that I cannot put my finger on as the result of the one visit.

Dragan led us to his office where a westerly facing window looked out and down across the coastal plain towards the Adriatic. On the opposite side of the room the wall was largely covered by a huge map that depicted both sides of the Confrontation Line while it was obvious, from the pile of them in a mug, that all the coloured pins had been removed for our visit.

Over coffee Paul questioned him at length, in English (which they both spoke perfectly) about his political beliefs *vis-á-vis* the RSK and Croatia from which, in addition to other personal revelations, it was clear that he was vehemently anti-German. I discovered later that he had a German wife or, rather, had had a German wife whom he still saw in Belgrade. He believed, passionately, that there should be a buffer zone along the Confrontation Line, a form of 'green line' patrolled jointly by the UN and the RSK but not Croatia (which might have been a flaw in his argument). He said that he would accept the green line being almost anywhere providing that his camp was not re-aligned into Croatia and that it stopped the killing.

In the wider context Dragan confirmed that all Serbs with money had quit the country, leaving a very low grade population to run the army and the Government which, he said, was why his country was in such a poor state. From all accounts Croatia had the same problem, indeed this fact was one of the more serious aspects hampering progress throughout the whole of the Former Republic of Yugoslavia. The RSK, Dragan suggested, was not interested in the Dalmatian coast or its ports although I thought this was unlikely as, apart from Karen Plaza, the country had no outlet to the sea for which, all knew, it was desperate to possess.

He just wanted independence from Nazi-influenced Croatia and the end of all Nazi symbols and signs. If, he explained, Croatia was to give up any pretence of returning to its *Ustaše*-style outlook—in his view, the catalyst to everything that was happening—then the RSK could accept being part of Croatia but unless that happened independence from Croatia was the only way ahead.

Dragan claimed to train the RSK's special forces and that he had, personally and 'proudly' taken part in 140 missions into Croatia. He believed that Germany would eventually take over the whole of Europe and that what was happening in the Former Yugoslavia was an extension of the Second World War by another means: former Nazis, with tacit German support (although I suspected that the current German government would most definitely not be approving the swastikas and other outward signs of quasi-Nazi influence) was supporting Croatia in its bid to subjugate the Krajinas, as well as joining the European Union.[6] He believed, further, that if Croatia continued to receive *materiel* support from Germany and the US in contravention of UN Arms Embargo 713—now I listened even more intensely—it could then crush the RSK through rigorous ethnic cleansing.[7] It would be Greece's turn next followed by the rest of Europe, at which point I nodded politely but thought he was becoming a touch carried away! Finally, he admitted that Greece was continuing to help Serbia, a fact that was to come home to roost very firmly with what were to become my far-from-delicate, seesawing relations with the new Greek monitor, Vassilis Dertilis.

After two most affable hours Kevin Brown returned us to our own transport and we set off for Knin in the ECMM Land Rover.

On the way back Paul asked for my initial comments but as soon as I began to state that Dragan spoke with a South African accent rather than an Australian one Paul immediately burst into Arabic telling me not to say any more in front of the interpretress, who also spoke a modicum of French. He would discuss the matter in private on our return.

In Paul's office I could offer no more information about Captain Dragan other than to confirm that he did indeed speak English with a South African accent: I never knew why this was important to Paul. My own interest, though, had taken a turn upwards and, privately, I determined to find out more about this enigmatic man. That evening I wrote to my SIS contact, a retired British army major and friend from the Falklands campaign, with whom, prior to this present posting, I had discussed his various requests. Now I asked him one of my own; could he offer any information about Captain Vasiljković if, indeed he had ever heard of him. Forgetting Dragan for a moment I wrote in my diary that evening:

All 'sides' are subject to UN Arms Embargo 713 but some European nations, that should be jointly enforcing them, are themselves breaking them to support their various favourite or aligned, Balkan states. Very puzzling that the very embargoes we—a cross section of European monitors—are supposed to be monitoring are being broken by the countries we represent. The main 'criminals' in this respect seem to be the US, Italy, Germany, France and Greece plus of course some Middle East and North African countries such as Algeria and Iran—and Russia.

Amazing thunderstorm which has flooded my bedroom to about an inch all over the floor. This will explain why all the wooden blocks have lifted off the concrete floor long ago and on which I am always stubbing my toes in the dark and why the room is permanently damp and mouldy. No electricity but luckily I had just boiled the kettle and I am able to write by candle light. At dinner I was joined by Adrian Brown of the Daily Telegraph in the motel's restaurant which is a grand name for a square room with a very loud TV hanging from the ceiling, faded newspaper cuttings on the wall and a noisy and very busy bar at one end and not much else. Sent messages to Max Hastings for fun, Robert Fox and Patrick Bishop (all of whom Adrian says he knows) but I don't suppose they will get them.

By 14 December Team November Three's transport problems had still to be resolved yet clearly they were not going to be fixed in a hurry if Jack and Jeff had their way.

I will be glad (I think) to get to Split where I will be (and certainly intend to be) more of my own boss. Raining. Still no transport again so wrote special report for DI 4 on the possibilities of the RSK using Karen Plaza as an outlet to the Mediterranean. I described the place as being useful for smallish landing craft if ever Croatia could guarantee safe passage through the two narrow waterways that lead to the open sea. I estimated the beach gradients above and below the waterline; the 'trafficabilty' for both wheeled and tracked vehicles; the beach exits for men on foot; any cover from defensive fire; the 'fetch' from the far shore and thus the possible sea state in a north-north-westerly wind and the nature and suitability of the anchorage.

Then it was back to planning for the future knowing that the work on the coast would be rather more political and economic than military for all hopes for the financial regeneration of Croatia relied heavily, if not totally, on the Dalmatian coast. It was there that we, in the ECMM, might be able to make a difference. I mused, too, on other matters.

The country on both sides of the Confrontation Line is lovely and the people are probably nice underneath but there is not much evidence now in 1993. They all see us as spies and 'on the other side' regardless of which side of the 'border' we are actually on: thus they are hardly likely to show us their true face. The often-repeated saying is that the Serbs do not know how to hate and the Croats do not know how to love. I am sure that in Croatia they are saying the opposite! My personal view is that everybody knows how to hate and few, if any, know how to love.

Writing this at lunch in the motel surrounded by armed RSK soldiers with me alone at my table dressed from head to toe in ECMM white uniform feeling extremely conspicuous while deep in Serbian-occupied Croatia. They are becoming very drunk and noisy.

Had supper by myself—I think they were goat burgers but it felt as though I was chewing my own teeth. The better culinary news is that my trousers are already beginning to fit more comfortably around the waist! Too many pistol shots outside the window in the very dim and flickering light of the restaurant/bar. All the locals left in a rush but I couldn't think of any reason to follow them; apart from that I was hungry.

Local matters were occasionally overshadowed by echoes from home. In the middle of one morning briefing a bigoted IRA-sympathising Irishman called Fergus offered a tirade about how his country had been treated over the years. This was an extra-ordinarily unsavoury outburst during which I learned that at a party the night before he had brought a present for me which, in my absence, he then left on the mantelpiece under a notice with my name on it. During the morning's outburst he pointed to an IRA training pamphlet and a rifle bullet which had been placed with it to 'tease me and to watch my reaction'. Had I been at the party I trust that I would not have reacted in the manner he hoped but I could not help reflect that had I done the same to him with a Loyalist training manual about how to murder 'Provos' he would have lost his temper with awful results. Of that I had no doubt at all.

I brushed aside Fergus's immature 'threat' and joined Team November Three. After stopping for Jack and Jeff to make the first of their daily calls home we called on an RSK army unit for some long-forgotten reason except that, as usual, I remember that it involved three tots of *raquia*, with two poured into my brief case, before we headed once more for the Canadian platoon and the civilian-despising Kevin Brown. However, on this my second visit he treated me from the start as though I was still a serving Royal Marines lieutenant-colonel, which I was not, and admitted that before our last visit he had mentioned my name to Dragan who seemed to know it from somewhere. The remarkable outcome is that I have been asked, by Dragan Vasiljković to call on him for a special one-to-one, private meeting tomorrow. I was instructed to wear civilian clothes.

My enthusiasm for moving to the coast took a tiny dent the next day. At the morning briefing it was announced that the outgoing Belgian Director of Operations, who, according to the piano playing Dane, Lennart Leschly, was a most self-important man, was planning to visit Split on Christmas Day and leave at 0630 on Boxing Day. All agreed this was bad news for the unfortunate Team

Split while they also knew that the major-general was not a man of action and would never venture to the Knin side of the Confrontation Line. He has ordered us all, I was by now regarding myself as a member of Team Split, to be in white uniform and lined-up for his inspection on his arrival.

> I shall, of course, (!) be as charming and polite as I can muster but, personally, I will either want to spend Christmas Day my way or at least with any British I can find in Split. I certainly do not want to spend it with a Belgian general who is expecting us (so I have been warned) all to stand rigidly to attention while we are talking to him.
>
> Interesting dinner in the motel for at the next door table in the dark (actually Šifko has a generator which he eventually got going) was the new President of the RSK, Milan Babić,[8] a dentist and, lately I believe, the Chief of Police in Knin. I congratulated him on his 'election' and was rewarded with a glass of raquia and a long, one-sided 'conversation' about how he saw the RSK's future although he was aware that 'Bosnia proper' was not about to come to his aid or take it into its fold.

On the morrow, and with Paul's enthusiastic agreement, I dressed in my white uniform, packed suitable civilian clothes for my visit to the Dragan's Lair, as I nicknamed it, and was driven in November Three's dodgy Land Rover to meet the now genial Kevin Brown. Jack and Jeff were left with an ideal excuse to do nothing all morning. As Kevin drove just the two of us in his own Mercedes 'jeep' through the shallow mountain passes I was uncertain whether or not I was being set-up for something altogether less than pleasant. Unhelpfully, Kevin, who was at least armed, was of the same view. As this was a non-ECMM visit and, as far as I was concerned, I was off-duty and now in civilian clothes, I had considered asking to borrow a 9 mm Browning pistol, or whatever the equivalent it was that Canadian forces carried as a side-arm but, reluctantly, decided against the idea.

Dragan was waiting for us at his main gate, still armed with pistols and grenades around his waist. Kevin dropped me with the promise that he would return in two hours. I was now alone and in the hands of one of the most unpredictable and—if rumours were correct—one of the most dangerous characters in Serbia!

To begin with, over coffee served in cups—with saucers!—Dragan told me that because he knew of my Royal Marines' background he was anxious to discuss our training methods. The *quid pro quo* was that in return he would be delighted to show me his camp, his training teams and the men under drill while keen to discuss his operational procedures and current operations. Although he never said so, it was obvious that he wanted all of this to be reported back to the United Kingdom, by-passing the ECMM's convoluted and unreliable communications: of which he was suspiciously aware. I received the clear impression that he knew I was not only answering to the European Community Monitoring Mission but also direct to my own Foreign Office. I made no comment and let him talk on.

Absolutely fascinating—his camp can see the sea and thus all the Croat land between. Dragan's men have so far (apparently) completed 116 missions into 'enemy' territory and have suffered no deaths or casualties due to enemy action. He is unpaid—I think—and runs this specialist camp with about 1,000 men under training although I have to say I think that this figure has to be a vast exaggeration. Every night patrols are sent from the camp to reconnoitre enemy artillery positions as we are, Dragan says, just outside 155 mm artillery range of Croatia. This seems unlikely to me but I will check the ranges on the map now that I know where we are.

By RSK standards the men are drilled and trained very well and on passing the course as specialist infantryman are awarded a red beret. He has difficultly with his own senior officers in Serbia for they are suspicious of his overall motives but it does appear that he is slowly building up a cadre of junior officers who have reached a standard higher than any formal Serbian army training. He also runs the Dragan Foundation for, he claims, the wounded of all sides and on today's showing I have no reason to doubt his sincerity in this. A glossy brochure is well supportive of this Foundation but does only show, as far as I can make out, those from Serbia being helped—but, if only half true, it does seem to be a noble gesture and, coupled with what I have heard elsewhere, explains why he is very much a hero in his own country if not, rather obviously, in Croatia.

Everything in his camp is done, built, acquired or made through self-help. He is even given soldiers on punishment from the RSK to train them into better soldiers but not, in their case, into red beret soldiers. They are here as punishment and are employed only in the menial tasks. Ten months ago the whole area was a burned-out clothes factory—funny how everywhere we find people living in old buildings that turn out to have been ex-clothes factories! It is a quite remarkable set up. All his red-beret men are trained as scouts—for which read 'reconnaissance' troops. Helicopter drills are practised I am told but I never saw a helicopter and as some of his descriptions of helicopter operations did not quite ring true to my understanding of such affairs I doubt that they existed. The men are also trained in photography and I was shown some of their results—assuming they are true. He uses GPS a great deal (which someone must have funded). He also has some Passive Night Vision Goggles which will certainly need to be funded by someone. He also has (he claims) thermal imagers and laser target markers although I was not shown these. It is, though, the most spotless place I have seen since arriving out here and that includes our own quarters and HQ and Hotel 'I' and so full marks to Captain Dragan for his attitude to cleanliness. As he explained on my first visit he has a great hatred of the Germans and an exceptional allegiance to our own Queen.

He claims that he himself has led a very large number of patrols into Croatia although he insists that they were mainly to recce and destroy the guns that were firing into the RSK. Interestingly he can see the sea from his camp and must be within range of Croat artillery, despite his claims. The Croats must know where he is and yet he has never been targeted by Croat guns. Odd, as I don't give the Croats that much intelligence to be playing a game of double bluff or that they have worked out that by not killing him it will do the Croat cause a greater deal of good. In the same way that Paisley has never, as far as my limited knowledge of Northern Ireland affairs is aware, been killed by the IRA!

Eventually, on the way back to the main gate and my lift home, I was shown a cadre of 'foreign' soldiers under training. They were, I was told with no hint of conspiracy, from the Italian Garibaldi Brigade. This mechanised infantry brigade had (and still has) at its core the 1st Bersaglieri Infantry Regiment, who formed (and still form) one of the elite infantry corps of the Italian army. This extraordinary sight, in the middle of 'Serbian occupied' Croatia, could not have been fabricated and was a fact that I decided to keep from the ECMM but relay direct to my SIS contact.

And what lay behind Dragan's desire to produce better-than-average Serbian soldiers? I asked the question but his answer was, perhaps understandably, evasive. Perhaps his real motive for excellent training lay beyond his own country and is best described in part of a letter of mine that was published in *The Daily Telegraph* on 20 November 2000:

> Why, when as an FCO-employed European Community monitor in the Republic of Serbian Krajina, was I shown, in some secrecy by one Captain Dragan (whose name cropped up recently in Belgrade) in his mountain camp overlooking Croatia, a section of regular Italian soldiers being trained by him 'against the day Italy decides to take back that part of northern Dalmatia lost to the Germans at the end of the Second World War?' Dragan knew well that his revelations to me would reach the outside world but not via the European monitoring system.

One incident I did tackle Dragon on in answer to his clearly stated view that the RSK was totally innocent of any war crimes was the shelling of school children evacuated to an offshore island. I must have touched a nerve because he vehemently denied that he himself had committed any war crime although he also admitted that he was accused of doing so. He made it plain to me that as he had no artillery, and certainly no weapons capable of reaching an offshore island, he could not be responsible for such an atrocity. It certainly seemed to go against all that he told me about his foundation and the desire to do, in Serbian eyes, good works.

Later on I was to send a report on this visit to my SIS contact but it is necessary to paraphrase it here.

> Dragan received me in a very friendly manner and provided me with a short introduction, followed by a thorough tour of the camp including parade grounds, operations rooms, briefing rooms, kitchens, the medical centre and even a

prison. The camp was built by Captain Dragan's soldiers and is well organised, orderly and clean. The soldiers appeared well disciplined.

Dragan is an educated, English-speaking Serb who, he told me, had lived most of his life in Australia (although his accent is more South African). He has adopted many western military traditions as I believe that he served as a captain in the Australian Army's Royal Victoria Regiment.

His motivation for serving in the RSK appears to be pride as a Serb and not for monetary reasons. He feels deeply that the world community has been treating the Serbs unfairly and that Croat propaganda (supported by Germany) has succeeded in creating a common opinion of the Serbs as bad people.

Dragan informed me that he joined the Serb army in 1991. In 1992 he established a foundation in Belgrade, which supports victims of the war and has thus gained great fame. In March 1993 he returned to Krajina in order to establish his special training camp to produce the 'red berets' of specially trained soldiers for he is convinced that Krajina needs a small army of disciplined soldiers with better basic skills.

Dragan appears to have a great influence, both in Krajina and in Serbia where he is, in his words, 'popular among the common people'. He is about 45 years old is very fit, articulate, logical—and convincing.

Training is at a basic level. A 14 day course [there was some confusion over the length of the various training courses] is conducted in specialist skills such as scouting (reconnaissance in depth) anti-tank, sniper and pioneer duties up to corporal level. This training includes practical exercises along the Confrontation Line. On completion of the training the Serbs are awarded the red beret which they wear with pride. Captain Dragan tries to raise the basic qualities of the soldiers and JNCOs to make the RSK's military more effective and efficient.

Captain Dragan believes that the RSK army should be cut to approximately 15,000 well-trained soldiers rather than 90,000 amateurs and, again in his words, who are little more than uniformed bandits.

A possible solution to the present stalemate, as (perhaps naively) offered by Dragan, is to establish a green line between Croatia and the Krajina occupied only by a strong United Nations force. This would permit both governments to stop the hostilities for the international community would not, then permit any armed hostilities from either side. Any violation of the green line would be met with immediate response from the strong international military force.

Deep in a plethora of mixed and opposing thoughts I retraced my circuitous route to Knin where Jack and Jeff were waiting to conduct an afternoon of telephone calls and when, once more, I was horrified by the team's attitude towards the hapless civilians.

Jeff van Haven's treatment with the people whose names did not appear on the lists to make telephone calls was shameful. I knew it was a 'free' service and they should not have had to rely on it—but nothing should be set in so much cement. Many of the people were very simple, terrified and cut off from their loved ones and families—and I did not give a damn whether or not they were Serbs or Croats. I felt very sorry indeed for the last two women denied their calls and felt the need to distance myself from Jeff's behaviour.

It is galling to be number three of a team such as this.

I knew I had not been in Knin long but this was a simple case of humanitarian behaviour and it was no wonder to me that the ECMM had a bad name in some quarters. Such displays of bad manners did not help. What maddened me was that Jeff and Jack telephoned their own homes at least twice and sometimes four times a day for no apparent reason that I could ascertain from listening to their conversations.

Much shelling to the west of Benkovać and a certain amount of high velocity automatic fire along the south of the town as we were conducting the telephone service outside the Orthodox church which I visited with the communications girl from, I think, Denmark. She is a new signaller that has arrived in the HQ. In her other life she is a nurse with the Danish army who has been sent to the ECMM as a signaller which seems very odd indeed but there we are.

I am beginning to think that the ECMM is not very dynamic and is a poorly organised affair as far as some of the individuals in Knin are concerned. Most are here to serve out their time and clearly some are here because they are too old for service elsewhere in their own armed forces while others are here because they are too inexperienced and have been sent here to get some 'time in' before returning to their parent units.

The UK is one of a few countries to send retired, experienced military and diplomatic people to the ECMM.

I had supper by myself that night as Larry, the new Canadian monitor, and Lennart had returned to the HQ so they could follow the details of the latest prisoner of war (POW) exchange. Neither of them had any part to play in this operation but were inquisitive although, as the HQ's Operations Officer, perhaps Lennart felt he should exercise a passing interest! By 1700 there had been no word from the POW exchange team and as no POWs had been swapped by that time either, there was an ominous mood in the HQ for the monitors' safety.

The early evening of my penultimate day in Knin was marked by more shooting of high velocity, light machine guns outside my window than had been the norm but this time these bursts were accompanied, when I could hear them in a lull, by low velocity pistol shots.

But I suppose it is Saturday night!

Later in the evening, as I was preparing to turn in, an almost continuous amount of automatic, belt-fed bursts forced me to bed wearing my pheasant-shooting, ear defenders in order to get some sleep. Just as I was dozing off more belt-fed firing broke into my near-dreaming state until, just when I reckoned they must have run out of ammunition what sounded like, and probably was, a 3 inch mortar round exploding very close. As my window remained intact I did not look out and finally drifted off.

Apparently the POWs were exchanged at about 0100 this morning—19 December—but as they were not all being handed over at the same place the numbers from each side to be returned at a number of different locations had to tally which must have been a nightmare for the placid and phlegmatic Tony Smith, a retired Royal Artillery officer who had also seen service in the Oman. There are three ex-Oman army officers in Knin itself and probably more among the British throughout the ECMM. Patrick Brook had commanded the Sultan's Armed Forces armoured regiment and I had commanded A Company of the Northern Frontier Regiment.

Despite having had a long and tiring night Paul Ortholan summoned me to his office early the next morning and, behind a firmly closed door, gave me a very full brief on what I would find in Split and what he wanted me to do about it. Following these revelations—for they were nothing less—he offered some hints and ideas for the future of monitoring along the coast that he would like me to consider once I had had a week or two to understand the situation. The current state is that the leader of Team Split, Peter Noppeneau a Danish naval commander who is also 'frogman' trained, has been accused of 'spying' by the military authorities in Split.

A Danish frogman has been caught gathering 'amphibious' information in Split … what on earth the Danes will do with the sort of information he has been collecting one can only imagine and laugh.

Additionally, Paul was unconvinced that Peter was carrying out his ECMM duties in accordance with our guidelines while Noppeneau's second-in-command of Team Split was Willy van der Bossche, a captain in the Belgian infantry, who was forging a relationship with one of the married interpretresses. Paul confirmed that he was sacking Peter from the ECMM and not just from Team Split and, rather surprisingly I thought, making Robert Lekeu, the elderly, Belgian air force lieutenant-colonel the Team Leader. Robert, who I suspected with good reason to be verging on senility, had left a few days earlier to take over his new 'command'. As I knew that Robert's only aim in life was to hand out teddy bears that were being sent across 'in bulk' from Croatia for distribution among those few remaining Croat families in the RSK, I tried not to raise an eyebrow.

Added to all this Paul had been given permission to double the size of the Split team by forming a second team to cover the coast south as far as Dubrovnik, including the adjacent offshore islands. However he knew that the current composition at Split was too small for such expansion so his longer term plan was for me first to establish, then command a new Coordinating Centre in the town. When fully complemented I would then lead this second team in the south. He appreciated that although I would be the most junior monitor in the ECMM pecking order in Split I was to prepare myself for rapid promotion! 'Indeed,' he said quietly, 'I need you to start influencing events as soon as you arrive in preparation for this exciting future'.

What a strange place—responsibility with no mandate or power or is it power with no mandate or responsibilities! We shall see but it is clear from Paul that he has no time for the outgoing Team Leader, Noppeneau, while Robert Lekeu's only aim is to distribute teddy bears to the children. If that is all he does for the rest of his time out here he will be supremely happy but this does not bode well for our work on the coast which is, or will be, the most important area if peace ever comes to this part of the world. Anyway while I agree with giving out teddy bears that is not what we are here to do as there are plenty of NGO aid agencies doing that sort of thing. As a very minor part of our life when we visit villages and refugees camps it is nice to give the children something although the adults keep on telling us they would rather we gave them peace.

The Greeks are going to change many things to mask their territorial problems with Macedonia and to make things difficult for the Germans who will take over from them in the summer.

Packed in afternoon with yet more shooting as I did so. A continuous 'fire-power' demonstration. Also many explosions. While changing, much LMG firing and banging all around, continuing while I am trying to listen to Mozart's Clarinet Concert.

Paid my bill which was interesting as I seemed to have made a profit and don't understand why or how but as long as Šifko is happy I suppose all is well. Oddly, very oddly, I sense a certain sadness at leaving Knin but excited by Split—I hope this is not a false hope.

Bed, accompanied by much shooting, at 2300 although it seems like 0300.

4
Suicide (or Murder?) in Split

Monday, 20 December 1993.

Up early to finish packing in time for the 'shuttle' to Zadar.

Paul Ortholan joined me in the back of the cramped minibus on his way to Zagreb and leave. This was helpful as with my appalling and his fluent Arabic—a language rarely spoken in the ECMM, unlike French which might have been easier but less secure—he continued to brief me about the 'goings-on' in Hotel Split.

In Zadar we enjoyed a lunch of fresh salad and vegetables—a forgotten experience—before Paul continued north and I headed south to Split in another minibus. As before, I had been acutely embarrassed to be eating so well in front of the refugees and displaced persons: a feeling that, rather surprisingly, was seldom shared by my fellow monitors.

As the Dalmatian pelican might fly, the distance to Split from Zadar is just under 80 miles but as the ECMM shuttle travels around the coast, via the resort of Šibenik, it was more like 100 and took a good three hours. Had I known the greeting that was awaiting me I might have wished the journey had taken rather longer. Hotel Split[1] considered itself one of the finest five-star hotels in the city but in reality it had become a 'five-star hotel without the stars'. It was, though, still regarded by the smart set of Split to be the place to be seen and, indeed, its basement or 'downstairs' Café Riva Restaurant overlooking the Adriatic struggled, surprisingly successfully, to maintain a pre-war standard with 'gala dinners and dances'. The hotel boasted a grand entrance leading to a wide foyer, part of which was taken up by an astonishingly well-stocked bar and beyond, a swimming pool and the Riva Terrace Bar while, above, 280 comfortable but standard-shaped rooms across six upper floors supplied the accommodation. On the two seaward-facing corners these were *en suite* apartments with their rooms' wide windows facing across the six-nautical-miles wide *Brački Kanal* towards that island.

I humped my suitcases into the foyer to 'book in' and while doing so was confronted by an unfriendly Willy van den Bossche and an even more hostile Peter Noppeneau. Without bothering to shake my offered hand they both made it clear that I was not welcome in Split; indeed, in Peter's case, and as soon as he could, he made it obvious that I was the reason for his dismissal. As I had not known of him until a few days earlier I was puzzled by this sudden attack. Excusing myself from this unexpected unpleasantness, I navigated my way to Room 519.

A comfortable room with a view of the Adriatic and a plug in the basin and, so far, hot water. I took the shower head to bits to clean it out so that it sprayed more than two tiny dribbles. Now working pretty well. It hasn't taken long to realise that my room overlooks the entrance to Split harbour and therefore Split naval base which I will find very useful indeed for my 'other' work.

My first evening in Split continued to be thought-provoking! Via a circuitous route I eventually found my way to the 'upstairs' ECMM dining room, a soulless, high-ceilinged 'space' on the ground floor whose west-facing windows looked across a crumbling terrace of near-slum, two-storied dwellings. Along the windowless south wall was a lengthy, help-yourself table of cold meats and huge bowls of green and black olives that, I was to discover, would form the staple to my future diet! These 'delicacies' surrounded three cauldrons that contained the 'dish of the day' but to my then-untrained eye looked more like thin soup in which floated small meaty 'croutons': but whether they were fin, feather or fur would remained unsolved. This cafeteria arrangement was only for the use of the ECMM and was partitioned off from the remaining three quarters of the large room that was never used by the monitors. The room itself was at the end of a wide passageway that led from the lobby, along which lines of refugees and displaced people queued for a form of 'gruel' and bread. This 'pot mess' they took across the car park to their desperately overcrowded apartments.

Dinner with Robert Lekeu was difficult as he has very strange ideas of what we are to do on the coast and they very definitely do not tie in with what Paul has told me to set up and then 'get under way'. The immediate future may be tricky as Paul has given me unofficial powers, as it were, and yet I am, again, number three in a team of three. Noble gesture though it might be the distribution of teddy bears is not what the ECMM is about.

On my way to bed via the staircase, raised voices were arguing vulgarly and vociferously by the Foyer Bar. I turned and watched two men dressed in Croat army combat clothes, screaming at each other across a table. From the expletives and accents I guessed they were drunk American mercenaries. My first reaction was to intervene, as I would have been obliged to do had I been the duty officer in a military establishment, but my diary explains otherwise:

Considered helping but decided that it was not the job of an ECMM monitor to get involved.

A single pistol shot had me turning my head again in time to watch one of the men fall to the ground. As he did so a hand gun, probably a Croat army issue HS95 9 mm pistol, dropped to the carpet between the two. The women at the bar started screaming while a number of similarly dressed soldiers fled towards the hotel's revolving front door. I was new to the Split 'scene' and wisely continued to the staircase guessing, rightly as it turned out, that the hotel staff knew how to deal with what was probably a normal, if not an everyday, occurrence.

That is how I saw it but the two protagonists were so close together, face to face, that it could well have been murder although I was sure, then, and am sure now that it was suicide. The next morning, following the best sleep I had had since arriving in the Balkans, I walked across to the Foyer Bar on my way to breakfast to stare at the bare floor where the bloodied carpet had been cut away. This exposed patch of stained cement served to highlight the incident rather than hide it. Noticing my interest, and my white uniform, a Croat policemen asked me if I had seen the 'game' of Russian roulette that had been played the evening before.

Heard that the drunk last night was apparently playing Russian roulette but as I pointed out to the Croat police, who were investigating the incident, you can only play Russian roulette with a revolver and not a 9 mm Browning-type, automatic pistol. The police had no idea of the weapon used and the surviving soldiers had long since fled the scene, as had the weapon. A piece of carpet where the victim fell and bled—dying—has been hacked out with a blunt knife, so now there is a large ragged-edged piece missing. The police took my point and my suggestion that they should look for an American mercenary but they replied that there are simply too many of them. Nevertheless, I suggested that as they now knew the deceased's nationality it should not be too difficult to chase his friends and colleagues. I left them to it.

In November 1993, Robin Powell, then a young TV reporter on his first overseas assignment, was producing a series for ITV News about the UN operation and particularly the role of the Royal Logistic Corps. In 2018 he wrote to me:

In your novel *Death's Sting*[2] you refer to an incident at the Hotel Split in December 1993 in which a soldier was killed in the hotel bar in what may have been a game of Russian roulette. It actually happened right next to me.

The cameraman and I were relaxing in the bar at the end of a long day of filming. I was conscious of a group of soldiers at the neighbouring table. All of a sudden, there was an almighty bang and one of the soldiers slumped to the floor, literally right by my feet.

I remember my colleague saying, in the stunned silence that followed, that he thought it was a wind-up. And then he saw what I'd seen and obviously realised that it wasn't.

At that stage we didn't know what had happened or who had fired the shot so we got out of there pretty quickly. It wasn't until the following morning, after an almost sleepless night, that I was informed by a receptionist that the dead man was thought to have been an Irish mercenary, and that the group had been playing Russian roulette.

I'll never forget how matter-of-fact she was or how the hotel staff just seemed to carry on as normal. Guests were tucking into their breakfast around the very spot where the man had died, albeit with the blood-stained carpet tiles now removed from view.

Sadly, of course, many Croats, including hotel receptionists, were used to such sights and thus immune to the more normal, human responses to a sudden and very public death.

Before getting dressed to face my first full day in Split I had double-checked Paul's three priorities for the future monitoring on the coast which he had dictated to me during our last meeting at Knin:

Political monitoring with a view to reaching a negotiated settlement on the Krajina issue. Thus it is necessary for us not to be hindered in our military or civilian contacts by the Croat authorities.

Economic monitoring in order to prepare the rebuilding of Croatia through the assistance of the European Union when the war comes to an end: and to implement as soon as possible economic confidence-building measures. The bulk of any aid will come from Europe (which is where we come in—advising on needy areas) as is currently happening for humanitarian needs. Thus we expect to be given full freedom of movement and co-operation by the Croat authorities to identify the country's future economic needs.

Humanitarian monitoring in order to orientate and coordinate but not to handle directly: to include plans for the exchange of prisoners of war, the dead, and the reuniting of families through personal contact.

This all was in addition to our standard military monitoring duties of assessing the effectiveness of the United Nations Arms Embargo 713; observing ceasefires along the confrontation line or, more often, their collapse; tracking troop movements across the country and reporting cross-border activities such as patrolling and shelling. These last were also the duties of the United Nations Military Observer (UNMOs) but these gallant teams tended to be in static positions without the freedom of movement that we were supposed to enjoy. We were to liaise closely with them throughout my time in Croatia and always found each visit to the UNMOs on the Confrontation Line to be a most uplifting, and always humorous event, despite their privations. Although unspoken, I knew that military monitoring was not the same as military intelligence gathering which, as non-combatants was most definitely not in our ECMM remit. What I sent back to the FCO was, of course, a very different matter.

Later in the morning I was introduced to the Team Split office in Room 506, a converted bedroom a few doors along the corridor from my Room 519. All of Hotel Split's fifth floor was taken up by ECMM offices, storerooms and bedrooms as well as the Croat Liaison Officer's office that was, rather conveniently for him, placed in the room next to mine.

Occupying the suites directly overlooking the Adriatic to the south were the administrative offices, communications centre and accommodation of the ECMM's Forward Logistic Group or FLG. A number of other fifth floor bedrooms were kept ready by the FLG for monitors passing through on their way from Zagreb or on their way to Zagreb from Serbia, Bosnia–Herzegovina, Montenegro, Albania, Kosovo and Macedonia. As its title implied the FLG kept us all (or should have kept us all) across the Former Yugoslavia supplied with serviceable vehicles, working communications, flak jackets and helmets, stationary, and 'administrative and logistic' supplies other than food and personal clothing. Admission to this fifth-floor, ECMM enclave was guarded (it was never 'controlled') for twenty-four hours a day at the common entrance that led from both the lift and the staircase by a permanent section of bored, not always sober and not always awake, armed Croat police.

The initial 'briefing' by members of the still-unfriendly Team Split was noticeable by their absence, and for the only two smiles I had yet to see since leaving Knin. The cheerful interpretresses who were to be central to my life for the next months were the mercurial, thin, angular-faced and serious Vinka and the sometimes-laid-back, occasionally 'woozled' and 'rather more well-rounded' Sandra. They were—as I was to learn—from opposite ends of the behavioural scale and, if there was such a thing in Croatia, opposite ends of the social strata as well.

The briefing on the Split area was, of necessity, given by Robert Lekeu for as I entered the Team Split office the outgoing Team Leader and his second-in-command stated that they had better things to do and immediately left to do them! As Robert had been in office for less than a week and had yet to undertake a patrol I did not expect anything too earth-shattering or professional in either delivery or content and I was right. Apart from having my already-formed view confirmed that work on the coast would generally be less humanitarian and more political and economic than inland, the other snippet that I gained was that Paul Ortholan's wishes for a second Team Split to cover Dubrovnik was very much 'on the cards'.

Following a rudimentary 'map reconnaissance' of the area on the large wall map Robert suggested he drove me round around Split with Vinka, the duty interpretress, as guide. I agreed with enthusiasm although I learned little from this exercise other than that:

> Robert's driving is so appalling that I wanted to ask him if he had ever taken a test as he is uncoordinated and totally unaware that there are others on the road; rather like a sixteen year old beginner on his first driving lesson. I think he is prematurely senile.

On our return to the fifth floor I was surprised to find that, unannounced, the British Ambassador to Croatia, Bryan Sparrow, was waiting to speak to me. In Split to visit the Honorary British Consul, Captain Aleksi Mekjavič, Bryan asked for a brief on conditions in Knin and the RSK in general for which he retained responsibility for it was, in international law, part of Croatia and thus within his FCO bailiwick. So, in the doubtful security of my room and despite my suspicions that it was bugged directly into the CLO's office next door, I gave Bryan an off-the-record account of monitoring Knin-style, including the activities of Captain Dragan. Once he heard that the Serb was training Italians from the Garibaldi Brigade he became even more interested than he had been up to that moment.

> A good start, professionally, to the job here as the Ambassador's visit surprised the other monitors and did no harm to my street cred! Pleasant supper with a Dutch monitor on his way back to Zenica in Bosnia–Herzegovina, plus Robert and Willy (who has begun to accept my presence in Split) but not so Peter Noppeneau who refused to join us—or, rather, me.

If I had thought that the minimal-work ethic endemic in Knin was a thing of the past now that I was in Croatia, I was mistaken for at the end of my second day I wrote:

> No work today as everyone in Split seems to be on leave—we must not be seen to be shirking our own work just because the country is on holiday but I detect a lack of interest in work by the present incumbents of Team Split.
>
> With me driving I was guided round the town by Vinka—just the two of us this time which made a delightful change. The town is very old and very beautiful in those parts that have not been destroyed by the dreadful, all enveloping communist concrete.

That evening both Vinka and Robert, separately, came to Room 519 where, over a glass of white wine, each asked me to edit lengthy papers they had written in English: in Vinka's case rather better and more accurate English. Hers was a fascinating thesis on the local sardine fishing industry's current and predicted problems that had been written by her sister for forwarding up the ECMM chain.

This extra-curricular work was precisely the monitoring required by Paul for the future economy and I was most happy to tidy up the near-perfect prose. Clearly the declining sardine fishing would be, when peace returned to the coast, due for rejuvenation and this treatise was a fine blueprint for that day.

Robert's paper was an altogether different matter that I began correcting with a growing sense of embarrassment and anxiety. It was a wholly RSK-supporting diatribe against Croatia and while I might have agreed with some of his personal sentiments they had to remain just that—personal. If we were to maintain a sense of impartiality Robert's views could not be used in any context whatsoever within Croatia, and yet it was towards that country that his highly-critical, inflammatory paper seemed to be aimed. I told him that I could only continue my editing on that basis. He appeared to see my point and agreed that it would only be sent to his Belgium 'foreign office'. I was to be naïve in my trust.

The good news is there were no suicides in the Foyer Bar this evening. At least, not before I turned in.

Two days before Christmas and at last I was off with Willy and Vinka on what might have been called our first, proper patrol. Heading for the village of Sinj, close to the Confrontation Line, we had been called to meet representatives of the Local Red Cross (LRC) to discuss with the Croat army's Military Liaison Officer, a Captain Marco, the collection of an unknown number of dead Croat civilians from within the 'no-man's-land' that straddled the Confrontation Line. These unfortunates had been killed crossing a Serbian mine field and their putrefying remains were still lying where they fell. The meeting was cordial, as expected, and 'chaired' by a lady from the LRC who had been approached by her 'opposite number' in Serbia to help move things forward. As this discussion was, on Willy's own admission, beyond his competence, I was 'allowed' to lead the negotiations for the ECMM and, between us, we suggested that if the Serbs could recover the bodies we would swap them for three dead Serb soldiers that I knew to be lying on the Croat side of the Confrontation Line.

On the face of it a sensible, pragmatic plan but there was, inevitably, a snag. The Croats suddenly announced that as the Serbs were 'terrorists' they were not covered by the Geneva Convention. Our understanding, supported by the LRC, was that soldiers, in a recognisable uniform and killed in battle, should be covered by the Geneva Convention and, in this case, their bodies repatriated. Unfortunately, after a long morning involving much *raquia*, coffee and dried bread we remained at stalemate with the Croatians and their repeated mantra that all RSK soldiers were terrorists … and that was that, the bodies would continue to rot in the fields with no exchange. It was a deeply disappointing outcome but, as Willy explained on the way home, fairly typical. I was at the foot of the learning curve.

In contrast to those hours of intransigence our visit to the United Nations Military Observers was an eye-opener of international cooperation. The UNMO's large house stood by itself on the edge of a plain that bordered the Confrontation Line and housed, at any one time, at least eight different nationalities from across the globe. Most 'members' of this international team were from Africa, the Middle- and Far-East and not only did this make for interesting meals as each pushed his own national dishes, but it also made for a far more harmonious existence than existed in the ECMM's monitoring teams with our internecine, European squabbles.

Interestingly, on our return from the patrol and while I was showering, both Vassilis (the Greek HCC Zadar designate, whom I had yet to meet properly) and Willy van den Bossche banged on my bedroom door. Under Willy's guidance I was then led, dressed, to the Foyer Bar where, for the first time since the Knin castle dinner, I actually exchanged words with the Greek.

'You've got to take charge of Robert and not let him speak at any meeting!' Caught out by this collective demand, my first thought was that that had to be Willy's job. Not only was he Team Split's second-in-command but he was also the longest serving monitor in the area. Conscious that not only was I new to the ECMM and its procedures but I also had no idea who in Team Split was, in practice, running the show. Nevertheless, I explained that this would not be easy and suggested to Vassilis that, 'If you are that worried why not demand that Paul sack Robert for it was Paul that appointed him. As he is the new Team Leader and you are the new Head of the Zadar Coordinating Centre it will be wrong for me to usurp Robert's position so openly. Anyway,' I continued, 'according to the ECMM pecking order Willy is the number two monitor so why ask me to do his dirty work?' Despite my arguments I was secretly delighted that Robert's behaviour had been highlighted. I wrote that evening:

> There is something odd going on here as no one seems willing to make a decision and I am not sure that I should be part of that progress. It will be better if I sit back and wait.

While this could have been the herald of good news as far as my own employment was concerned even better news was the delivery, the next morning, of my first mail since leaving England.

> Over one month's worth of mail has been sitting untouched in Zagreb. Also one month's worth of Times newspapers which was a bonus. Late night after all the catching up. Included was a letter from my SIS contact stating that Captain Dragan was known to them as Daniel Sneddon.

Through Christmas Eve morning I corrected Robert Lekeu's subjective essay while becoming yet more horrified at his judgements on Knin and the RSK *vis-à-vis* relationships with Croatia. Added to a growing fear that, despite his earlier assurance, his essay would somehow find its way into Croat hands, I pondered whether or not to continue. His views may have been, just occasionally, apposite but if made public and coming from the Team Leader in Split, they would undermine the ECMM's vital impartiality and I did not want to have played a part in that potential embarrassment. However, life moved on; slowly.

After lunch in the ECMM dining room of, incongruously, frogs legs I worked on the 'sardine project' for Vinka and her co-author sister. The Belgian major-general did not, as expected, make it to Knin (lucky Knin!) so he is here instead (unlucky Split!) which might be why the Greeks showed some form during dinner, and probably why we had dinner in Café Riva—again. They are taking over the running of the Forward Logistics Group and the presidency in Zagreb.

Sat next to Roger Castle a British monitor and retired Territorial SAS officer whose presence was an all-too-brief breath of fresh air. Long streamers of tracer fire outside and across the restaurant windows added to the occasion but I don't think they were aimed at anyone or anything in particular. At one stage we were obliged to eat by tracer light as there was a power cut of a few minutes.

I tried to make Christmas Day as traditional and as personal as possible while remembering some others I had spent away from home over the years: at anchor in HMS *Anzio* off Kuwait; with 45 Commando at Dhala, up-country from Aden, or with the Northern Frontier Regiment on the Yemen/Oman border—all riotous! During this quiet morning in Room 519 with a bottle of Croat white wine I opened presents from Patricia and Jan Adam while listening to a recording of last night's 'Carols from Kings'. But it was a morning that was unexpectedly spoilt by being ordered to change into white uniform for lunch with the Belgium general. Later I managed to tune into the Queen's speech on a wild, wet and windy day with a short steep sea running down the Adriatic.

Christmas is Christmas and a day of my own routine so I didn't change into uniform which is just as well for the Belgium major-general, having ordered us all to be in our white clothes to entertain him for lunch and dinner, did not bother to turn up. Over a glass or five of wine I asked his ADC what was going on. He said, rather tellingly, that the general had decided to eat out for both meals!

Boxing Day's weather was no better but the wind, rain and cold were not the only unpleasantness's of the day.

Dinner by myself in the ECMM dining room as the incoming FLG Greeks, the outgoing FLG Belgiums and various Dutch from heaven knows where, plus the rest of Team Split and the two interpretresses, are having a farewell drinks party for Peter in the Foyer Bar followed by a dinner party in Café Riva. I was not invited and was even 'ordered' to leave the bar by Peter as, 'You are not welcome.'

Oh well … Patum Peperium on toast as a late-night savoury in Room 519 which is a lovely treat as compensation.

The outgoing Head of the Forward Logistics Group was a Belgium, Walter de Keyser, and whatever else I might have thought of others of his nationality he had done a quite excellent job. His overall expertise, unflappability and professionalism were about to be missed—badly—for his Greek successor was the opposite in every possible way.

Machine gun fire about 200 yards away. Not the first I have heard since arriving in Split but it is definitely more rare than in Knin although single pistol shots are definitely prevalent.

Early on, and now on the Croat side of the Confrontation Line, I thought it sensible to make contact with my intelligence service friend in London and the only secure way I knew was by letter:

I thought that our mutual friends might be interested in the enclosed brochure about Captain Dragon, whom you told me in your recent letter, is called Daniel Sneddon. The brochure is interesting and self-explanatory—and self-publicising. What is particularly interesting is that this week we heard that Dragan has been appointed Inspector General of the Serbian army of the Republic of Serbian Karina.

While I am about it. Is there any possibility that our friends could tell me about two people? Our Croat government liaison officer in Split is one Dino Genda: a young, very self-assured person who enjoys a position that appears beyond his apparent experience and (dare I say it) his intelligence. I think he may, in the end, be harmless but something on his background might be useful. The second person is an ECMM monitor who is causing more than a little stir: a Greek naval captain called Vassilis Dertilis, at least, I think that is how he spells his name. I know that he attended the Royal Naval Staff College at Greenwich a few years back and now claims to be the head of Greek special forces—but then every foreigner claims to be in the special forces for it is very important to them, whether true or not! VD is clearly here with a hidden agenda and is not very good at hiding it which is already beginning to cause the ECMM some embarrassment.

Despite Christmas now being well behind us monitoring was slow to re-start. A delay not helped by Robert ordering our lives around in the most idiotic, pedantic, fussy manner which did not bode well for the future of monitoring the coast. Mindful of Paul's unwritten, but crystal clear, remit to me to 'do the dirty-work for him', that evening I determined to be rid of my Team Leader. But before that happy day we continued delivering parcels—and teddy bears! With little else to occupy my mind I noted, rather pathetically, that I was going to return to England speaking pidgin English, then went on to write:

> There is, undeniably, a great compulsion to help despite the fact that on both sides of the Confrontation Line (and even among some monitors when drunk) the Second World War is believed to be continuing and has yet to run its course. Germany is supporting Croatia as it did in the 1940s. The Greeks, and as far as I can make out the Italians as well, are supporting the Serbs while Iran and Algeria are supporting the Muslims on all sides. God knows how the French fit into this nor the Danes: the departing—sacked—Danish head of Team Split was spying on the coast but for what purpose must remain a mystery.

On 28 December Robert and I called on the Italian Vice Consul who instantly struck me as being one of the few genuinely sincere people with whom we were to deal. It turned out that he was a Catalonian and keen to assist the ECMM with any questions or favours we asked. These were based around how far Italy would be prepared to help in the eventual reconstruction of the tourist industry along the coast. Unfortunately, just as I thought we might be conducting one of the more serious discussions Robert Lekeu excelled himself by, quite out of context, asking why Italy was training its soldiers in the 'enemy's country'. Hiding well the fact that he must have been considerably taken aback the mild-mannered Italian Vice Consul replied, quite truthfully I suspect, that he did not know that Italy was training any soldiers anywhere in the Balkans. The clear impression being that the Italian knew nothing of Captain Dragan and his Garibaldi Brigade's trainees. I imagined the wires between Split and Rome were about to begin humming the moment we left the Consulate!

How did Robert know as I never told him? Paul? If so, why?

Glad for an opportunity to escape Robert's company I dumped him in Hotel Split and that afternoon, drove Vinka to her parents' house where we drank serious quantities of *raquia* but this particular 'home brew' had been distilled with herbs and was very pleasant, but enough was enough! Vinka had been keen for me to meet her father, an old-style, proud communist and supporter of President Tito. He regretted the break-up of Yugoslavia, believing passionately and lucidly, that, 'In the good old days Tito taught us that we are all Yugoslavs….' I should not have driven back! Then, to emphasise the extremes of our existence, five of us—one Croat, one Greek, one Frenchman, one Belgian, and one Scot—visited the glorious Split Opera House where we had hired the Royal Box for the price of three bottles of beer each. This was, and remains, a stunningly beautiful building with adjoining ball room and music hall. The opera we watched was the annual performance of

Splitski Akvarel, a form of musical based on the history and the culture of Split. As none of us monitors had the slightest idea what we had come to see I was not sure if we would last the pace for two and a half hours but at the precise moment that the curtain rose a Croat girl slipped into the back of our box and leaned over my right shoulder. For the whole of the evening she translated the not-very-difficult plot into flawless English. Sadly, at the intervals and then at the end, she slipped away without my hardly seeing what she looked like other than having been offered a fleeting glimpse of a more-than attractive face and figure … and long, nylon-clad legs.

Dammit!

The 'opera' was a beguiling mixture of classical opera, music hall farce, straight play and even ballet all presented through what I could only describe as the format of American-style burlesque. The evening was, though, more than just a cultural outing for during one of the two intervals I met in the bar the Italian and British consuls both of whom greeted me as an old friend.

The city comes alive after dark and at 2300 the streets are packed full off fun-seeking people, quite different from those that we tend to meet in our daily work. Watching everybody it seems incredible that there is a war and that there is no money. Much dancing in the streets and laughter—but then perhaps some of them do not have to wander through minefields by day although all families must be affected by some tragedy or other. There is supposed to be no money but everything needed for living—when available—is so cheap that what little there is goes a long way. The shops are full of luxury goods but no one buys them so the merchandise does not shift as there are no tourists.

Monitoring, Robert Lekeu style—while I attempted to monitor Ewen Tailyour style—continued, including a visit to two refugee villages that were full of Croats 'ethnically cleansed' from the RSK. I believed, although Robert did not, that it was important for us to check that they were as comfortable as possible and had access to food and medicines. Sadly, as I mentioned earlier, they do not have refugee status for they were regarded by the Croat Government—their own government— as displaced persons. Thus a more than usual reliance had to be placed on the ECMM monitors to ensure their well-being, albeit at a subsistence level.

Pathetic sight, seeing them living in such squalor but the Croat Government doesn't have either the money or the inclination to make things better. I think it supplies them with basic subsistence but not much else. Most are not farmers but professional people forced, with no experience of living off the land, to exist in these ex-holiday camps while scratching their own living from the soil.

Returned to Room 519 to find a message from Admiral Sir Hugo White, the Commander-in-Chief Fleet, asking me to contact the Royal Naval Liaison Officer responsible for British ships in the Adriatic with a view to my briefing him on the situation ashore.

That same evening was spoilt with the sudden appearance in the Foyer Bar of Vassilis as he affected a 'Hollywood-style' entrance, swaggering in through the hotel's revolving front door not in the white uniform of an ECMM monitor but with a mauve fedora—of sorts—balanced over the back of his head and a dark, woollen overcoat hung loosely across both shoulders. To add to this spectacle he was accompanied by a 'private' lady interpreter wearing a short, black mini-skirt covering just the top few inches of her thighs above her long, stockinged legs. This was the first time that I saw Vassilis in his 'true colours'.

'Peter Noppeneau,' he announced loudly, 'is to be reinstated as a monitor.'

'Surely,' I replied quickly, 'the Head of our Regional Centre sacked him so on whose authority will this happen?'

'Mine! As Monsieur Ortholan is now on leave I am making the decisions.'

If this was true, and I prayed that it was not, it was going to make things awkward for the Croats as well as for the ECMM's credibility. But my hope that Peter would not return was not shared by Vinka which was, perhaps, a clue to another reason for his unhappiness at being dismissed. I should have spotted this. I looked across at her. Her deep blushing confirmed my suspicions.

It was not the time to embarrass Vinka but Vassilis, now the Head of Coordinating Centre Zadar, needed to be challenged.

'In many ways this is nothing to do with me but I am pretty certain that his reinstatement will not be met with approval in Zagreb and I am equally certain it will not be met with acclaim by the Croat military here in Split.'

'Ah, but that is where you are wrong. As Greece is taking over the Presidency we will be making the decisions not the Belgians,' he paused to add haughtily, 'nor the French and I think I can handle the local military.' Vassilis then dropped another bombshell, 'You, Ewen, are being appointed as the Team Leader!'

'Over Robert's head. Not very tactful.' Luckily the Belgian was not present. 'When will this happen?'

'As soon as I have confirmation from the new Greek Head of Mission.'

During what could only be described as an 'interesting' conversation I explained that I was not sure my sudden appointment was a good thing for two very clear-cut reasons. Peter would make life extremely difficult while I was, anyway, under the impression that I was only in Split until the time was right for me to move to Dubrovnik to establish a new team, as proposed by Paul and confirmed by HQ ECMM. This second factor, the Dubrovnik aspect, cannot have been known by Vassilis for he expressed genuine surprise, and seemed quite pleased by the idea.

If Peter is to reappear in Hotel Split, will he work as a junior member of Team Split and thus be answerable to that buffoon Robert, or am I really to take over in which case Robert cannot stay. The worrying side is that if Peter does return it will be an appalling piece of man management which will do nothing for the image of the ECMM in Split.

Even without the benefit of hindsight I could, at the time, detect the beginnings of a rift and contradiction of values between the French and the Greeks but, regrettably, none of us in Split had the clairvoyance to see trouble looming. Nevertheless I wrote in my diary for 29 December:

Peter wrote very good reports but was too heavy handed and too 'military' in his monitoring, according to Paul. This was the reason why he has been sacked after complaints from the Croatians—apparently—but the Greeks do not follow the Croat's wishes as they, the Greeks, support Serbia. I should tackle Vinka about the situation as she knows/knew Peter rather well and that, too, might be why he has gone! In which case why is Willy still with us as his relationship with Sandra is hardly a secret either!

The next morning Team Split, still under Lekeu's 'leadership', attended the weekly meeting of the United Nations High Commission for Refugees (UNHCR). We were expecting a large convoy of Italian trucks loaded with aid for the interior of the Former Yugoslavia. This had been promised by the Italians to compensate for their lack of involvement ever since that country had removed all its drivers from the ECMM leaving the Mission embarrassingly bereft. By some earlier agreement, Italy had then supplied the majority of the Mission's drivers but stories of their vast telephone bills, mostly to 'pop stations', might have been one of many reasons behind their removal.

In fact we arrived late at the UNHCR meeting, not that we took any part but merely noted the expected convoy's timings so that we could ease its passage through Croatia to the border. As we were leaving a party from *Jeunesse Sans Medicine* called on us unexpectedly. It was always a pleasure, although often, as on this occasion, a sad pleasure, to meet the *JSM* team for they had with them a young Muslim boy aged, I guessed, about 14. His parents had recently been killed in Bosnia following which his brother and sister had been removed to refugee camps 'somewhere'. This miserable young lad was being taken to France, a country of which he knew nothing and certainly not any word of the language. Understandably, he was not happy yet, on the other hand, was expressing a deep desire to get away from it all despite being desperate to see his brother and sister and was frantic to know where they were and how they were. Another large part of his unhappiness was his uncertainty over whether or not he was now in safe hands and in this respect he had every good reason for his misery to be compounded for Croatia was not well disposed towards Muslims.

However, salvation—and a demonstration of 'safe hands'—appeared in a timely but temporary form.

Vinka, at her unusual best, befriended him but we could not get him to eat anything even when we took him for a good meal in a Split restaurant. An act probably against all ECMM regulations, but sod it!

My view was that the *Jeunesse Sans Medicine* team was better placed to help him so on our return to the hotel he was swept away as the party moved on. Wretchedly, we heard no more, despite attempting various 'follow-up' procedures.

Work of a different nature in the afternoon found us back at the UNMOs' house near Sinj from where we endured a rocky drive to one of the observation posts overlooking the confrontation line. The only available shelter from wind, rain and artillery was a wooden hut exposed on the edge of a steep-sided promontory. The morale of these remarkable men was exemplary, encapsulated by their view that any 'local' shelling was almost certainly inadvertent. Inadvertent or not, I could not help thinking, an artillery shell kills just the same and a wooden box is scant protection.

These UNMOs observe, two at a time, for two hours at a time over a 24-hour period on a day on, day off routine. The off-duty member of the duo hunkers down for rest, come freezing rain or burning sun, alongside the hut.

Not a good existence.

There were all types and characters in this team: Malaysian, Indonesian and Norwegian for example. One of them—a Belgian—told me about the restrictions placed on them by the Croat Army (CA) with whom, otherwise, they seemed to have a respectable relationship. Nevertheless the CA made it very difficult (for lesser men it might have been impossible) for them to reach their observation post (OP). This struck me, and them of course, as odd since the reporting of ceasefire violations perpetrated by the RSK must have been very much in the Croat Army's interest. On the other hand, the attempted prevention of reports of their own ceasefire violations only added to our suspicions that there might have been something afoot. I had been to their OP before but this time we had to approach via a very long route through the hills on unmade up, rocky tracks. In our tiny Peugeot motor car, uncomfortable even on a tarmac road, the journey was close to torture and especially for the two in the back with no seats—and no windows.

This already interesting day ended in a bizarre fashion. As I was typing out our daily report for transmission up the line through the various intermediary headquarters to ECMM HQ in Hotel 'I', Robert, as was his habit, was leaning over my shoulder while I compiled the day's events. For some reason, inexplicable at the time and certainly now, without warning he took exception to an innocent military expression I was typing. The first sign of this was a fist slammed hard into my left ear. This full-bloodied punch not only momentarily stunned me but, once recovered, made me bloody angry. I wrote simply and rather more calmly than I felt:

Lekeu had a mental flip while I was typing Team Split's Daily Report.

Sanity reappeared later that evening in the form of Rory Ormsby, an amusing and lively British monitor who had served as an officer in the Gurkhas and who was then on his way back to Tuzla from leave. Determined not to eat in Lekeu's unstable company we bucked the rules and had what I remembered as an 'amazing dinner' in the Café Riva Restaurant.

Rory would like to come to Dubrovnik with me which would be very good news indeed—if that is to happen, which still seems on the cards.

New Years' Eve—Hogmanay—1993/1994:

Not much on today! Tried unsuccessfully to telephone the British army battalion in Gornji Vakuf about a driver for some Italian journalists who seems to have been captured. By whom?

Much shooting and explosions around the hotel in the afternoon and evening which I assume has all to do with the New Year and very little to do with the war.

Gave Rory my hand-held emergency alarm that is actuated by the slightest movement and about the size of a box of Swan Vestas matches. VERY noisy siren indeed. This had been given to me by a security organisation based in Reading. They use them for putting behind their hotel bedroom doors when they are asleep and Rory lives in a hotel at Tuzla which suffers many thefts by Bosnian Serbs. His need is greater than mine—at least I sincerely hope so as Hotel Split is not quite the same.

The New Year brought no certainties over Team Split's status for 1994.

Under Robert Lekeu's continuing 'leadership' we were now responsible for the Airfield Monitors whose duties included every airport and landing strip south to, and including, Dubrovnik. With these monitors now under command I hoped that an order for Team Split to assume responsibility for monitoring that far south would surely follow. It certainly made sense and was what had been discussed so often and was precisely what Paul Ortholan required. Yet 'so often' I had been told that 'next week' I would take a new team and base ourselves in Hotel Argentina in Dubrovnik where—I knew—there was much anti-English feeling.

That can be circumvented by describing myself as Scottish!

An 'old fashioned', semi-retired Croat general had established his quarters in a form of 'grace and favour' residence in the Hotel Argentina's annexe from where he had recently reported that the Serbs were massing in the hills above the badly damaged town of Dubrovnik. (According to the town's Press Releases, now to have been rebuilt, 'older than before'.) The general was also predicting that the Serbs would attack in force 'once and for all as soon as they can'. Additionally, the view that Dubrovnik should declare itself an autonomous state, á la Monte Carlo, had much backing in the town and immediate area but, naturally, not nearly so much support in Zagreb. As all traffic, by foot or motor, had to pass through Bosnia–Herzegovina to get to Dubrovnik, it did not seem like a bad idea and indeed was *de facto* the then current situation. In practise it was possible (indeed mandatory in those days) to bypass Bosnia–Herzegovina by taking the ferry from the port of Ploče to Trpanj on the near island of Pelješac.

Hogmanay had been rather a quiet affair compared with what the Tailyour family was used to. In accordance with our tradition I rang '16 bells' on my father's yacht's bell that had been used at my christening. It always travelled with me and had been rung, in my presence, at every Hogmanay since. However a few minutes into 1994 I was summoned from the dining table. Paul had just arrived from leave and, having been briefed about Robert's behaviour as he passed through Zagreb, was anxious to know more. This meeting in a side anteroom was accompanied by:

Much tracer along and outside the great windows of the Café Riva Restaurant. Quite impressive really especially as it did not seem to be aimed at anyone in particular although like all such shooting, the bullets have to come down somewhere. I saw a man killed by a similar spent round in the Oman as he was standing next to me.

Briefed Paul in some detail on Robert's behaviour ending with a plea to have him removed so that we can get on with our work. I also raised the likelihood of Peter's return. Paul's one word reply was 'Rubbish!'

Later during the celebrations there was another altogether more pleasant diversion when a small girl in her mid-to-late twenties caused 'quite a stir' for she was wearing white knickerbockers beneath a black 'ra-ra dress': at least I think they were called that in the 1990s. Everyone had their eyes as wide open as was medically possible watching her as she danced like a dream: both classic and modern. It turned out that she was a friend of the Croat Liaison Officer's secretary and had been in a car crash, then a coma for two months. Marika, as I was later to learn, had trained as a dancer but because of the scars on her legs could no longer become one professionally. Nevertheless she was 'quite a gal'—and still a mesmerising performer.

The evening ended with an interesting talk with the CLO in his office (next to my bedroom) with a glass of whisky, some Greeks—and the spellbinding Marika.

I intend to develop my working relationship with Dino for monitoring purposes as I believe that he holds the key to any such success. Ask no questions—let the CLO do the talking. Already it seems to be working.

Apart from the diversions it had been an amusing supper with Rory Ormsby despite being joined by the Greeks who we made welcome for they had managed to buy, on the Forward Logistic Group's hotel bill, a case of St Emilion. As they appeared not to have the slightest idea what they had bought, Rory and I helped them dispose much of the claret with clear consciences.

Up at 0900 on New Year's Day. Weather very much better and with the whole of Croatia still on holiday there is not a great deal we can do at the moment except sort out the signals and make yet another outline plan for the week ahead based on who can now see us and who will not. As I am discovering, fixing patrols and visits is a very moveable feast that changes hourly, making planning a nightmare and in some cases slightly pointless. It also shows how little we can do within our guidelines to the point that I wonder what on earth we are supposed to be offering in the form of serious assistance. Especially as we cannot actually promise anything anyway. Both sides, Croat and Serb, look upon us as spies for the other. None of this is helped by Greece—which has held the Presidency for all of two days—helping Serbia and the Germans, who will replace the Greeks in six months' time, openly supporting Croatia. This will probably explain why Vassilis is making promises to the Croats in order to build up credit on behalf of Greece before the Germans come in only to find that that they will not be able to honour them. Most intriguing.

Walked along the beach into the old town and through the port of Split. Incredible filth everywhere even stumbled across an elderly but smartly dressed lady defecating by the railway line in full view of the pedestrians on the street above—her husband than followed her in this rather public activity! I have to assume that they have no running water at home.

There was the odd hardy soul swimming in the sea. Very brave of them for even though the communists may (and I only say may) have had a sewage treatment system before, now everything is pumped directly into the sea. With all these holiday camps, resort hotels and villages inundated by refugees and with very few services working I do not think the water colour in many places is a fact of nature; more a fact of raw 'manure' and 'the war'.

All the beach cafes and restaurants are closed with many little more than piles of rubble daubed with obscene graffiti—and although I don't understand the words I can certainly understand the drawings!

One can imagine this urban stretch of coast in its heyday. It would not have been very lovely then either as it is, and was, a mass of concrete bathing areas looking rather like the old Nazi fortifications along the Atlantic seaboard of

France and the Channel Islands but in minute detail. Now there are not even the tourists to give some life and colour to the coastline that stretches for a few miles south of Split—desperately depressing. The marinas are full but few, if any, boats go to sea—mind you it is not the season as the Bora often blows.

Nobody takes any notice of the machine gun fire that punctuates the air throughout the day and the smaller explosions of fire crackers and pistols—not always easy to differentiate between the two—at night. There are few smiling faces among those one passes which is hardly surprising although they see themselves as the aggrieved party vis-á-vis the RSK. I am not so sure, certainly the Croat record of war crimes is considered by some, who have been here considerably longer than I, to be rather worse than the Serbs. Coupled with the fact that they are openly being supplied against all international rules by Germany who is finding ways of breaking the embargo and the open use of Nazi symbols and names cannot do their case with the international community much good. Certainly not their cause with the Serbs who have, I believe, every good reason not to trust the Croats.

It is quite easy to see why so many regard the present situation as a continuation of the Second World War by other means. Sadly those other means could spill into a continuation of the divisions that then held sway in this part of the world in the early 1940s. i.e. *Ustaše—Vs—Četnik*.

On 2 January a disturbing number of stickers began to appear all around Hotel Split's fifth floor corridor expressing support for Macedonia while the Greek drivers were sporting 'over large' brassards on their arms announcing to the world that they were Greek. This went very much against the spirit of the ECMM where our individual nationalities were not outwardly advertised. Knowing that their country—Greece—was supporting the Croat 'enemy', Serbia, was far from tactful, but the new head of the Forward Logistics Group did nothing to stop them. Philipos, a corporal in a Greek army logistics organisation, was a permanently worried little man, always nodding his head like one of those toy 'nodding dogs' sometimes seen on the back shelves of motor cars. He spoke no intelligible form of English which, considering his position in the ECMM, was indicative of the contempt that Greece held for the ECMM's objectives. So appalling were Philipos's mannerisms, coupled to his lack of any known language other than his own excitable version of Greek, I was often forced to ask him, through one of his staff, to stop nodding, 'Otherwise I have no idea whether you mean yes or no.'

The previous evening I had spoken directly to Patrick Brook, Deputy Head of the Knin Regional Centre, about the future of Team Split. He confirmed my worst fears and my best hopes. If we were to establish a team in Dubrovnik (and he hinted that there could now be some doubt about that) I would be the Team Leader with no line of authority through Lekeu but direct to Zadar. My view was that if the new team's responsibility stretched from Dubrovnik to the northern border with Bosnia–Herzegovina where by reaching the sea, it divides the south of Croatia from the north, then, I argued, we need a second Team Split to cover from Split south to that *de facto* border. The current Team Split could then face inland from the coast and to the north as far as Šibenik. We agreed that while the possibility of the new team existing remained extant I should go to Neum and Ploče for a week or so to establish indigenous contacts, a *modus operandi*, lines of communications and confidence-building measures between the southern civil dignitaries and businesses and the ECMM.

On the face of it, my conversation with the unruffled, sensible and professional Patrick encouraged me to look forward with enthusiasm. I did, though, suggest that a useful beginning would be the removal of Robert. 'Not possible unless we have firm evidence of his inability.' I thought I had given it!

Then, on 4 January, I conducted what I hoped would be the first serious monitoring event of many and one that, if successful, would pave the way for a productive future. Prior to the meeting with the Split Chamber of Commerce (SCC)—and what better place to start—my only reservation was that I had to take Robert Lekeu with me so prayed that he would keep his mouth shut. He tried to intervene but as he had no idea what was really happening keeping him quiet was not too difficult. Hence, as he took no sensible part in the meeting my subsequent Special Report was written in the first person singular.

As I understood it, there was a difference between our regular Daily Reports and the occasional Special Reports. I may well have been wrong for I never knew what actually happened to either document once they left our desks. Special Reports were written for transmission beyond the ECMM and concerned themselves with, but not restricted to, longer-term strategic issues worthy of reaching the higher levels of the European Community. More often than not, on the coast, they dealt with the financial, commercial and social regeneration of the country. Daily Reports covered the mundane, tactical level of our work, although some did contain snippets that, too, deserved forwarding beyond the ECMM, but that was up to those further along the chain. They reported visits to local police stations, isolated villages, the distribution of mail, medicines and the making of cross-border telephone calls, the violation of whatever cease-fire agreement was in force at the time, the repatriation of dead bodies and the exchange of prisoners of war.

We must be very careful not to make promises that neither the ECMM or the EC can ever meet. One of our duties, as explained by Paul Ortholan, is to establish where EC money will best be spent when (if) peace comes to this benighted part of Yugoslavia. Our meeting with the Split Chamber of Commerce will be a good start and one which I have insisted we set up, although not without opposition from Robert who could offer no facts to back-up his opposition.

Robert managed a wonderful and rather public tantrum as we were leaving the hotel. The moment he heard that our Croat Liaison Officer was joining us at the meeting he exploded as we passed the Foyer Bar. As the CLO had set the meeting up and had gone to some lengths to get the SCC to meet us Dino and I both felt that he should be there to introduce me, start the proceedings, and then leave. We, or more truthfully I, relied on the CLO for much. Without him we would not have any meetings established and would be forced to spend our time simply patrolling the border which, although important, was only a third, and a low third at that, of our then priorities.

Once the CLO had bade us farewell (or, in Croat, *dovitzenia*,)[3] in the SCC's offices the meeting with the Chamber of Commerce could begin. Sadly, though, Lekeu once again excelled himself by pushing a piece of paper in front of Vinka the interpretress, sitting between us at a table, and asked her to translate a passage into Croat for the benefit of our 'hosts'. I looked down at what Lekeu had given her and was, once more, horrified to see that it was a page from Paul Ortholan's report of a recent meeting he had had with the Zupan of Split: a functionary that was roughly the equivalent of mayor, military governor and head of commerce. It was marked *For Monitors Eyes Only.*

This paper also included Paul's views on the Zupan of Zadar and various other strictly confidential matters that the interpretresses—and anyone outside the ECMM—were not supposed to know. What the hell had, once more, got into Robert I did not know either but I swiftly removed the piece of paper. Apologising for my 'friend' I tried to change the subject but this sparked Lekeu to lose his temper.

'Shut up, Robert!' I ordered loudly only to be answered with vulgar Belgian abuse. When he stopped I told him I was taking over the meeting and that it would be best if from now onwards he remained silent. Surprisingly he did as I asked, thus allowing me to apologise once more to our hosts.

The SCC members seemed highly amused by this little vignette but it was better that they saw Robert lose his temper than that they knew what was written on that piece of paper.

We really do have problems with Robert and I think we have reached the end … indeed we must have reached the end.

In the afternoon I wrote a tactful Daily Report for the various HQs up the line (to which Lekeu was obliged to put his signature along with mine) but I then typed a rather more informative Special Report on the visit to the SCC to which Lekeu was not privy. In this second paper I highlighted the manner the the direction that I believed our future monitoring should take—which the SCC members had agreed earlier and for which they had promised every help—with one vital caveat that had been put to me in private as the meeting had broken up. It had then been suggested, manna to my own ears, that our monitoring would be infinitely better and more acceptable to the Split establishment if it could be conducted without Lekeu.

While I heartedly agreed, although loyalty to the ECMM prevented me from actively saying so, this would not be easy for we were supposed to monitor in pairs. Lekeu was also, *de jure*, the Team Leader with his name publicised as such to the Split community.

But there must be ways round this and for the sake of ECMM's reputation we will have to find them.

As will be seen from my report, the visit to the Split Chamber of Commerce was a fascinating one and one that I had high hopes would be the perfect springboard to my time on the coast. I paraphrase it here to set the scene. I did, though, add some personal, relevant thoughts afterwards in italics which were not on the original:

INTRODUCTION

Following a request to our Croat Liaison Officer a visit was arranged by Team Split to the Split Chamber of Commerce (SCC) … The last visit had been made by UNPROFOR Zagreb but we have no reports of Team Split ever visiting. The SCC was represented by Mr Berislav Buselić, Head of Foreign Relations and Promotion of Croat Industry. He was joined after the start by Mr Drnjevićm, Head of Infrastructure, Roadbuilding, Traffic, Investment and Reconstruction, and by Mr Mayer, Head of Industry and Energy.

ORGANISATION OF SCC
Up until 1 January 1994 [*just three days earlier*]. The SCC had been responsible to the Zagreb Chamber of Commerce for all commercial dealings from Šibenik to Dubrovnik but now both towns are responsible to Zagreb for their own commercial affairs and will each mirror the arrangement now in Split. The SCC, as the others will be when they have settled down, is subdivided into eight well-defined sectors:

Industry and Energy
Trade, Tourism, Food, Ports and Shipping
Light Industry and Agriculture
Infrastructure, Roadbuilding, Traffic, Investments and Reconstruction
Foreign Relations, Promotion of Croat Industries
Statistics and Information Technology
Business Education
Macro Economic Analysis of the Industrial System—this is conducted from Zagreb.

Before the war the main industries within the SCC were, in order of economic importance:

Tourism
Shipbuilding
Cement Production and Export
Manufacture of plastic goods, toys, clothes, boots and Macintoshes
Aluminium production and export

DISCUSSION

I began the meeting by thanking the SCC for agreeing to see us after which I explained the purpose and aims of the ECMM. This was new to the members of the SCC who, by their comments, appeared delighted that someone from outside Croatia is worrying, not so much about the present but, in particular, about their future.

One of the members asked what the ECMM was doing to stop the war, not in the Republic of Serbian Krajina but in Bosnia, as he believed that until that was solved any talk of reconstruction in Dalmatia was pointless. We were very politely reminded that they were commercial men and did not want us to talk politics. I reassured them that the aim of our meeting was the economic present and future of the Croat littoral.

One question I put to the SCC was: Is it possible to manage both the tourism (if it can be regenerated) with the large number of refugees now living in many of the hotels and camping sites. The reply was a strong yes. During this particular conversation I learned that they are expecting no less than 60,000 tourists this coming season through the tour operator, BEMEX, which has its headquarters in several European Community countries. 12,000 of these tourists are expected to arrive from Germany. The SCC expressed a great desire to see more British tourists as they tended to come in the off-season when others do not. This influx used to prolong the money making period in any one year and was always welcomed.

The SCC identified a number of reasons why tourists do not now naturally come to Dalmatia:

One.   The fear of the war

Two.   The difficulty passing down the coast, due to shelling at various
          bottlenecks

Three.   The difficulty in obtaining, or the added expense of, insurance premiums

Four.   The supposed lack of suitable accommodation

Discussion on the above points produced the agreement that in many places the war did not affect life at all [*This is not my view*], and especially on the islands. [*I hope to establish this fact for myself.*]

A lack of positive advertising or public relations exercises throughout the rest of Europe that explained the reality of the situation along the coast is a contributory factor affecting would-be tourism. The lack of merchant shipping was blamed on the arms embargo plus the huge insurance premiums. I agreed that this should be brought to the ECMM's notice.

[*One thing I can agree on and with which I can personally help is the absence of British yachtsman.*] A plea was made for British yachtsmen to return to the coast as many used to sail here in the summer and, of economic significance, during the 'off' seasons to winter their yachts here. I explained that I knew many in the British yachting establishment and would, with the ECMM's permission, contact the British yachting press and yacht charterers together with the professional bodies covering yacht building, brokerage and yacht insurance. [*Inevitably, the ECMM took no notice and so on my leaving the Mission I did as promised; although, as will be seen, this caused the 'gentle' ire of the Croat Ambassador to the UK.*]

There was, though, some good news such as the extra ferries expected to sail from Ancona in Italy bringing in the expected 60,000 tourists. [*Where they would be accommodated was not discussed!*] It was difficult on this first meeting to gauge the accuracy of the statements and the reliability of the members present but there seemed to be an air of optimism: and even if this is all we achieved it makes a marked change from so much pessimism we meet. Particularly good news is the fact that Brodosplit has recently received an order for ten oil tankers of an unknown tonnage. I asked to visit the shipyard and was given permission provided I made the arrangements through the SCC.

Brodosplit is an interesting case in optimism and positive forward-looking planning. It was founded in 1992 by joining together several smaller Split yards. Currently they claim to have built ships for Argentina, Brazil, the UK, Finland, Sweden, Norway, Greece, India, China, Liberia, Libya, Mexico, Nigeria, Poland, Pakistan, Panama, Switzerland, Venezuela, Russia and the USA.

Jadrolinya (the national ferry company) has expressed a strong desire to build two ferries for inter-island work as the present fleet is, on average, 30 years old. There is a need for one ferry to carry 200 motor cars and 1000 passengers and a second ferry to carry 30–60 motor cars and about 600 passengers. However due to the lack of money (i.e. tourists) there are no means by which they can design and build these ships—and without these ships the tourists will not come. Nor will they will come if there is no accommodation. (But see below.) The SCC is looking at ways to break this endless cycle but the earlier optimism seemed to fade at this point in the conversation. In the absence of national assistance a very strong request was put to me for foreign investment. [*I can only forward this special report but I doubt it will get further than the Croat-despising Greek in Zadar.*]

As a measure of how the SCC sees the present small regeneration of tourism the SCC has set up three independent customs zones to correspond with points of departure in Italy: Bari to Dubrovnik, Pescara to Ploče and Ancona to Split.

HUMANITARIAN

The SCC expressed a need for government help in building refugee settlements so that the tourist centres can be released for their proper purpose. This is particularly important for the SCC as they are very keen to welcome tourists with good facilities but as with the proposed ferries they are in a vicious circle. They are worried that the estimated 65,000 Croatians still in Bosnia will very shortly try to come to live in the Split area with even worse consequences for the (hopefully) re-invigorated tourist economy.

FUTURE

I asked that I might be allowed to call on the sector heads (designate) of the future Chambers of Commerce in Šibenik and Dubrovnik and while they have not yet been appointed this was agreed in principle ….

CONCLUSION

While I accept that during an initial meeting of this type it is impossible to assess the reliability of information (and its source) I believe that the most important factor was the friendly and cooperative spirit in which the meeting was held. It was openly and freely expressed by those members of the SCC that attended that if they had known of my aims and aspirations (to be positive and not just to listen with no result) they would have come better prepared with facts and figures. As it is I will now be sent brochures of various organisations useful for my background knowledge.

It was a morning very well spent and the feedback already via the CLO confirms that the same was felt by the SCC.

Naïvely as it was to turn out I came away from this first serious session of monitoring encouraged that I had at least begun what I had come to do; help make a tiny difference. However, as I was to discover all too soon, no report I, or anyone else as far as I was aware, ever despatched, Special or Daily, was acted on by the ECMM, even if they reached as far as Zagreb. I suspected then, and became more certain as time moved on, that few ever did: the assurances I—and other monitors—made to our 'host' countries across the Mission were worthless and if the Serbs and Croats had known this then the ECMM would have ceased to exist.

Throughout this and all subsequent meetings and visits, my views on Croatia were not important and, indeed, were irrelevant. On this side of the Confrontation Line I was required to monitor the re-generation of a country. I was being paid to be impartial—and to predict!

5

The Duplicitous BBC

At 0300 on 3 January a Russian-built Mi8 helicopter landed on the hospital landing pad overlooked by my bedroom window. Built as 'aerial tanks' these aircraft flew higher than 10,000 feet (above ground level) into the interior to avoid Serb surface-to-air missiles. Not fitted with oxygen, it was hardly surprising that the pilots were seldom fit to fly on reaching their destinations: I hoped I would never embark in one.

Ostensibly they were carrying casualties back from the war in the interior but as the pilots were cheating the whole time the airfield monitors were kept very busy. Even the seriously wounded had to be searched for weapons and indeed two people lying on the same stretcher pretending to be one in an attempt to escape from Serbia was not unusual. I was never quite sure what was actually going on except that if a Serbian Croat managed to infiltrate into Croatia proper he, or she, would not, presumably, be treated as a displaced person or refugee but, inevitably, be considered a 'spy'—and almost certainly 'punished' as such.

With no patrols or visits planned and precious little likelihood of Lekeu planning any for the foreseeable future, it was high time to take some serious 'long distance' exercise, at least, as much as was possible under the conditions. My idea was to spend a long morning walking around the coastline visiting the marinas and civilian docks in a journey that, had I been a crow, would have been about three miles. However, without wings, the distance was four times that along a much-indented route.

Strolling through the marinas was a sad exercise. 'Real yachts' were rare and with little sign of the type of vessels one associates with Mediterranean resorts, serious money and a hedonistic life it was an unexpectedly depressing morning. This had nothing to do with the war but the general, downmarket lifestyle of the Croatians. There were, of course, exceptions, some beautiful exceptions, one of which I was to get to know reasonably intimately for one purpose of this first 'recce' was to identify a number of candidates as escape vessels should one be needed. This was not such a far-fetched plan as it might appear now, twenty seven years on.

There are few sea-going vessels in the marinas. In the immediate Split area most are small motor boats for day fishing which in the heat of the summer would be very pleasant. Sadly, graffiti has spread onto the hulls of all the vessels that are laid up here (which seems to be most of them) and that is sad. Nobody seems to care about anything very much although, as I have said earlier in these notes, a happier life of some sort seems to emerge at about midnight when the younger element take to the streets and cafés.

Due to the lack of any pre-planned monitoring prior to my arrival in Split I had time on my hands and so it struck me that a useful visit should be made to the ex-Jugoslav National Army's Divulje Barracks 15 miles or so west along the coast. The reason was entirely personal for I was keen to see Richard Perry, a lieutenant-colonel in the 11th Hussars whom, I had discovered, was stationed there with Headquarters British Forces (HQ BRITFOR) within the United Nations Protection Force. It was a pity that neither of us had known of the other's existence as we were good friends of many years and it would have been pleasant to have been among kindred spirits over Christmas and the New Year. Earlier I had been invited by the British RAF's liaison officer to a New Year's Eve party but in a misguided sense of loyalty had decided that I should be with the ECMM. As it happened, my absence would not have mattered one jot.

I found Richard on his expected excellent form for which he was renowned and invited him to dinner on the morrow in Hotel Split, determined that if the Greeks complained that he was eating 'ECMM food' I would remind them of all the unofficial guests, mostly single girls, that they regularly entertained in the far more expensive Café Riva. As Richard was the head of the British Army's public relations team I reasoned, rather mischievously, that giving him dinner would be a more acceptable charge to the ECMM than a collection of young ladies with dubious reputations!

Later in the afternoon, Roger Sugden and his colleague Günter, a retired German air force pilot, called in to the office. Günter was a quite superb gentleman whose character and professionalism belied any other thoughts some of us might have had about his country's nefarious involvement. He was excellent not only as a monitor but also as an unofficial 'ambassador' for his country. Open, honest, a thoroughly 'all round good chap' and, along with other German monitors in Croatia, he was proficient, charming and straightforward. As I was to learn it was his government that was breaking United Nations Arms Embargo 713 while the monitors themselves were as embarrassed as the rest of us. The airfield monitors were now part of Team Split's organisation and although their work was separate we would be called upon to supply the occasional 'helper' and transport in time of need or crisis. How they would take to having Lekeu as their *de jure* boss I was soon to discover.

As Roger and Günter had little time I suggested they came back at 1730 when we could talk at length about our mutual involvement and this they did but for some unexplained, and certainly inexplicable, reason when Robert Lekeu heard they were in the hotel he 'blew his top' and ordered them to leave. They did not!

That same evening a meeting was held in Team Split's office chaired, apparently, by Vassilis Dertilis. Philip Watkins, the Head of the Coordinating Centre at Mostar and Tony Smith the Humanitarian Officer at Knin also attended. I say Vassilis 'apparently chaired the meeting' for as always with these gatherings there was no actual leader and thus no guidance: it was simply a free-for-all discussion without an agenda. However, whether with or without authority from further up the chain of command, one or two 'decisions' were made.

Team Split, under Lekeu's non-existent leadership, was now to be responsible for monitoring the Dalmatian coast as far south as the point where Bosnia–Herzegovina reaches the sea while I was to set up a new Team Split to be known as TS2 in Dubrovnik.

'Is this an official ECMM decision, Vassilis?'

'No, but I am eighty per cent certain that it will be.'

'So,' I continued, 'in reality we do not actually know what we are supposed to be doing.'

'It will happen.'

Not yet convinced of Vassilis's authority I was not so sure.

Certainly Philip Watkins, an experienced monitor and retired Royal Artillery officer, said that as he only had eyes looking inland he would welcome the removal of Dubrovnik from his Area of Responsibility: after all it was actually in a genuinely different country.

To set things in motion, despite Vassilis's word being the only authority we had as a guide, it was agreed that I should establish Team Split 2 prior to Robert Lekeu visiting Philip Watkins's adjacent teams based on Mostar (and thus the other side of the internationally agreed border between Bosnia–Herzegovina and Croatia) to decide demarcation lines. Of course these decisions were, correctly, also the responsibility of the Team Leader, Lekeu: who was not present! Lekeu had purposefully not been invited to this meeting by Vassilis for he would have messed things up. In strictly 'legal' terms this was, perhaps, rather odd but also rather typical of the low-grade anarchy endemic throughout the Zadar Coordinating Centre.

> Vassilis does not like Lekeu and does not consider him to be the Team Leader—indeed he hardly acknowledges his position as an ECMM employee! This whole way of working is what my marines would have called a real 'cake and arse' party and I would heartily have agreed with them.

After supper I had a long chat with Patrick on the far-from-secure public telephone line to Knin.

If I go to Dubrovnik to get that team under way then I might ask to extend my six month contract to nine months. Then the ECMM might ask me to complete a full tour which I would be happy to do providing my work in England can be put on standby for another six months but this will depend on ABS Hovercraft, VSEL (now BAE) and Swan Hunter's decisions on the expected Ministry of Defence's 'invitation to tender' for the new 'landing platform dock'—the replacements for HMSs *Fearless* and *Intrepid*. However it is an interesting proposition worth thinking about. Additionally, the SIS might like me to be in Dubrovnik so I see no problem there.

The next day, 4 January, with Roger Sugden in the front of the Land Rover and Lekeu in the back with Vinka I drove the eighty or so miles to Zadar for a meeting with Vassilis, the Head of the Coordinating Centre and Patrick the Deputy Head of the Knin Regional Centre. Normally I preferred not to drive but I would, we all would, do anything to prevent Lekeu from doing so.

While on our way Robert handed Vinka the paper he had written about his time in the RSK and asked her what she thought of it. The moment I realised what was happening in the rear of the Land Rover I stamped on the brakes in order to drag Lekeu out and throw him into the ditch. Sadly, I did not carry out my plan which was a pity for it would have saved us much trouble.

Instead I released the brakes, tried to keep a straight line on the road, and thought, 'Vinka should not see that even though it is a private view.' I might have agreed with much of what Lekeu had written but it was not for Croat eyes and particularly not for this individual Croat's eyes with her links to the Split 'establishment' and perhaps even to the Zagreb political hierarchy. Nevertheless, it was too late and short of an unseemly tussle across the back seat she read on.

After ten minutes, horrified at Vinka's obvious distress and near tears, Roger read the paper himself. Following a long silence while his frown intensified he asked, 'Who wrote this stuff? It's dynamite.'

'Robert!' I replied.

'Bloody hell, Robert,' Roger twisted in the passenger seat to look over his shoulder, waving the papers in the author's face, 'what on earth or you doing showing this to Vinka?' There was no answer. Roger switched to the interpretress, 'Vinka, this is terrible. Believe me, this is a private view and not that of the other monitors.'

There was nothing more to say other than for both of us in the front to express a sudden and strong desire for a hefty slug of the dreaded *raquia*!

I knew the contents of Lekeu's paper well as I had helped correct the English. Despite stating at the time that it should not leave his possession due to the explosive nature of his views I had no idea at all what on earth he was going to do with it. He had only made a vague intention of offering it to some Belgium glossy magazine. Showing it to a Croat interpretress was about as bad as it could get.

The Zadar meeting was fairly typical for the ECMM … Little of any value or even use came out of it other than, on a personal level, I was told that in five days hence—9 January—I would be appointed (not for the first time, or the last!) Team Leader of the new monitoring team, to be known as Team Split 2 (TS2) with responsibility for the coast and islands to the south of Split. This team would not yet include Dubrovnik but it was definitely a move in the right direction, geographically. Robert Lekeu would be remaining as Team Leader of TS1 covering Split itself and the coast to the north. The better news would have had him sacked altogether but apparently that is still not possible.

On our return to Hotel Split Geoff Beaumont, a retired officer in the Prince of Wales Own Regiment, from the Mostar area within the Zenica Regional Centre, was waiting to speak to me which he did over drinks in Room 519. Eventually I had to kick him out, nicely, for I was anxious to change for dinner.

My rush was to meet Richard Perry in the Foyer Bar before we moved downstairs to Hotel Split's main dining room, the Café Riva Restaurant, rather than along the ground floor corridor to the monitors' un-inviting 'eating hall'. As the head of the British Army's public relations team across the Former Yugoslavia Richard enjoyed professional and social access to all representatives of the media, be they print, wireless or television. This evening he was bringing with him one of the many BBC correspondents assigned to the Balkans and had given me advance warning so I was looking forward to a good evening with a rare chance to listen to sensible, balanced points of view. However, as it happened …

The reporter talked about himself nonstop which I suppose is natural for people of his calling. He was only interested in his own opinions and while Richard and I tried to tell him of other matters that were going on in this awkward part of the world he would not listen. He just kept expounding his theories which did not seem to be based on reality but merely on his personal views as a news reporter. He was obviously bored and, on his own admission, was searching for scandal rather than hard news. Over the three or four hours that Richard and I had to listen to him it was clear that he had made his mind up about the general situation long before he arrived out here. I thought, and I'm certain Richard agreed, that this was a pretty poor form of reporting. He even asked Richard why it was that the Coldstream Guards had the nickname in the UNPROFOR as the Cold Feet Guards. There was no known cause for this insulting and probably slanderous slight so Richard gave him a seriously hard time for trying to invent stories from unsubstantiated rumours that had no basis in truth. I rather went off Richard's guest—and the BBC—then for if he/they has/have nothing better to do than invent rumours or 'sex up' existing rumours then he had better go and find another war more to his/their distorted liking. A great pity really and so unnecessary of our national broadcaster and its employees.

It was, though, fascinating listening to Richard giving one of the BBC's apparatchiks a hard time as there is not much he does not know about this place. Richard's astute and perceptive mind is able, very coherently, to offer a most balanced exposé of both the overall and the detailed situation. He gave the reporter a good run for his money and in a far more intelligent manner than, rather obviously, the reporter was capable of doing himself. My strong and abiding impression is that this BBC man comes across as rather a fraud! He clearly had no time at all for the ECMM and was not in the slightest bit interested in our work. I argued with him that it should not be right for him to make up his own mind on our work and usefulness without interviewing any ECMM member—which he admitted he has never done. He is not interested in knowing what our mandate actually is and so I doubt that he cares.

However the BBC's representative did confirm one or two interesting snippets that I already suspected. The Greeks were supplying arms and fuel to the Serbs while the Germans were supplying the same to the Croats. This was much as my friend Peter Seldon, a top-rated, international business man with an engineering background, had also told me before I left Plymouth.

I did not tell Richard's guest of Italy's position *vis-à-vis* training troops in the RSK with the idea of taking over the northern Dalmatian coast: I thought the BBC could do without that highly explosive fact.

To add to the underlying confusion of ECMM politics it was well known on the monitors' grapevine that the Germans had begun planning for when they were due to hold the Presidency of the European Union in six months. Already they had identified which key posts would be taken over by new German monitors who would arrive with little, if any, understanding of the political, military and economic situations. Apparently they had been planning the takeover of these key positions even before the Greeks themselves moved in, while the Belgians were still in situ. 'So,' I had to ask myself, 'why are they so keen?'

One aspect of German concern must have been their fear of taking over from the Greeks, of all European nations, for they, the Greeks, were already, after little more than two weeks, doing everything to ensure that they injected as much influence and promises (even propaganda) into Croatia as soon as possible. In this context I had to ask, too, 'Why is someone as well connected as Vassilis already the HCC of Zadar—the only coastal HQ in the ECMM?' He had moved straight in to that position without ever having been a monitor in the field. Was it relevant, indeed was it true, I further wondered, that he had commanded Greek Special Forces? Even Sir Martin Garrod, the retired Commandant General of the Royal Marines and twenty-times Vassilis's calibre, started life as a 'simple monitor'. Certainly from almost his first day, during 'that' dinner in Knin castle, Vassilis was offering guarantees amid an overt and grossly 'over the top' exercise in 'buttering up' the Croat hierarchy, both civilian and military. This cannot have been an accident: it was not long before I was also to learn what the French part in this hugely suspicious saga was.

An added complication was lying in wait.

Have now been told that Robert Lekeu has given his personal report on the RSK to Dino. That is precisely what the ECMM does not want—to the Croats the RSK is an enemy, breakaway territory and for a monitor to expresses, in public and without apparent shame, views such as his are abhorrent to both sides. What on earth has got into the man? We have to get rid of Robert before he does any more harm and destroys what little work we are achieving—heaven knows, we are allowed to do little enough as it is without that little being destroyed from within our own organisation.

… And now, seriously down to earth, I have just heard on Sky News that Ermington (a mile from where I live in south Devon) has had a traffic jam with a broken down lorry on Town Hill. This would be a bizarre news item nationally, let alone internationally, as it is a tiny village in a darker corner of Devon with two pubs, one church, one Post Office stores, no bus route and a population of hardly three figures: it is very much off the beaten track. I feel this has to be a coded message for me in the manner that the BBC sent cryptic communications to the French Resistance in the 1940s! 'The geese are flying tonight,' that sort of thing!

Monitoring of a sort began with a visit of myself and Willy van den Bossche to the mayor of Omis whom I found to be the most pessimistic of any man I had yet to meet this side of the Confrontation Line. His mantra, for such it was, believed that it was the ECMM's job to tell the world that his town did not have a war. All he wanted, understandably, was to have his tourists back … but that was apparently our responsibility and indeed our job. I suggested, in return, that it was the job of his country, now that it was a sovereign state, to start acting like one and to use its embassies for what they were, partially, intended: publicising his country abroad. He could attract tourists to his town on his own if he bothered to think positively but he just sat there, rather weakly, moaning that it was his government's problem and until it did something he would just have to let his town collapse.

This was a very different view from other areas on the coast that, according to my predecessor's reports, had decided that as the government was not going to do anything they would do it for themselves. These more optimistic approaches may not yet have been working but at least they were based on the worthwhile principle that God helps those who help themselves and God certainly was not going to help Omis unless the useless mayor got off his miserable bottom of self-pity and started doing something positive. My advice, put rather more tactfully, fell on decidedly un-receptive ground. Finally after considerable tedious discussions I reiterated my offer of help. 'Any help,' he moaned, finally agreeing that it was not Team Split's job 'must come from my government.' And that was that: end of visit. Team Split's job, as I saw it, was to highlight his plight and pass it up through the ECMM's channels. Thank goodness Lekeu had not been with us.

On return to Hotel Split I spoke on the telephone to Vassilis's surprisingly-receptive ears about Robert Lekeu. Later in the conversation Vassilis told me that my Special Report on the Split Chamber of Commerce visit was being circulated throughout the ECMM as an example of how monitoring should be conducted and how such reports should be written. I explained that I thought this was embarrassing and suggested that he was trying to soften me up for something. He laughed in denial but I remained unconvinced. In fact I did not think it had been written at all well although the content had expounded some fair- (and far-) sounding hopes for the future. Nevertheless the Directing Staff at the Royal Naval Staff College Greenwich would have been amused for I had not been their most erudite student in 1979.

The rest of the day was spent preparing maps and programmes in advance of my move south with Team Split 2 although, as I noted in my diary that evening, there was bound to be a delay to any such deployment for a second member of my embryo team had yet to be appointed.

During the evening the Greeks invited all the British and French army vehicle fitters from the UNPROFOR workshops to dinner in the Café Riva which was either rather brave of them or incredibly foolish. Some of the private soldiers and junior non-commissioned officers had not changed out of their working overalls and all began to drink their beer out of the bottles. Torn, oily jeans and armless T shirts were not quite what the richer, in comparative terms, members of Split society, who ventured to the Café Riva on special occasions, would have expected as dining companions. Nevertheless, despite their dress, they were impeccably behaved and a huge credit to their organisations and regiments. In the end the mechanics turned out to be an amusing bunch of lads who made the evening a noteworthy success. A noble gesture of thanks by the Greeks that was, in the end even appreciated by the locals.

In the middle of dinner a voice whispered in my ear, 'Can you please come to my office immediately?' I turned to find that a clearly agitated Dino had crept up behind my chair and was kneeling on the floor. From then until well after midnight Dino and I talked about Robert Lekeu which is probably not a conversation an ECMM monitor should have conducted with a Croat liaison officer. Be that as it may, the CLO was worried about the status and standing of the ECMM in the Split/Croat community which—if true and genuine and I believed it was both—was very good of him. Certainly without his support we would get nowhere while, for his part, he seemed to think that we did have something to offer. Which is more than I did for much of the time!

Eventually we came to the real purpose of the summons. Dino had been handed a copy of Robert Lekeu's paper, the contents of which saddened him greatly. He was not naïve enough to think that the paper represented ECMM policy nor the ECMM's views on the *de facto* situation although he probably thought that much of what Robert said might be true. We both agreed that that was not the issue: the issue was that the controversial views of a Team Leader were being made public to the Croat establishment.

I apologised, formally, on behalf of the ECMM, which I may not have had the authority to do but took it upon myself anyway. Knowing that Lekeu was my Team Leader Dino expressed the view that this might be awkward for me but I was happy to assure him that it was not!

I knew that Dino regarded me as 'a spy' working for the British and not the European Community especially as I had taken over from a Danish 'frogman' who, he was convinced, definitely was a 'spook'.

'After all,' Dino explained, 'Peter was 'caught' measuring the lengths of Split's public jetties and the water depths for what-ever reasons a country like Denmark needs to know!' I had no answer.

Moving the subject on, Dino produced more evidence to back up his opinion of my activities. Earlier I had told him about his country's shipbuilding programmes with contract dates, ships' tonnages and potential owners, allied to the latest details of the last ship to have been launched by *Brodosplit* shipbuilders.

'There you are,' he had riposted, 'you are a spy! Otherwise how on earth do you know so much?'

'Actually Dino, everything I have just told you was in day's *Slobodan Dalmatia*, your local daily newspaper. The girls translate relevant bits of it for me over breakfast each day!'

He was amused at that although surprised, perhaps understandably, that I had retained all the technical information in my head. I told him that, being professionally interested in nautical matters, it was not very difficult, but he remained unconvinced!

Before heading back to the restaurant and the tail end of the evening's 'entertainment' I guaranteed Dino that I would be speaking to the ECMM HQ about Lekeu although I had to add that I really did not know what could be done. All I did know, but I kept this from the CLO, was that Robert had to go before he did any more harm to what little we were achieving in this part of the Former Republic of Yugoslavia.

Meanwhile, work was slowly trickling back into our lives as monitors.

Patrolled with Sergio the male, weekend interpreter, to Podgorna then visited the stunning mountain passes, with quite amazing scenery, before stopping for a beer in Vrgorač. Then back through an equally striking valley, like some parts of west Scotland, with weather very much to match that of the Highlands and Islands in autumn.

My undeclared aim had been to get a feel for the countryside over which, I was becoming more sure, fighting would eventually take place. In theory, I hoped that the presence of an ECMM Land Rover in rarely-visited communities would be a form of confidence building—one positive facet of our work.

> The Croats are clearly preparing for an attack on the RSK despite what the FCO thinks. But the FCO does not hear the rumours, or is ignoring them, that UN Arms Embargo 713 is being broken almost daily. I wish I could find out how and where as the heavier arms must be coming in from sea. Ploče? When the attack does come it is possible that the main thrust will be up through the Drniš valley towards Knin. Something is definitely happening as rumours from along the coast keep mentioning various small, apparently unconnected movements at sea and on land. I hope someone up the line is putting all the snippets together to see the wider, overall picture.

Dinner was in Café Riva (again) and (yet again) I wondered who was footing the bill as our food was paid for (in advance, as it were) in the upstairs, monitors' restaurant whether or not we ate it. Meals in the Café Riva Restaurant were charged extra and were, supposedly, only sanctioned by the FLG for 'special occasions'. Who was paying I could only guess but it had to be costing the ECMM an un-costed bomb and so I pondered, as I often did, how the Greeks were getting away with it: not that we complained. The hotel was clearly making additional money which, equally clearly, had to be pleasing the hotel owners. It also made them better disposed towards the Greeks! Nevertheless, it could only have been a matter of time before the ECMM auditors, such as they were, in Zagreb would start questioning the finances of the Greek-run Forward Logistics Group.

That evening, fully fed, we moved from Café Riva to the ECMM's drab dining room for a party of some sort which I knew would be, in reality, nothing more than a beer drinking competition. So, on our way upstairs I bought some local wine, more palatable than the over-fizzy, continental lager that would be on offer.

> At dinner I sat next to a charming Swedish Air Force Major called P. G. Wiik. An excellent man from Team Gospić. He had been in Knin with me briefly. Now he had with him his delightful French lady driver—lucky bugger. There are some excellent men and women here but we all wonder what we are trying to achieve especially when what little we do accomplish is let down by a very few idiots such as Lekeu.

The next morning included another fascinating, not to say interesting, visit to the UNMOs of Sinj who live in their house on the edge of the plain. Inevitably, I supposed, they existed in some squalor with a communal style of life that allowed little time for chores. With no money, indeed no financial pool from which to hire one, there were no cleaning ladies nor cooks so each off-duty UNMO undertook these tasks, plus the laundry and general cleaning. This might have had its doubtful charms for those involved but with little financial support (apart from their basic pay) from the UN for their comforts it was amazing, and heartening, to find them cheerful, happy and pleased to see us. That having been said the duty cook always managed to excel with his own national dish each day so eating, if not washing up, was always a joy for them.

Each time we called I would offer them meals and drinks if they could ever visit Split but their schedule was tight and, as they never seemed to be up to strength, they found it impossible to get away for any length of time. To us, and I have no doubt to them, this was a huge pity for they had a difficult and, more often than not, a dangerous job which they conducted with great good humour and utter professionalism. Following this latest visit and coupled with my own observations I wrote:

> There seems little doubt that the Croat Army (CA) is planning something and that something seems at the moment (and after discussions with the UNMOs) to be a two-pronged assault into the RSK ... or at the very least a form of military pressure on the RSK by threats backed up by real troop movements. One of the CA's aims, which is openly discussed with those officers whom I meet, is an attack on Knin with the objective of capturing and holding it to ransom. For instance I watched yesterday about 160 soldiers being bussed into the southern areas from some undisclosed starting point in the north. From my bedroom window I also recorded a 385 ton, fast patrol boat of the Kralj Class Type 400 leaving Split harbour at speed. These craft are fitted with up to eight Saab RBS 15 missiles with a range of 38 nautical miles at Mach 0.8 with a 330 pound warhead: also carried on board are one 57 mm Bofors; one 30 mm Gatling; two Oerlikon 200 mm guns while they are also able to lay four AIM-7 magnetic or eight SAG-I acoustic mines. She was heading south-eastwards along the coast towards the southern borders doing about 25–30 knots which is close to her maximum speed of 32 knots. I have never seen this type before in Split although I knew that they had existed within the rump of the Croat Navy's order of battle.

On my return to the hotel I discovered that Vassilis had, that day, returned from Dubrovnik and thought this odd considering that I, as the potential Team Leader of that area, had not been allowed to conduct my own similar reconnaissance. Consequently, I had to ask myself what the real purpose of Vassilis's visit was although I had a sneaking suspicion that it had precious little to do with ECMM work and all to do with his winsome Croat interpretress. Anyway ... he stated that he was certain that 'the enemy' were once more overlooking Dubrovnik and in a position to attack. My suggestion was that any enemy intent on dominating Dubrovnik would need a commercial port and the obvious, indeed the only, candidate was Ploče just under 40 nautical miles to the north-west in a straight line measurement. Certainly if they owned that an enemy would really be dividing Dubrovnik from Croatia … but then Dubrovnik wanted to become an independent state in the manner of Monte Carlo. Such action would encourage that view but, conversely, by cutting off Dubrovnik from outside help would, in practical terms, only ensure its eventual demise.

> I have the very strong feeling that Dubrovnik may not be a haven of peace although that may be a question of timing. There are indications that things may hot up there again but on the other hand the whole area could go quiet—there never seems to be any rhyme or reason for events out here. At least I shall have my back to the sea and in a strange way I shall feel happier for that but whatever lies ahead I hope I am there and not sitting impotent in Split with Robert Lekeu as a rather dubious companion. The important thing is to keep Vassilis Dertilis as a friend no matter what I think of his methods.

Vassilis had some more rather disturbing information. Team November Three (the team I was with when in Knin) had been stopped the day before by two RSK soldiers who, with cocked weapons and stinking of alcohol searched their vehicle. Eventually these two drunks let the monitors go with the excuse that theirs was the wrong vehicle: they were looking for an UNPROFOR Land Rover. 'Rubbish, Vassilis,' I said, 'You can't possibly believe that. ECMM vehicles are white, clearly marked and manned by white-clad monitors whereas UNPROFOR vehicles are blue, equally clearly marked and manned by armed, uniformed personnel. Even to a drunk there has to be a difference.'

The interpretress had been terrified out of her wits, certain, as were the monitors, that they were about to be led away and shot. Apparently the UNPROFOR vehicle the soldiers said they had been looking for had been shot at recently. Heaven knows what would have happened if N3's Land Rover had been their target … except that at least the UN personnel were armed which is a damn site more than the monitors were.

This incident reminded me that before I came to Croatia I was told that a monitor who had not served in the Gulf War was not considered to have any relevant military background! As it happened, now in theatre, I only heard the Gulf War mentioned once. The Falklands, the Oman and Northern Ireland seemed of more interest to the other 'foreign' monitors than events in the Middle East. The only person who mentioned the Gulf was Roddy de Norman, a delightful, retired 9/12 Lancers officer whom I had met in Zagreb and who had been a tank commander during that conflict. On his own admission, though, he had not seen much, if any action and was very funny about it. The other abiding memory is that it seemed vital in the eyes of every non-British monitor to have been 'special forces': every 'foreign' monitor, on first meeting, would find some excuse to mention his part within his country's 'special forces'. Even the incompetent Lekeu liked to boast that his job in the Belgian Air Force logistics department had been part of 'special forces'. I found it impossible not to laugh at him. For my part I denied any involvement with 'special forces' saying simply that I had been a Royal Marine despite it being beyond the comprehension of, for instance, the Belgians that the Royal Marines were not special forces. I would argue, correctly I believe, that they were elite but not 'special' in the military sense of the word.

10 January was an 'absorbing' day which saw three of us—myself, Willy and Sandra—driving to Imotski on the Confrontation Line to the south and east of our Area of Operational Responsibility. Here we were to visit a wine-producing 'factory': vineyard would be too fancy a title. There was, naturally, a serious side to this apparently frivolous visit for wine production, or the lack of it, was of great concern to many as it was one of the few 'industries' still surviving. It was imperative to Dalmatia that it continued to do so.

Sandra knew the mayor, which was just as well for on our arrival he denied that we had made the appointment, despite it having been fixed through the CLO's office. With peremptory introductions over we were quickly escorted into the bowels of the factory with, I had little doubt, the aim of getting us back on our way as soon as was possible. I have not visited many factories but I can't imagine that this one was different from most. The only obvious dissimilarity being the end product: from all the pipes and machinery came wine rather than washing machines or tinned cat food. Then, without once stopping to take in the mechanics of wine production it was back to the mayor's office for our farewells. He visibly regarded himself an eligible, or even an irresistible, bachelor with a keen, a very keen, eye for the girls: which is why I suspected that Sandra had managed to resurrect our meeting and why it was not over quite yet!

Expecting to be dismissed back to our Land Rover we were unexpectedly herded into the barest of rooms that, in another life might have reminded me of an interrogation cell for there was nothing in it beyond the absolute basics. The grey walls were cold and un-adorned, one plain wooden table sat in the middle with a collection of odd chairs set around it on a concrete floor. This 'cell' was lit by a single broken window and one bare bulb hanging by its flex two feet below the ceiling, from which once-white paint was shedding. There was nothing else at all in the room.

Rather self-consciously and perhaps even a little nervously we sat, where instructed, in silence and waited. Abruptly the door was flung open and in were carried trays laden with plates, glasses and bottles. Accompanied by relieved laughter on both sides we were offered, and unashamedly devoured, a remarkable array of delicious ribs of beef complemented by every category of wine that the 'factory' produced. These were rough, raw and hardly advanced from the original grape juice that I found surprisingly delicious—although some samples were more 'delicious' than others. In smaller glasses we 'chased' the wine with 'tasters' of the spirits also fermented 'on site' and, in particular, a selection of fiery 'brandies', one of which was 'manufactured' from grass. This latter spirit was, to be polite, not pleasant. As the 'meal' progressed the obese—a gross understatement—production manager, whom we had met earlier, became more and more drunk ... and the more he drank the more argumentative he became and the more argumentative he became the less he could accept any logical, counter arguments to balance his extreme views. He expressed, vehemently, a deep-seated hatred of the ECMM and everyone else in Europe except the Germans: he particularly hated the British while proudly admitting that he was a committed communist who believed that his country should never have thrown off that particular yoke.

> His varied and sometimes contradictory arguments did not hold up and so I was never quite certain where his loyalties really lay. 'Oh well', I kept thinking, 'He is very generous with his company's booze so just relax and enjoy this bizarre experience!' They all think the UK/UN/ECMM/UNPROFOR is here to win the war for them against the RSK and because we are not they despise us. I tried to explain why the various non-governmental organisations were here across his country but it became more and more pointless as he became more and more drunk. I gave up and helped myself to another 'grass' brandy which was beginning to creep up on me.

As we left the factory with all its unsold vats of wine we were stopped, rather aggressively, by the security guards at the broken main gate, once more uncertain what was about to happen. Before we could get out to ask what the problem was the back door of the Land Rover was wrenched open and copious bottles were loaded into the vehicle with, according to Sandra, the compliments of the general manager who was, she translated, embarrassed by his colleague's behaviour.

Willy drove the three of us home despite, unnoticed by Sandra and me, having been drinking heavily. I thought it had been lemonade in his glass but not a bit of it. Nor was his mood helped by Sandra who, in her own words, was also 'pissed'. Forcing Willy to stop on the road she suddenly climbed into the back seat where, after a few miles, she fell asleep with her head on my shoulder. As I knew that not only did Willy fancy her but that she was actually sleeping with him I refused to drive and let him suffer his jealousy in silence.

In the end Willy had his revenge, by proxy, for during the night I was extremely ill: at both ends as it were. Certainly, the factory's hygiene would not have passed an admiral's annual inspection and thus, equally certainly, I was suffering from acute food poisoning.

I was to learn later that when our Daily Report was received in Knin our fellow monitors commented that after weeks of 'doing nothing on the coast' we had 'finally got up from the beach and carried out a patrol to a wine factory'. If they hadn't meant it so seriously it might have been amusing but the trouble is that life in Split was seen as a holiday and although I agreed that our routines were certainly not the same as that experienced inland there were serious issues at stake that would bear fruit if and when peace came.

It is towards that day that Team Split is working—the economic recovery of the coast.

While I alternated between bed and bathroom throughout the next day, Team Split planned a visit to the island of Hvar. This had been 'on the cards' since my arrival for it was always accepted that much of the regeneration of Dalmatia, Croatia's powerhouse, would begin with the near islands. However two days before the visit to monitor the future economic situation the other members of Team Split decided that we should cancel the appointment until I was better. To me it was unthinkable that, having made such a fuss about the lack of monitoring over the Christmas period, we should cancel or even postpone our visit. As two monitors were required I asked one of the airfield team, Peter Sugden, to take my place.

From a personal view this was sad news but more than compensated for by the sudden and welcome vanishing of Robert Lekeu. No doubt fed up with being side-lined in all our activities Lekeu quite suddenly was not with us and disappeared without telling anyone he was going, thus, obviously, giving no hint of when he might return. I was delighted, relieved and was certainly not about to miss him and his senile influence within the ECMM. Inevitably there was a downside: he, quite illegally, took our more-than-precious Land Rover! So we were back to begging from the FLG.

At long last we can get on with serious and worthwhile monitoring, or we could if we had something to go monitoring in without having to creep cap-in-hand to the 'nodding dog'.

6

Escape Plans with *Eloise*

With Team Split's absence on Hvar I was able, from my sick bed, to catch up with events a little further afield.

News is that UN/NATO will use aircraft to bomb Serb positions if they continue to shell Sarajevo or fail to allow the airfield at Tuzla to open or prevent the changeover between the Canadian and Dutch battalion at Srebrenica.

We have been told that this will mean retaliation against the softer targets of the EC community such as the monitors in the RSK and Bosnia–Herzegovina so the rapid evacuation plans for the teams in, for instance, Knin are being dusted off. We have also been warned that as the UN/NATO threat includes, rightly, any organisation—be it Croat, Muslim or Bosnian Serb—that attacks the UN I have confirmed to the CLO here that this could mean the coast being targeted by the UN. We have, equally understandably I suppose, been told that we will become legitimate targets in Split if that occurs—fair enough and one of the risks that we live with. I can't help feeling that there are quite a few Croats who are longing for the 'legal' chance to get at us for they are angry with the EC for not supporting their country to the exclusion of all the others.

In the view of the majority of Croatians, as they are now a sovereign nation we (the rest of Europe) should support them against the illegal RSK. Actually if I was a Krajina Serb I would have done the same once Croatia started resurrecting the old Nazi symbols. But the holier-than-thou Croats don't see that.

At least the drunken production manager of the winery will be satisfied if the UN attacks the Bosnian Serbs although nothing will satisfy him until Knin has been flattened as well.

I was, though, roused from my bed when a Serbian man was ushered into Team Split's office. He owned a flat close to the hotel but had been bodily thrown out on Saturday night by a Croat Army soldier. The Serb's father, the legal owner, was in his 90s and still in the RSK so the poor chap that sat across the table from me now lived in a motor car despite the flat being his. The ECMM could of course do nothing directly but part of our remit was to bring cases of humanitarian interest to the notice of the authorities so that the Croat policy of 'even-handedness and innocence in the RSK problem' (tell that to the marines!) could be shown to be false. The Croat police would then be forced, on pain of international exposure, to do something about it. The authorities were terrified of adverse publicity of this nature getting out but would actually do nothing while pretending to do much. They wanted their cake and they wanted to eat it while it was part of our job (as I saw it) to see that they did not have any cake in the first place!

I could do little in this sad episode except take the details and pass them onto the Humanitarian Monitor in HQ ECMM who could, if he felt he had a solvable case, bring them to the attention of the Minister of the Interior or whoever the equivalent of our Home Secretary was. I also gave the Serb the telephone number of the Chief of Military Police to whom he should go with his complaint but I also knew that absolutely nothing was going to happen because of his nationality. The chief of police would just say that the Croat Army soldier had every right to commandeer an ex-JNA flat. After all, it would be explained, he is a serving soldier who has priority whether or not he is the legal owner—which of course he is not.

What a warped and immoral society!

As it happened this was one of so many such 'cases' that managed to breach the non-effective security and reach Team Split's office. These visits were always occurring despite the two civilian police stationed by the lift and staircase on the fifth floor. Their duty was to prevent such unsolicited visits and yet, daily, hugely deserving cases were getting past the 'guards'. In fact I kept telling the police that while it was our duty to meet these people it was, paradoxically, their duty to prevent them from meeting us. I'm glad to say that no one in Team Split ever complained about this police inefficiency: how could we when the cases were so deserving despite being so insoluble.

Following this latest incident I felt well enough to join Sandra for lunch after which, and in the cool sun with a stomach-settling *Prošek* or two—a form of sweet wine we drank in place of port—in the Riva Terrace Bar. Here Sandra poured out her heart to me about her rather difficult love life …!

At one stage I rather impolitely stopped her to express my surprise that any monitoring was done at all and, unsurprisingly, she replied that she wished there had been no monitoring to get in the way of her relationships.

Martin Garrod regarded this behaviour as 'sleeping with the enemy' especially so as it was expressly forbidden by ECMM rules although I never saw this 'in writing'. The other aspect that emerged from this lengthy, *Prošek*-fuelled, one-way discussion was that there could be no doubt that all interpretresses were working for two masters. This former communist country still retained a considerable sympathy towards that style of government—and Vinka's father was a prime example and one who had fought as a partisan. I was not sure how that tied in with Croatia's support of Germany but let that lie for the moment.

Now that Vassilis, our intermediate boss in Zadar, was living with his 'civilian' interpretress I was surprised that we were getting anywhere—maybe we were not.

Richard Perry called in which was a good bonus especially as he brought some of the maps I had asked for as we cannot get any through our own impoverished logistic system.

Later that evening, in answer to a signalled request, I telephoned Patrick in Knin who had some rather interesting news. Robert Lekeu and his wife were staying in the motel for his holiday while continuing to use 'our' Land Rover.

I must say Knin is the last place I would take anyone for a holiday, let alone my wife even if the transport and petrol are 'free'.

Earlier I had discussed Robert's behaviour with Patrick and faxed him a copy of his, Robert's, paper although not before both French and English versions had already been sent, quite understandably, to the Zagreb government by our Croat Liaison Officer. Patrick's initial comment was to ask, not for the first time, if Robert had been drunk. Sadly the answer was 'no' for it might have helped explain his behaviour.

One unexpected bonus of Robert taking his leave in Knin was that he had his misdemeanours paraded before him by Patrick. Apparently Lekeu was, then, more than non-plussed on being told that his behaviour in showing everyone 'that' article had not been well received by the Croats. Apparently (although I was not in the least surprised) it had, by then, been shown to General Govina, the military commander in Zadar, and while we agreed that it did not contain anything that was not known it was very definitely not good for the ECMM's image to have that sort of thing, coming from a monitor and a Team Leader, being publicly broadcast. Comments such as the following, although true, were not conducive to Croat perceptions of our impartiality:

It is extremely difficult for the Serbs, who are in the majority in almost all towns and villages of the Krajinas to envisage a peaceful life in an independent Croatia where they would remain in the minority.

The renewal of Croat nationalism and the reappearance of the Ustaše symbols make the Krajina Serbs fear further genocide. Croat promises to guarantee the rights of the minorities are not believed.

Lekeu was, of course, spot on. We discussed this all the time, and we were proven correct in August 1995, but that was not the point at the time!

While our colleagues in Knin brushed off their barely-viable evacuation plans it was sensible that I did the same for Team Split. Given enough warning we had two options. The one I preferred, naturally, was to take one of a selection of yachts that I had already noted in the Split marina and sail her across the Adriatic to an Italian port ... or hop along the coast to HQ BRITFOR at Divulje, where, I doubted, we would be made welcome in what would be the middle of a serious drama. The second option was to go by road to Divulje Barracks but I reckoned we would need more notice for that move and, to add a complication, we could not go in a ECMM white vehicle while a taxi was out of the question. I considered cold-starting a civilian car from the hotel car park, or hiring one in advance—but could we guarantee that it would be 'free' at no notice and who would pay, up front? So it was back to the maritime option.

> Must see the Split Marina harbourmaster and ask to look over the most suitable candidates by pretending I might like to buy one of them. I already have one in mind. It strikes me that any yacht owner will be happy for a sale under the current circumstances. What I need to know is how to get on board, where the sails might be kept (assuming they are not already bent on) and how to start the engine.... Will she have enough fuel and so on? The nearest largish Italian port with a marina is Pescara at 114 nautical miles, although San Benedetto del Tronto is a touch closer. Both a 24 hour sail given a fair breeze.

As it happened, during one of my walks around Split's marinas my eye had been caught by a beautiful, traditionally-designed and built, wooden sloop of about 36 feet in length. Unlike almost all of the other sailing vessels moored in their untidy and crumbling berths, *Eloise* seemed to have been maintained; at least, she had not been allowed to fall into total disrepair. My initial thought had been to seek out her owner and ask if he would like a weekend crew but as the threats to our own existence became greater I decided that it was best not to give an inkling of my ulterior motive.

At last, and with the final vestiges of Robert's behaviour behind us, I was able to turn my ideas for escape into action. Calling on Captain Maroje Moroević, Split Marina's harbour master and, by chance the Foreign Port Representative in Croatia for the Royal Cruising Club, I learned that the yacht that I had in mind, *Eloise*, had been abandoned three years earlier by her owner who had not been seen since. He had been, according to Moroević, one of the *intelligentsia* that had fled the country, probably never to return. As a member of the RCC I felt it right to take the harbourmaster into my confidence and was met, not only with understanding, but a guided tour of *Eloise* that included the 'secret' place where a spare set of keys would be kept. Moroević also instructed me on starting the engine. The fuel tank was about a third full, and thus offered a good range should we have to motor the whole way. The state of the diesel, having lain for so long lying undisturbed in the tank, had to be an acceptable risk. The mains'l and genoa were in bags below and could be bent on once we were under way. The sailing side of affairs I could work out for myself.

Encouragingly, Captain Moroević believed that if *Eloise* were to be left in a safe Italian port she might, yet, be reunited with her owner. He was, therefore, happy to be a party to this scheme!

Reconnaissance of Brač's 'Secret' Airfield

Encouraged by the Greeks' use of Café Riva for just about anyone, I asked a number of officers from the HQ BRITFOR at Divulje Barracks to dinner on the following Saturday, 15 January. Although I planned the party to include pilots from 845 Naval Air Squadron—the 'junglies'—for a straightforward, naval style, 'run ashore', inevitably in that part of the world there was an ulterior motive. I needed to get good intelligence about events in the Split area, as seen through military eyes, while at that same time hoping to glean snippets about what was happening across and along the Confrontation Line. I needed rather more honest and factual opinions than those I read in the ECMM's Daily Reports that originated in Knin before being sent on their way to Zagreb and thence, much watered down, on to Brussels.

Due to the lack of transport I had, too, time to ponder on the interpretresses, without whom nothing could happen, yet through whom much that should not have happened did happen. Their part in the overall saga was always confusing. Although they could be fun—not all the time by any means—and were professional—not all the time either—they often let their personal lives get in the way. After all, through their interpreting we were seeking the truth in our work whether we or they liked what we heard or not. They usually thought only of themselves to the point that many a patrol's route and timings had to be altered to suit their social plans: this was fine, in a way, for we had to live together and the interpretresses were an integral part of our small, supposedly close-knit, team. Indeed we could not work without them but, compared to their non-ECMM friends in Split they were paid a fortune and should have tried to conform to the rules of those who employed them. It may seem odd or even unprofessional of us but we had to acquiesce often to ensure their cooperation.

Some patrols cannot happen until we have collected children, delivered children, been to the dentist or stopped to shop for trifles. It sometimes can be difficult to balance the patrolling as there is great jealously between them. Our two, Sandra and Vinka, are so totally different in style, temperament, looks and background that nothing is interchangeable. One is good for some things and the other likewise for different aspects of our work such as areas of expertise or knowledge of a particular village. Of course there are some overlaps and we have to juggle these and the patrols' aims with the interpretress' whims very carefully indeed. No interpretress can be asked to do anything without risking some petty jealousy creeping in with regard to the other; fascinating stuff but it can be tedious.

The more the Greeks/Belgians/French/Croats get excited about 'small beer' stuff the more I try to become relaxed and quiet … which is very good training for me in self-control, often a self-control I did not know I possessed. This is monitoring unlike monitoring in the interior where a real military threat engulfs the teams all the time.

In the Republic of Serbian Krajina they are monitoring the present whereas here on Croatia's Dalmatian coast we are monitoring the future.

By 0830 on 13 January I was fit enough to take part in the second island patrol for which myself, Sandra and Willy set off on the one-hour car *Jadrolinja* ferry voyage from Split to Brač. With Lekeu still 'on leave'—and we were not feeling the loss especially as by now our Land Rover had been returned—Willy was the 'senior' monitor in post but, according to Paul Ortholan, I was the *de facto* Team Leader. In practise this suited Willy for he was not interested in very much except Sandra and, anyway, he was not good at conversing—in any language!

It was a beautiful, cool day with an oily calm, pale-blue sea which, I guessed, was the Adriatic at its winter best: I longed to be hauling on sheets and halyards rather than sitting in a ferry's stuffy café. Luckily the beauty of the day was still with us on our arrival at the island's terminal.

The 'capital' village of Supetar was, and I hope still is, stunningly attractive in an old-world, Mediterranean-style way and was very much how I imagined all the island villages would be. The contrast with most of what I had experienced on the mainland was marked for it was clear that they were very different communities.

As we were early for our visit with the mayor, we sat with hot chocolate in the almost-warm sun reflecting in intermittent bursts off the clear Adriatic water. Interestingly, the lady owner of the café was, too, coming to the meeting in place of her brother, the mayor, who had been suddenly 'called away to Zagreb'.

That old excuse whenever we turn up.

Once ushered into the deputy mayor's office, and even before we had sat down, he was explaining in pleasant but direct terms that his absent mayor was fed up with answering 'all the usual questions from equally bored monitors'. He continued by expressing his hope that we would not keep him long for he, too, felt that we conducted these visits simply to keep our records up-to-date and not because we, the ECMM, were interested. 'Neither you or the ECMM can do anything about our problems so why do we bother to greet you, knowing that you never offer us anything.'

Having seen the lovely, old, fishing port unsullied by the war and tourists and un-alarmed by this opening salvo, for it was quite usual, I decided immediately that a new beginning, a new approach to coastal monitoring, was in order.

Actually the lack of tourists, especial as they were mostly German or Italian, allowed the place to be seen as it really was and not as a down-market tourist trap as was the case with all of the mainland's coastal towns. Here was a beautiful Adriatic fishing village that I wished, silently, could remain that way if it could only find some other source of income. I was to discover shortly that the village was already intent on specialising in the netting, canning and exporting of sardines; a reasonably far cry from their all-purpose catch that supplied the near-empty restaurants and hotels.

Thinking on the hoof as it were, and emboldened by the statutory injection of *raquia* into the bloodstream, I began by telling the deputy mayor that I owned a fine sailing vessel and wondered whether or not she would fit alongside one of his quays.[1] At this he and his mayor's sister perked up. Soon we were discussing *Black Velvet's*[1] size and draught and the number of bunks before slowly moving on to discuss a wider collection of eclectic subjects. We were encouraged to overstay our welcome and as we had nowhere else to be until the afternoon both 'sides' allowed the meeting to develop into a thoroughly pleasant experience. By the natural and unforced end of our conversations I was happy that we had not once mentioned the ECMM, refugees or displaced persons. Yet we had gleaned everything we needed to know about the state of Brač's economy and how the local establishment was planning to overcome its significant problems without the help of the central government in Zagreb.

At one point the deputy mayor remarked that during the two World Wars his island's inhabitants had lived off sardines and that if they could survive on sardines in those days then they could do so again—now. A number of fishermen, he explained, had already returned from taking non-existent tourists on day fishing trips to netting these ubiquitous and plentiful fish. Our conversation had also, for me, brought to life Vinka's English language essay on the future of sardine fishing that I had edited during my first days in Split.

'We will survive as an island community without money. We have fish, olives and wine.'

As we left his office the deputy mayor's farewell remarks were unexpected and welcome. 'It has been pleasant to meet ECMM monitors as friends for once.' He continued, 'I have much enjoyed our talk about all manner of things to do with my island. An island that I love and want to see prosper again.'

For my part, and for the first time since my arrival in the Former Republic of Yugoslavia, I felt that we may have actually achieved something. I was not quite sure what that 'something' was other than that our presence seemed to have given the deputy mayor and his entourage, for others had joined us throughout the morning; a grounding for encouragement. That was all we could have asked although I did hope, privately, that they would not be disappointed for, in truth, we had done nothing—altered nothing—in any practical sense.

Apart from sardines another aspect of economic revival had been discussed. Interestingly, and of significance, the white stone, or marble, quarries at the eastern end of the island (according to the islanders the United States' White House was constructed from Brač stone but I fear this was wishful thinking) had seen an increase in exports since the war started. Nobody could explain this phenomenon but obviously this brought in welcome revenue.

I had, earlier, been invited by my SIS contact to confirm that rumours of an airfield on the island were true yet in answer to my innocent-sounding question, centred around future tourism and trade, the deputy mayor replied that currently all had to travel by sea as that was the only way on to or off the island. If an airfield existed at all, and following the deputy mayor's denial I was beginning to have my own doubts, it was certainly not used, at least not by civilian aircraft: which might have explained his reluctance to confirm its presence. So, not believed to exist even by the deputy mayor (who I suspected was not quite telling the whole truth but I refrained from making such an accusation) and thus built for an un-revealed purpose, I was even more determined to continue with my planned visit on the morrow … and if it did exist it would prove to me that life on Brač could only get better in time.

Neither Willy or I, had—outwardly anyway—been regarded as spies, so it was gratifying that the deputy mayor and his mayor's sister, made no effort to hide their satisfaction, indeed their pleasure, with our visit. The one thing I could do, I explained, was to make a recommendation that Brač was an ideal place for European Community money to be invested when the time was right. Unlike the miserable mayor of Omis, who had complained incessantly about the plight in which his town found itself, the elected representatives of Brač believed their island had a future that did not depend entirely on hand-outs from central government. The island deserved any assistance we would recommend. Brač's deputy mayor could only look forwards and that he was doing in the most positively enterprising manner. This was a boost to Team Split's morale and so we came away knowing that we had, at least, made friends while perhaps even enhancing the ECMM's image by listening and not questioning.

A lesson for the future which we must cultivate.

The only downside to this visit, thus far, was the message from the mayor himself. He had not wanted to see us which, naturally, made me think he was not in Zagreb at all. Nevertheless there was little doubt that his deputy would pass on a positive report of our visit. Then, maybe, he would tell his fellow mayors in Makarska, Omis and the other mainland coastal villages that there was a different atmosphere in Team Split and that we should all meet—maybe even together—for a dinner or lunch in the Café Riva.

We were due to stay in an hotel in the village of Bol on the southern coast so it was to there that we drove through the magnificent, wooded hills until finally dropping down once more towards the Adriatic. The view from the top of the escarpment was wonderful, enhanced further by the enticing site of Hvar, in the background across the *Hvarski Kanal.*

I could live here very happily!

During the Second World War Brač, and a number of the other islands including Hvar, had been occupied by the Nazis until a partisan-led initiative, guided by the Royal Navy and Royal Marines, fought the enemy across the island and, from these same hills, then launched raids against the Nazis on the mainland.

Unfortunately, when I needed it most, my modern Leica camera (not my mother's 1934 version that I had left in my bedroom) had broken that afternoon after just five rolls of film, most taken in the RSK.

I should have brought my water colours but sadly they, too, are in Split.

Having checked into the Hotel Kasstil the three of us enjoyed a meal of octopus and steak. With no tourists these were offered at a high, but affordable, price. As the hotel stayed open purely for the inhabitants of Bol the menu had to be within their reach and while there was 'old money' still left it must have been running out. The rough red wine was delicious in its expected rough way.

During the afternoon I walked with Willy to the end of Zlatni Rat, a remarkably symmetrical, triangular spit of land jutting south at right angles from the coast, a mile to the west of Bol. This was, and still is, a place of beauty that had once been one of Dalmatia's prime tourist attractions. I could not argue. A pine wood runs down the spine of the spit which is fringed with startling, white shingle (not sand as I was expecting) where people had camped in the better days. From the photographs covering the hotel's walls, Zlatni Rat was always packed with Germans but not this afternoon. The only activity, on the eastern side, was a small fishing vessel towing a seine net in a wide circle out from the beach. We watched for half an hour until the land-based crew hauled the net ashore but our patience was unrewarded so, empty-handed but better for the fresh air and exercise, we walked back. Following an early evening kip I woke for dinner to find the other two had disappeared. Sitting alone in the vast dining room, of necessity lit only by candle-light, and with a bottle of red wine and my laptop, I mused:

Luckily I am happy with my own company otherwise this job really would be depressing. I always bring my portable word processor with me so I can dive into writing whether it is for a magazine or one of the books I am working on. It is a great source of comfort (wrong word!) in this strange environment and keeps me sane if not always sober. After about three hours of writing I have probably drunk at least one bottle of the rough wine … And this with little effect but it is a rather nice way to ease the mind if not the fingers on the key board which become more clumsy as the imagination grows more vivid.

Eventually Sandra turned up without her 'lover'. The remnants of the stomach bug, that I had had a few days earlier, were still with me (maybe the unaccustomed, large lunch had not helped) but I was game for a light supper in a nearby café where the interpretress had agreed to meet two girlfriends. My plan had been to beat a retreat to bed after managing delicious, still-warm bread and a bowl of spicy, fish soup but I became reluctant to leave for the café was quickly filling with Bol's 'attractive young things'. Another cause for my reluctance to leave was Sandra's elder friend. Here was a whole gale of fresh Adriatic air who, with her boyfriend, had established a 'sea-adventure school' that offered limited nautical expeditions coupled with 'water sports'. When asked about the lack of clients she agreed it was making the embryo venture difficult: nevertheless they were beginning to attract a nucleus of locals boosted by a growing trickle from the mainland. This was typical of the islanders' determination to get on with life to the point that I could not think of them as Croat. Indeed, whenever possible, they would, sometimes quite vehemently, distance themselves from that tag.

Tackled over the comparatively high prices they charged, the response was illuminating. In Sandra's friend's near-faultless English she explained, 'This is especially on purpose so that we can keep the 'fish and chip brigade' out!'

Quite a sacrifice to make under these poor economic circumstances yet nice to know that just because they might need money now is not the time to lower standards—what an uplifting attitude.

I learned, too, that the island also supported the hunting of *mouflon* (of the mountain sheep family) in the hills while their spring lambs were a pronounced delicacy: 24 pounds in weight being the upper limit for them to be killed as such.

The lambs only eat herbs and, so I am told, taste superb. It is not the season so maybe when it is I can return.

The probability of a 'secret' airfield on Brač puzzled me more now. The SIS thought it existed 'possibly in a low lying plateau somewhere above Bol' which was a good enough excuse for me to go and have a look. The deputy mayor seemed to think it did not exist or was he implying that it did not exist as far as civilian traffic was concerned? If this was the case, what was the purpose for its existence? I had in mind the breaking of the UN arms embargo. Days earlier, when planning this 'patrol', I had mentioned the airfield to Sandra as a monitoring project. Intriguingly she had stated that it was not a secret so much, it was just an unused military airfield and, as such, she advised against wasting our time: by which she meant wasting her time! I had disagreed and responded with the view that that was precisely a good reason to find out what it was, in truth, being used for and what, perhaps, it could be used for in the future. I had, too, reminded her that the Croat Air Force had barely existed since 1991 when the Jugoslav National Army had 'left' for Serbia: building a military airfield for an air force with no aircraft had to be questioned.

At 0900 the next day, 14 January, Willy drove us via a rather peripatetic journey to the airfield, retracing our track several times. There were good reasons for this: neither Sandra or Willy knew where it was although her assessment of the approximate position did, obviously unknown to her, coincide with that of the SIS. The airfield was not marked on any map despite construction having begun a few years earlier and, as we were eventually to discover, it was over one mile from the nearest marked track and over one-and-a-half miles from the nearest formal road. Once we found what had to have been the route taken by the construction lorries, now very much overgrown, we actually covered a further two-and-a-half miles until, quite unexpectedly the very rough path, for it was by now little more than stone-filled ruts, opened into a small, tarmacked car park below the control tower. Another reason why it had been difficult to find was that Willy, with his hangover found driving 'confusing' nor was he helped by Sandra's map reading. I suspected that she did not want us to find the airfield for she kept suggesting the least likely turning wherever there was a choice. In truth, she was so hung-over that I do not think she cared whether we found the thing or not!

I was not surprised by the state of their health for earlier that morning, at about 0300, they had created a considerable noise in the corridor outside my room which lay between theirs!

To reach the airfield we had driven along a switch-backed, boulder-strewn (on purpose?) track between wild olive groves to find a modern but simple complex of aluminium-clad sheds, a baggage store and rudimentary 'control tower' perched on top of a wobbly-looking, large metal pole around which an equally unstable, metal, spiral ladder twisted upwards. There was not a soul around and although it was clearly 'operational' it was not actually in operation. I was, though, conscious that what I was about to do exceeded my ECMM mandate and could only be classified as intelligence gathering: nevertheless I was suspicious and decided that the need to know 'why it existed' outweighed the risk of being caught. Anxious to get a feel for the place, the length of the paved runway and its possible uses it was a simple job to climb the perimeter fence and drop down the other side. Although glad that there was no one to prevent my snooping I would have liked to have asked one or two, quite correct, monitor-style questions about the airport's real purpose for it had a very military feel to it. I was not to know, as I paced just over 4,700 feet of pristine runway,[2] that it had been visited fourteen days earlier, as a subsequent article in the Croat weekly magazine, *Nacional*, described on 24 May 2005:

> Considering that the US was more interested in the situation in Bosnia–Herzegovina than in Croatia, they asked Croatia to permit them to install a military base with unmanned aircraft. The basic condition was that this be the best kept secret, so that it would not appear that the US had taken sides in the war. The island of Brač was selected, as it could be well protected. There all the equipment and personnel led by the CIA experts, with the long-range unmanned aircraft which could cover the entire territory of Bosnia–Herzegovina to the Serbian corridor on the Sava River, were based. The entire Krajina region in Croatia was also in its range. At that time no-one had any idea what was going on and what was being hidden on the island of Brač. Nor did the US's allies, the Germans, have any idea. They sent their military attaché there on 1 January 1994. He hired a car and drove the outer fence of the base and began taking pictures, thinking that the alertness of the base would have faltered on New Year's Day. However, he was quickly spotted and arrested. Only when he was brought in for questioning was it learned that he was the German military attaché in Zagreb, Hans Schwan.

I was obviously lucky for, unlike the hapless Hans Schwan, there was not a soul to apprehend me although I could not help feeling that Sandra was longing for me to be caught and locked up! As the result of Schwan's arrest—and release—I was to learn much later that the airfield's security was then boosted in preparation for the arrival of the American, *Predator*, unmanned surveillance aircraft prior to the invasion of the Republic of Serbian Krajina during *Operation Storm* in August 1995.

> Dry scrub and olive trees are scattered across this stony, undulating plateau which is surrounded on all sides by the low hills above Bol, screening the runway from any casual observers. No roads leading to the airfield are marked on the maps that we have.

Happy that I had all the intelligence I was likely to get and as neither the canning factory nor the stone quarry managements would see us, despite these meetings having been set up by our liaison officer, we headed home.

> If they do not want help we should not try to force it upon them for they then become suspicious of our motives. On the other hand they are fed up with visits

that produce nothing so we are chasing our tails. I suspect they know that as well and that is why they refuse to see us. This is a huge pity and will remain so, even on Brač, unless the deputy mayor can spread the word. We took an early ferry back although I could have remained there, willingly, but without Willy and Sandra, to explore the island.

In Hotel Split Vassilis and John Georgiadis, the Mission's Greek Head of Logistics and Personnel, were staying for dinner in preparation for Croat independence celebrations on the morrow. John, a large, floppy-faced, unfit major-general, had studied the Falklands campaign at the Greek Staff College which was, perhaps, unfortunate for over dinner he talked endlessly about nothing else. To shut him up, I promised to send him a copy of my *Falkland Islands Shores*[3] and that should bore him into silence!

15 January was the day that Croatia celebrated the second anniversary of its recognition as an independent, sovereign state and I was not looking forward to the mayor of Split's reception for my limited experience had shown what turgid occasions these could be. The second reason for my reluctance was that I would be accompanied by Philipos, the Greek head of the ECMM's Forward Logistic Group. He was the man with the 'nodding dog' head and a permanent air of inferiority. In his remarkably limited English this middle-aged, Greek army corporal had, on his first day in Split, taken me aside to declare, in an oddly conspiratorial manner and in 'nursery' English emphasised by much wringing of hands, that I was under his command and must obey his orders from that moment onwards. This was, of course, a nonsense for, although living in the same hotel we were, most emphatically, not in his chain of command: no more than any other monitoring team throughout the Mission across the Former Republic of Yugoslavia. He and his men existed to supply 'on-demand' logistic support to monitors in the field; no more and certainly no less. However, at 1030 Philipos and I, accompanied by the corpulent Sergio, the one male interpreter in our team and employed only at weekends, set off for Split's ornate Town Hall dressed, tactfully, in our best white clothes. Although I hated wearing white when not on monitoring duties in the field I felt I should, on this rare occasion, be in 'uniform'. On arrival I was glad to be correctly dressed for all the military personnel from just about every nation participating in UNPROFOR were also in their best uniforms with medals and 'all the trimmings'. This made it even more surprising when one of the British brigadiers appeared in tired-looking, crumpled combat dress—what I call camouflaged pyjamas.

Why can't a senior British army officer behave and dress correctly on such a civic occasion: it looked very bad and uncivilised while proving nothing.

We hung around with Sergio who had insisted that we come early. A great deal of embarrassment as nothing was ready. Oh to be in charge of my own affairs on occasions like this. Eventually we were ushered along the receiving line towards a tray of champagne which was rather a surprise as I was expecting coffee. Introductions were followed by a twenty minute harangue (there is no other word) in English from the mayor about how Germany was the only country that had had the foresight and strength to push for the recognition of Croat independence. We all, Croatians and foreigners alike, found this acutely embarrassing. He then continued to tell all the military that it was about time they attacked the Serbs in the RSK. The captain and various naval officers from HMS *Invincible* were there too but no German military that I could detect: just as well considering I know but cannot prove—YET!—that they, along with the Americans, are breaking the UN arms embargo in support of Croatia.

A final quote from the mayor: 'It is about time the international community punished Croatia's enemies'.

Anyway, in a thankfully-short speech, the brigadier refrained from telling the mayor that UNPROFOR was not there to fight Croatia's wars—which of course they were not—but he did emphasise the fact that they were there to ensure, among very many other aims, that any aid convoys passing through the country reached their various destinations.

After the speeches a number of former colleagues from the Royal Navy and British Army were anxious to question me about life as seen from the perspective of a monitor while I was equally keen to learn of their business. Sadly, these enlightening conversations were nearly brought to a premature halt by the Greek corporal losing his temper while insisting that he and I left before the end of the party. I suggested he took a taxi back to Hotel Split or even walk but unfortunately this did his humour even less good.

It's not my fault if the 'nodding dog' does not like parties, champagne, senior officers or cannot speak English. He screamed a 'military' order at me in his farcical English and in front of the others as though I was his minion which wasn't very wise of him. Anyway, he was forced to stay and sit by himself at a table in the corner sipping from a glass of lemonade.

This evening, to wash away the memories of this morning's goings-on, the ten officers I had invited (including four pilots from 845 Naval Air Squadron—one of whom was John Pentreath, David Pentreath's[4] charming son) came to dinner bringing with them their RAF Liaison Officer. Squadron Leader Martin Sinclair has a very keen eye for the girls and is most amusing about it. Hilarious evening and a hugely fun oasis in this otherwise barren social life. A light-hearted occasion in the midst of so many stilted conversations with boring, uninterested Croats which is probably our fault for being so turgidly boring with our questions: a fact that I am altering as quickly as possible. As first practised at Brač, 'no more questions' is the order of the day—there are other ways of getting what we need. Much useful background information about 845's work here with their Sea King helicopters.

Paul Ortholan and Patrick Brook called in for lunch the next day having driven across the Confrontation Line from Knin bringing with them a new monitor. When I heard that an Irishman called Fergus was joining Team Split my heart sank for I thought it had to be the arch republican, Fergus, who had been at Knin on my arrival but, thank God, Fergus Marshall was not at all like his namesake. This Fergus was an emotionally-balanced, lieutenant-colonel in the Irish Army, a professional logistician, and an offshore yachtsman. He was to be great fun and a magnificently supportive ally. He also wore a tie! The not so good news was that there was no update about Team Split's status and whether or not we were to be two teams and whether or not we were now responsible for the coast to the south. As nobody else was monitoring this major area, which included the strategic port of Ploče, it had to be about time that an unalterable decision was made.

Following lunch Paul took me aside to discuss the problem of Robert Lekeu. It was now that I first learned that well before my arrival in Knin he had already been causing trouble. At one point he had been reported crossing, unlawfully, various borders, both international and 'self-proclaimed', and at some previous stage had also 'gone missing' by himself for 48 hours with an ECMM Land Rover. While speaking, Paul was crafting a signal he would send that evening in which Lekeu would be told that he was no longer a monitor while hinting that he might be sent back to Knin. Although glad that Lekeu had finally been sacked from Split I saw his removal to Knin, rather than back to Belgium, a poor idea. It would show the Croats that the ECMM had given him a second chance of serving in the RSK, a place he clearly supported. Apparently Headquarters ECMM did not wish to send him home in disgrace for he was close to the end of his service in the Belgian Air Force from which, too, he would probably then have been dismissed. I did not really care, all I wanted was to see the back of him.

On the morning of my fifty-second birthday, 18 January, Vinka kindly unveiled from her ever-present, ever-full, wicker basket a bottle of rather delicious, sparkling Croat wine which we drank in the office before setting off—admittedly a little tiddly!—to patrol the Confrontation Line and the United Nation's Military Observers' Observation Posts. This surprise set both of us up well for an interesting day.

With nothing to report from the OPs we called in, by invitation, at the UNMO's multi-national dwelling to enjoy a superb lunch cooked by an Indonesian officer—the day's duty cook. Perfectly spiced meat and vegetables generously ladled on to equally perfect, dry rice, was the rarest of pleasures; tasting unlike anything I had eaten since leaving England. Around the table, if I remember correctly, most of the globe seemed to have been represented. Other nationalities that I recall came from Scotland, Ireland, Holland, Malaysia, Sweden, Ghana and Norway plus three from Middle Eastern countries and at least one representative from black Africa. After such an entertaining interlude the last thing we wanted to do was to spoil the day by interviewing yet more, uninterested Croat military personnel. Nevertheless, as it had been fixed well in advance, we drove to a Croat Army Home Guard unit where we were invited in to their officers' mess. This was little more than a half completed cottage in the bottom of a cold and damp valley that had been commandeered for the war. Quite surprisingly, the commanding officer knew it was my birthday and to 'honour that fact' (his words) he produced coffee and much *raquia*; or for once it might have been *slivovitz* for it certainly tasted considerably nicer. It was, rarely, a most relaxed meeting during which I felt it possible to apologise for Lekeu's behaviour during our previous visit. Then he had told the major in command that he, Lekeu, had spent his first months with the Mission in Serbia. When the Croat officer asked, 'Where in Serbia?' Lekeu had replied 'Knin'. This tactless remark was compounded further after the major countered, 'No, that is still Croatia.' Lekeu's instant reaction was so insulting that the interpretress and I had to physically manhandle him into the Land Rover. It had been a bizarre episode with the Belgian continuing to shout through the open window, as we drove away, that the major was wrong and that Knin was part of Serbia. We had driven home in embarrassed silence.

Now, the major took my apologies in good faith especially when I was able to tell him that Lekeu had, at last, been sent away. The many Croats of all ranks around the large table expressed their satisfaction that the ECMM had been seen to take positive action which, in a way, was almost as embarrassing.

Before we left, the major had one unrelated request. 'Please tell the Royal Navy helicopters to stop flying outside their agreed flight paths as I cannot trust my men not to shoot them down if they continue.' This struck me as odd for I was certain that 845 Naval Air Squadron's pilots were sticking rigidly to the agreed plans. Nevertheless I promised to speak to their commanding officer and that evening I was as good as my word. The pilots were intrigued to think that their aircraft had strayed into the no-fly zones; or even outside the agreed flight paths. There was little doubt in the British minds that the miscreants were actually Croat aircraft flying illegal missions into Bosnia–Herzegovina and if that led to a 'blue-on-blue' engagement, so be it! I doubted there would be many tears in 845 Squadron's aircrew briefing room.

In the evening and following many drinks in the Riva Terrace Bar I gave a birthday party dinner and as Martin Garrod was in the hotel he had joined me even earlier in Room 519 for tea and *Patum Peperium* sandwiches.

> Huge fun party in the ECMM dining room. Richard Perry gave me a 'Red Cross' birthday parcel containing a pot of marmite, a tub of honey and a tin of 'pussers'—government issue—marmalade.

Above left: Ewen S-T.

Above right: Ewen S-T at Makarska.

Hotel 'I' (Google).

Above: Chart showing the confusions, a rough version of this was issued to ES-T on first arrival at HQ ECMM, Zagreb. *Re-drawn by Tim Mitchell Design.*

Left: The so called Republic of Serbian Krajina in red, as issued by the ECMM.

Below: Ethnic divisions across the Former Republic of Yugoslavia as issued by the ECMM.

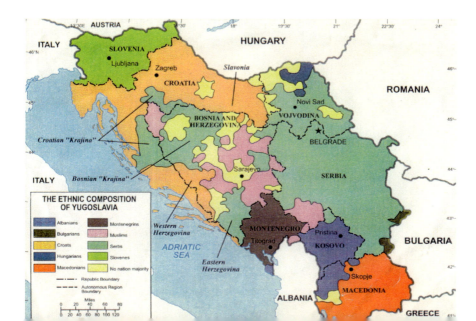

The Croat flag with re-introduced Ustaše chequerboard introduced in 1990, so feared by the Serbs.

Above: Knin.

Below: The Knin 'Motel'.

Karin Plaza beach reconnaissance.

Ewen S-T and Captain Dragan during the 'official' ECMM visit to his camp.

Right: Vassilis Dertilis.

Below: Hotel Split now named the Radisson Blu. (*Courtesy izvor fotografije*)

View from room 519.

Above left: The 'nodding dog'.

Above right: Vinka.

Fergus Marshall with Sandra and 'Roads of Peace' convoy lorries.

Jean-Pierre Thébault as French ambassador to the Republic of Ireland, during a service in Dublin to honour the victims of the Charlie Hebdo attack in Paris. (*Wikimedia Commons, courtesy Cqui*)

Fergus 'fully prepared' in helmet and flak-jacket while Lennart entertains in Team Split's office.

Port of Ploče, 23 October 2015. (*Wikimedia Commons, courtesy Quahadi Añtó*)

Eloise, our escape yacht.

Croat soldiers on the front line.

Split Opera House. (Croatian national theatre in Split), 29 November 2006. (*Wikimedia Commons, courtesy Kaiser87*)

Above left: Patrolling the Confrontation Line.

Above right: Serb couple in Croatia.

Above: A Royal Navy UNMO on the Confrontation Line with Hans, Ewen and Lennart. (He has even had his hair dyed white!)

Below: Šibenik Bridge, 25 January 2009. (*Wikimedia Commons, courtesy Ex13*)

The control tower of Brač airport in 2011, but from where the Predator was operated in 1995. (*Wikimedia Commons, courtesy Waerfelu*)

Members of the 11th Reconnaissance Squadron, Indian Springs, Nevada, perform pre-flight checks on the Predator prior to a mission, 9 November 2001. (*Wikimedia Commons, courtesy U.S. Navy photo*)

Above left: Operation Storm (*Time Magazine*)

Above right: Bill Clinton, photograph 1 January 1993. (*Wikimedia Commons, courtesy Bob McNeely, The White House*)

Franjo Tudman. An article from *The Sunday Times*, 6 August 1995.

Croat Air Force Mig-21.

Above: USMC EA-6B aircraft destroyed Serb communications prior to Operation Storm. (*USN library*)

Right: USN F-14A fighters destroyed Serb anti-aircraft defences prior to Operation Storm. (*USN Library*)

M-84 MBT during Operation Storm. (*Time Magazine*)

The ethnic cleansing of 200,000 Serbs from Krajina following Operation Storm. (*Time Magazine*)

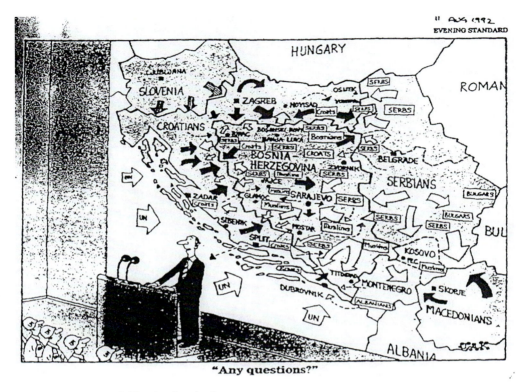

"Any questions?"

Any questions? (*Evening Standard*)

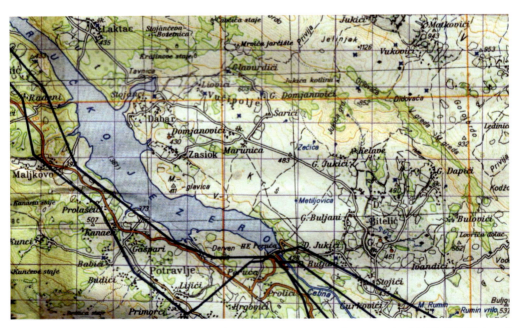

Sample of the issued maps acquired from BRITFOR. Peruca dam area. (*MOD/ BRITFOR issued map*)

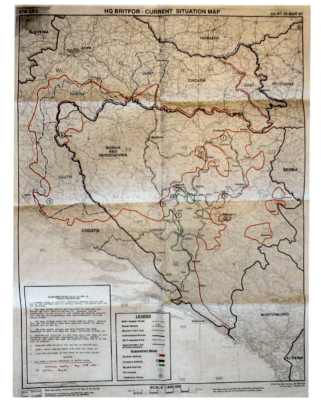

Above: Sample pages from my diary for 12 February 1994.

Left: BRITFOR Situation Map dated March 94. Shows not only the confusions across the FRY but the RSK border into Croatia. (*MOD/ BRITFOR issued map*)

It had been kind of him especially as I was due on my mid-tour leave in the morning. I stored them in a safe place to await my return. The next day the aeroplane was three hours late arriving at Split airport, due to fog at Zagreb, allowing me time to reflect on my surroundings. This was the airport that had been shot up by the departing fighter aircraft when the Yugoslav National Army had left the country after Croatia's declaration of independence two years before. All the pilots had been friends, indeed they were officers in the same squadron, yet when those leaving for Serbia took off they wheeled back to strafe the control tower and nearby buildings killing a number of their now ex-friends and colleagues. The bullet holes remained as a visual indication of some of the internecine hatred caused by Croatia's independence.

There was no transport at Zagreb airport for Hotel 'I' and when it did turn up, one hour late, it had to wait for another plane not due in for a further hour. It had been a long journey but one fairly typical of travel with the ECMM in the early 1990s. Over drinks in the hotel that evening I met again Steve Habbington, Zadar's Operations Officer. Despite my distrust of his loyalties I needed him as an ally of Team Split if we were to progress in the direction demanded by Paul Ortholan but …

There is something odd about Steve and his cynicism. I suspect his views of our immediate boss, Vassilis, might be personal rather than professional. Something odd is going on here and of that I am pretty certain.

My passing through Headquarters ECMM coincided with the monthly meeting of the Heads of all the Regional Centres throughout the Former Republic of Yugoslavia and thus included my own 'boss', Paul, who took the rare opportunity to brief me, face-to-face and not by signal, on Team Split's future. The move to Dubrovnik was not to happen—yet. However it had been agreed at Zagreb that Team Split would still be divided into two teams with me responsible for both as overall Team Leader while a fourth monitor would be appointed to help. We would then mainly be responsible for the Šibenik area to the north as well as the south down to and including the port of Ploče but, disappointingly, no further.

Paul confirmed that the official priorities of monitoring in the Split area were political, economic and military, in that order. We were to continue monitoring, in particular, those areas that could be helped by ECMM money once, and not until, the confrontation between the RSK and Croatia was over. Moving on, he asked me to contact my FCO, while I was on leave, to sign on for a third, three-month period. In return I asked for a proviso, to which he decisively agreed: I wanted Team Split's proposed arrangements to be inviolable for the foreseeable future. In reply he, in effect, issued a direct order to me to, in Royal Navy parlance, 'Make it so' ending with the promise that this would be cleared by the Head of Mission himself. He agreed that it was vital that we had a degree of permanence in order to get things going while he accepted that monitoring UN arms embargo 713 was to have an 'unofficial' priority. Whatever that meant! That evening I met also the Head of Mission, Mr Gerokostopoulos, a Greek diplomat with 'Ambassador' status who was dining with the new British Head of Delegation, Godfrey Garrett: both gentlemen were to feature in my life, but the former not very usefully, once I returned from leave.

My impromptu meetings were not yet over for the day:

Martin Garrod is here for the HRCs conference. He is fully convinced that the Greeks have a hidden agenda and are about to re-jig all the Team Leaders so I must keep in with Vassilis Dertilis no matter what. He is also here in the hotel and has somehow wheedled his way into the HRC's conference but was, tellingly, not included at their dinner which put his nose very severely out of joint. He went into town in a huff, no doubt looking for … …! He does, though, seem to have a great position of influence, or so he keeps telling me. Certainly there do not seem to be any Greek hang-ups about him living with his 'civilian' interpretress/driver, or for wearing civilian clothes when on duty. Nor does anyone in authority seem concerned that he is making undeliverable promises to the Croats that can never be honoured before the Germans take over or, of more significance, after they takeover. Without doubt this is to embarrass and wrong-foot the Germans once they hold the presidency. The Greek hierarchy turn a blind eye to him spending time in Dubrovnik, for no apparent 'official reason', with his female driver….

All very strange but I shall have to continue to put up with him taking our two interpretresses out for the night when he is in Split and swaggering through the Café Riva with a long, woollen overcoat across his shoulders, smoking a large cigar and with a wide-brimmed fedora either perched on the back of his head or pulled low over his eyes—like something out of a past and rather dodgy, black and white Hollywood movie! He is easily bored ….

Early night after a final brandy with Martin Garrod who is fascinating about Mostar for which he obviously feels a great affection but apart from his deep concerns over the re-building of that desperate town he gets very worried that the ECMM can offer nothing. 'We have nothing to give them, Ewen, nothing to give them.' He is smoking very heavily his small cigars and is even more gaunt than before. I and others worry about him. He works hard and that is to be expected of him in particular but he is overdoing things.

Yet more snippets of news, true and rumoured, reached me during my last evening in Zagreb with none of them encouraging me to believe that anything at all would be sorted out as far as monitoring on the coast was concerned, despite Paul's optimism. One rumour had it that monitoring in Dubrovnik would never be on the cards notwithstanding the Greeks (one of their more sensible pronouncements) saying that Regional Centres and their dispersed teams should follow international borders. Forgetting for a moment that the Confrontation Line was not an international border this meant that teams from Bosnia–Herzegovina should not be involved in coastal monitoring in the Dubrovnik area. This tied in with the views of those monitors in Mostar and Tomislavgrad who were more than occupied looking eastwards to worry about what was happening across a border to the west that was, in effect, dividing them from a foreign country 'behind' them.

As Dubrovnik's humanitarian issues were beginning to reach far into Bosnia I argued that we should have two teams with one, one man team in Dubrovnik for Bosnia-related humanitarian problems and a second, two-man team based in the town for the economic monitoring. On the southern Dalmatian coast, this monitoring task had to be vital for the future viability of the area. To divorce Dubrovnik's economic needs from the rest of Dalmatia did not make sense since the town was the largest jewel in the Dalmatian crown. If Dubrovnik wanted to go it alone then perhaps there were even more reasons for the ECMM to be in place, advising and discussing future economic aid. This had to be, I would have thought, much to Croatia's benefit.

Interesting talk with Godfrey who took me aside as I was trying to leave for bed. He was worried about my personal security because of something that has been said about me being a member of the British special forces! As I have studiously told everyone, I am probably the only person out here who does <u>not</u> claim to have been in special forces, this is rather an odd accusation. It is easy to see why it has been levied for everyone from the 'continental countries' claims to have been in their country's special forces: for some macho-inspired reason (and as I have said before in these notes) it is very important for certain individuals (no matter what they did in fact do when in their countries) to have been in special forces. Being able to claim such a background somehow projects a sort of virile image. A load of baloney as far as I'm concerned. I have met just a handful of 'foreigners' out here who would be, by British standards, a member of a special force but then continental standards in these matters are rather below ours.

It was high time that I was on leave and by the same time the next evening, I'm glad to report, I was preparing to enjoy, on the morrow, a day of pheasant shooting in deepest south Devon. Nice, safe, happy, secure Devon: no drunk sixteen-year old soldiers firing their AK47s across the front of my nose; no armed soldiers evicting innocent civilians from their legally-owned houses: no swastikas daubed on government buildings never to be removed; no excitable, screaming Greek corporals stamping their feet and nodding their heads; no minefields; no 'special forces'; no Confrontation Line or mined no-mans'-land; no duplicity … and no *raquia*!

As expected, the two weeks of leave were a wonderful break although certainly no rest. Among other excitements they included a very long lunch with three SIS officers in a 'safe restaurant' in Soho where one or two things were required of me on my return to Dalmatia. In reply, I asked them to conduct yet more homework on Captain Dragan.

While on leave I thought it useful to send a formal report of my first impression to Julian Metcalf now back with the Eastern Adriatic Unit at King Charles Street. My letter of 4 February 1994 read in parts:

> In common, probably with everyone else posted to former Yugoslavia, I was amazed at the length and breadth of the problem. In this current day and age when most people are able to accept differences in order to live in peace, the hatred quite openly expressed and shown between the people of both sides (Croat and Serb) is horrifying ….
>
> It is always difficult for a newcomer to understand exactly what it is he is supposed to be achieving and, in the case of the Former Republic of Yugoslavia there are certainly a number of anomalies which do not help in this respect: the very quick turn-round of monitors; the personal standard and commitment of some who are only here because they have been sent by their respective services to grow-up is an example. My first team, from whom supposedly I was to learn the ropes, were very moderate indeed, with no active service experience, although the Frenchman always insisted he was trained to kill and not to monitor. Their only aims were to telephone their wives the moment we entered the Land Rover, distribute aid then get home as quickly as possible …. Thank goodness for the FCO's vetting system and the fact that we (the UK's monitors) are all volunteers having retired following much foreign service and operational experience.
>
> Some monitors, usually at the beginning of a presidency, are appointed with no experience at all into key positions. The case of the new HCC in Zadar (a Greek naval officer clearly with a very different and hidden brief) started with no understanding of the problems at all and he was replacing an experienced British monitor ….
>
> Now for some constructive comments and observations: one thing that has become apparent to me in the RSK is that there are few if any people left with any understanding of international politics and relationships. On arrival in Split I found this to be just as relevant for Croatia.
>
> Money = higher education = political awareness = an understanding of international affairs and interactions between neighbouring states. People with money on both sides, have all left. Hence the dearth of sensible politicians able to know when to give a little. They do not have the diplomatic experience to know when to stop taking, to stop demanding … and to start listening.
>
> On the coast a different style of monitoring is required from that in the RSK and I would sum up our work as follows:
>
> a. Political monitoring with a view to helping international politicians and diplomats reach a negotiated settlement on the Krajina issue. This may expand if Dubrovnik comes under real threat again.

b. Economic monitoring in order to prepare the rebuilding of Croatia through the assistance of the European Union when the war comes to an end, and help the implementing of economic confidence building measures.

c. Humanitarian monitoring in order to orientate and coordinate and not to handle directly such aspects as the exchange of prisoners of war, the dead, and the reuniting of families.

While the present system of monitoring is well-established I believe that for some monitoring it is likely that we will achieve better results if we were not always dressed in white. I have noticed in intangible ways that when we walk into an office it is the uniform that often puts people on their guard. Because nobody on either side will never believe that we are here for their own benefit I see this as a hindrance. People who are unwilling to talk to us in uniform are happy to dine with us in the hotel during which we can talk as equals with a consequent benefit to both sides, but this is an expensive, time-consuming, and sometimes invidious way of doing business.

This throws up two anomalies—probably more relevant on the coast … In Split I believe that it would make more sense for monitors to have a background in economics and politics—and perhaps even commerce. Not only would this ensure a higher standard of monitoring, but would provide a more professional image among those whom we monitor. The second, but allied, aspect is that monitors, particularly those away from the war, should spend as long as possible in their area. Political and economic monitoring only becomes useful after a lengthy study of an area's local political and economic backing and filling.

However, as I am neither a politician nor an economist I have devised a style of monitoring on the coast that, I hope, hides these deficiencies in my background. I have developed a technique whereby I ask very few, if any, questions and treat the person to whom I am talking as a friend whom I wish to get to know better and, through him, his country. An example was on the island of Brač where I started by discussing whether or not I could get my yacht alongside the town quay. At the end of a fascinating morning I probably knew more about the island's problems than most of the islanders and was able to put them into a proper perspective ….

One final thought. There has been a move by the Greeks to have the whole of the Dalmatian coastline under one Regional Centre. This is now the case as far as Ploče is concerned. However, for reasons to do with the war in Bosnia it has not been accepted by some that the Dubrovnik area should be monitored by those on the coast. This is not understood. Dubrovnik is the jewel in the Dalmatian Crown and while it is accepted that, *inter alia*, aid moves inland from the area south of Ploče, where the Bosnian border reaches the sea (thus effectively cutting the coastline in half) the current monitors in that area do not, and I suggest cannot, cover the area of Dubrovnik at the same time. The monitors themselves admit that they are only interested in looking eastwards along the convoy routes.

This cannot be in Dubrovnik's long-term interests. The whole of the coastline is linked, despite being cut in half, through common policies on tourism, fishing and canning, cement production, light industry, such as the plastic factories and the ladies underwear factories. Internal Croat trade takes place either by sea along the coast or, in penny packets, along the coast road. One inland Regional Centre can, if necessary, cover the humanitarian work in the port area, undisturbed by the monitoring team from another coastal regional centre covering economic and political aspects. My suggestion would be to downgrade the Regional Centre at Knin (but for local presentation purposes call it something important) turn Zadar into the coastal Regional Centre with (going south) a Coordinating Centre at Split with three teams covering the north as far Šibenik, the centre around Ploče and the south covering Dubrovnik. As I may have mentioned, there's been talk of Dubrovnik becoming an independent state with a status similar to, for instance, Monte Carlo.

Julian Metcalf replied, in part, on 9 February:

Thank you very much for your honest, and perceptive, letter of 4 February .... Your comments, particularly those relating to the sense of hatred amongst the parties and the calibre of (some of) your colleagues chime loudly with my own impressions .... Your letter indicating the sense of reward, often achieved at an unexpected moment as in your account on the island of Brač, is deeply satisfying.

Your comments about the isolation of RSK politicians are, sadly, very apposite. I hear similar sentiments about local politicians from other monitors working elsewhere in the Former Yugoslavia. Each monitor needs to find his depth and judge how best to swim the tide. I'm not surprised that your own particular technique has proved to be successful. One of the drawbacks of the professional technocrat—and I speak as a professional economist—is that they tend to go in with far too many direct questions at the outset. For the ECMM this has led to particular problems. As you will know from first-hand experience, attempts by ECMM to glean economic information have often been misinterpreted by the host as interference in internal affairs, or worse. The roundabout approach is often more effective.

I have much sympathy for your comments about the division of Regional Centre responsibilities along the Croat coast. A letter I have recently seen from the Mayor of Dubrovnik is clear that the community there is determined to pursue their immediate interest in an imaginative manner. But the issue is complicated by the schizophrenic attitude of the Croatians towards the ECMM .... Croatia must accept that the ECMM's efforts to evaluate the economic situation and the potential of particular areas does not amount to spying.

Too soon, on 7 February, I flew back to Split airport where, as half expected, there was again no transport: the Greek Chief of Transport in the Forward

Logistics Group had made his usual cock-up. By sheer good chance the one pleasant (and English-speaking) Greek in Hotel Split, the permanently-smiling Aris, was eventually able to collect me. This was an unexpected bonus for on the way back to the hotel he mischievously, while amusingly showing no empathy for his fellow Greeks, brought me up to date on events that had taken place in my absence. On our arrival we continued this fascinating conversation over whiskies in Room 519.

Things had altered a little since I was last in Split and I arrived bearing permission from the FCO to extend my service by a third, 72-day tour: this was excellent news with which both Paul and I were delighted. Willy van den Bossche was no longer with us and the absent Lekeu had been dispatched to Zagreb—neither was a loss. At last a new team of three experienced monitors was in place and by coincidence all with a military background: myself, Fergus, Lennart Leschly the piano-playing Dane with a Dutch army officer, Hans Spijker, due to join the Mission that day to make the fourth. Inevitably, and naturally, it was not to be all plain sailing.

With some relish Aris also briefed me on the Willy saga.

The story is slowly being pieced together as I listen to various versions. Apparently his wife arrived for the leave he had planned to take in Split but she had suspected that Willy was having an affair—and any monitor who does that must be stark raving NUTS. His wife finally had a very public sense of humour collapse and gave Willy a bad time saying she would leave him unless he got an instant posting to Knin—which he did overnight leaving behind the most enormous telephone bill.

Now we are to be a team of four covering the large area from north of Šibenik to the northern limits of the Dubrovnik in the south but with two, two-man teams having to box and cox for the privilege of patrolling as we still only have the one Land Rover. This, of course, makes a mockery of the whole exercise: either all four of us patrol which puts off the people we are interviewing … four of us turning up to talk to one man is intimidating … or two will have to stay behind each day twiddling their thumbs in Hotel Split. It is not satisfactory and we collectively wonder why the Greek-controlled ECMM has bothered to set up this new arrangement without transport.

My first full day back was spent de-briefing Lennart and meeting the new Dutch monitor, Hans. Although Hans's English was rudimentary I believed that we had the makings of two excellent and experienced teams and (*pace* the transport problems) hoped that we could now get on and do something with them. Paul had promised that we would be left alone so I was now able to assure the Croatian authorities in our area, and particularly Dino, that for at least three months Team Split would remain unchanged. Consequently I now briefed him to spread the word: from this day onwards not only would there be continuity with no change of monitors but also there would be no repetition of pointless questions while we intended putting economic monitoring at the top of our list. I realised soon afterwards that experience should have shown me that that was a very naïve assumption!

What I did not tell Dino was that I intended to focus on the UN arms embargo.

The future looks good and interesting even if we do not yet, in practice, have Dubrovnik.

Nick Turnbull, a retired Queens Own Hussars officer, appeared on his way to leave which was fortunate for him as dinner that night was, for some reason known only to the hotel and not the Greeks, in Café Riva. Often the hotel needs to take over the huge ECMM 'dining hall' either for dancing or some political convention. During these evenings the ECMM drivers and signallers drink in the Foyer Bar to study 'the form' as it passes by. On the occasion that a Croat girl is seriously attractive then she is STUNNING—in capital letters. Regardless of any other features, their legs are, almost invariably, fabulous! They wear alluringly short dresses and often it is hard to remind ourselves that there is a war on and that during the day we might be on the front line among the minefields and shelling but by night we are back to witness these equally dangerous sights!

Which are 'equally dangerous' thoughts just before Valentine's Day.

On 10 February I made an interesting visit to the Peruća dam, escorting one of many newly-arrived Greek major-generals. The dam, holding back a lake 18 kilometres long by three kilometres wide had been badly damaged in January 1993 by the Serbs who placed 30 tons of explosive deep within the turbine compartments with the intention of flooding the plain below, putting at grave risk the lives of thousands of civilian Croats. This massive humanitarian disaster had been averted by a Royal Marines major, later colonel, Mark Gray who was working with UNPROFOR. Following an inspection, prior to the detonation expected at any moment, Gray, on his own initiative and far exceeding his orders, released water from the dam, thus reducing the level by fourteen feet. When the Serbs detonated their explosives the bulk of the dam held fast. Eventually Croat forces re-captured the surrounding area and repairs were completed by May 1996. Gray was awarded Croatia's highest award for bravery, the Order of the Duke of Domagoj.

During the day of our visit one of the three generators within the dam was operational and putting something into the national grid, although not much. We could see the RSK positions on a ridge overlooking the dam and knew they were watching us in our white uniforms. The RSK, having retreated a few hundred yards, shelled it every two or three days which is why it was not easy to persuade civilian contractors to conduct repairs and carry out the necessary daily maintenance. The 'other side' is an area where the ECMM from one of the November Teams, was not allowed to patrol or visit.

I invited the general to come with me down into the lower gallery but he refused to move which was a pity as I was keen for him to see deep inside the casement where Gray had earned his decoration. He stood at the top of the steeply sloping tunnel shaking with fear.

Then on to one of the UNMOs OPs where the two 'on duty' observers had laid on a delightful little buffet in their hut while overlooking their area and from where we watched RSK shells landing to our left. The general said he would not have come if he had known we would take the 'back route' close to the border as he was not in an armoured Land Rover. As soon as the shelling started he said he wanted to leave 'immediately'. This ties in with Martin Garrod's description when, the other night, he described how he could not get the general to visit him in BiH despite, then, being driven in an armoured, four-by-four. Martin described him as being a coward and a useless example to the monitors under his command who spend the whole of their time at risk and 'if the general could not visit them he was no leader'. He would not go to Mostar if there was shelling and has asked to travel only in an armoured personnel carrier if he goes anywhere. As we do not have armoured personnel carriers he no longer travels! Not quite sure why he agreed to come on our patrol. My guess is that his staff must have hoodwinked him over the safety aspects of his day. Anyway he was very glum about the whole experience!

8

Aid Convoys and a Greek Complaint

Confusions continued to reign and dictate our work, starting with the news that a mammoth 400-truck convoy organised by two Non-Government Organisations, *Roads of Peace* and *Love for Bosnia–Herzegovina*, would need to pass through Split. Here it would pick up much of its cargo from the docks before heading for the interior at the rate of ten lorries a day for forty days. Obviously Team Split had to be involved for if we failed to smooth the passage of such a massive amount of life-saving aid from the docks to the border with BiH we would be neglecting our humanitarian duties … and, anyway, there was no one else to do so, quite apart from the fact that the scruffy British brigadier had told everyone in the Town Hall that this was one of the main priorities of UNPROFOR and thus, by inference, the ECMM as the 'local facilitators'.

Having signalled a willingness to assist, Team Split prepared to monitor the loading of the first convoy bound for Zenica in Bosnia–Herzegovina. Although the distribution of aid was not our problem its safe passage through Dalmatia was. Once out of our clutches fifty per cent of the cargo would be delivered to Muslim enclaves with the other fifty per cent going to Croat communes in Bosnia–Herzegovina. This was to be the first mixed convoy of the war and one that had firm international backing. Apart from escorting the lorries our duty, as we saw it, was to verify the contents according to the manifests along with the credentials of the drivers and NGO escorts.

My signal to Zadar confirming our assistance fell on foul ground for no sooner had it been received then Vassilis telephoned me in an angry, Greek-style-shouting mode. I stood my ground. It was, quite simply, vital that we were involved with the success of the convoy for if there was to be a cock-up on our patch the Mission's reputation, not just in Croatia but across Bosnia–Herzegovina, could well be tarnished. Yet in Vassilis's view, the answer to our involvement was unarguably 'No!' while in our opinion the answer was, equally unarguably, 'Yes!' The Greek head of CC Zadar was obviously determined to wash his hands of this affair …

What the hell are we here for if it is not to help … and why is he against it anyway?

In a state of angry frustration I telephoned Paul in Knin. He was adamant that there was no argument: we were to continue monitoring the forming up of the convoy and then ensure its safe passage as far as the international border between Croatia and Bosnia–Herzegovina.

> Martin Garrod here again in the evening in a very gloomy mood and repeating his chant that we hear so often, 'We have nothing to offer the locals, Ewen. Nothing. We ask all the same questions but have nothing to offer while the Greeks are here to feather their own political, diplomatic and military nests and not for the long-term interests of the EU. They are doing all they can in advance to bugger up the German presidency in the middle of the year by making promises for the future that they know the Germans will not be able to honour.'

Over dinner Martin related a sad little incident that reflected badly on the British Army. I thanked God that the BBC journalist, with whom I had dinner earlier, was not with us to hear it! Martin recounted how the Coldstream Guards company commander (a major), unlike his more pragmatic and well-mannered predecessors from another British infantry battalion in Gorji Vakuf, was refusing to allow any ECMM monitor into his officers' mess—which was hardly Chelsea barracks!—when passing through. One recent evening, Martin had been turned away unexpectedly and obliged to sleep on the floor of a nearby, roofless barn.

> He is far too nice to have made a fuss.

We were further appalled when Martin explained that he had received neither sympathy nor an apology from the battalion's commanding officer, a lieutenant-colonel. This sad news eventually reached HQ BRITFOR where the rather more senior officers were equally un-amused on Martin's behalf, nevertheless we reckoned any reprimands handed down to the Coldstream Guards company commander and his commanding officer would have been simply water off the backs of two arrogant ducks. All of us around the table that evening agreed that regardless of who we worked for—ECMM, UNPROFOR, BRITFOR, UNMOs, NGOs—we all had to pull together and support each other.

The next morning the two airfield monitors, Roger Sugden and his German colleague Günter, held a briefing in our operations room for the Deputy Head of Mission (Operations) which was a 'classic'. The reason why this was held in Hotel Split and not in the airfield monitors' own operations room was due to Vassilis Dertilis muddling the planning. Now he sat at the back in civilian clothes smoking his cigar while DHOM Ops sat in the front with a very far-away look on his face.

Deciding that he had had enough the mild-mannered Günter woke-up the general before rounding on Vassilis, demanding to know why he never behaved like a monitor. Saying nothing the Greek stormed out in a cloud of smoke.

With Vassilis's absence Fergus and I tried to bring some military order to the event by not only keeping the general awake but briefing him on our area, emphasising that it was the most vital of all for the regeneration of Croatia when the war was over. We stated our firm opinions that neither the RSK nor the Croatians were really interested in lasting peace along the Confrontation Line and that all the signs were in place for more bloodshed. 'Maybe as soon as this summer,' I finished, 'if the obvious Croat re-armament continues.' As it happened Fergus and I were to be exactly one year out.

DHOM Ops agreed our views and that there should be a Regional Centre Zadar to keep the whole of the RC on one side of the Confrontation Line although he believed that the Croat government would try to prevent this as they do not see the Confrontation Line as anything but a Serb-made illegality. However, I argued, we must face the de facto position rather than the de jure one. I raised the proposal that Paul and I had agreed and suggested that Split should be a Coordinating Centre with three teams—the third in Dubrovnik.

It is quite possible this may happen for it is DHOM (Ops) who makes these decisions and by agreeing with everything Fergus and I proposed, based on Paul's wishes, he has given us cause for hesitant optimism that this may occur sooner rather than later. I reminded him that I would like it to be soon as I had extended my service and it would be useful to have the whole new show running before my final tour ended in order that a real going concern could be handed over in June or July. He concurred and we came away feeling that we had achieved something positive. He even said that a second Land Rover would be despatched from Zagreb as soon as he returned to the HQ. Better and better and rather amusing that Vassilis's sudden departure had given us the time to state our case.

At the briefing's end we found Vassilis in the Riva Terrace Bar from where, and un-wisely still not in white ECMM uniform but swaggering around in his dark woollen overcoat and fedora, he escorted the Greek general back to Split airport. Here Vassilis was refused entry by the pistol-waving Croat authorities who saw him simply as a civilian muscling in on a military occasion and had him removed, quite physically, from the premises. Sadly, no one from Team Split was there to jot-down the shouted, fiery conversation that took place across the security barriers and x-ray machines between the general and Vassilis but we were told it was worthy of the finest Hollywood scripts.

That evening's discussions ranged wide with Martin Garrod here again and this time with Rory Ormsby.

These are interesting times especially as an ultimatum has been given to the Bosnian Serbs stating that all weapons heavier than Medium Machine Guns must be removed to outside a 20 kilometre circle around Sarajevo. If NATO bombs them there will be no turning back over this watershed and we must be prepared for a war between NATO—v—Serbs and possibly NATO—v—the Croats and Muslims if they, too, decide to attack UN or the ECMM. The Serbs have said they cannot guarantee the safety of UN personnel or foreigners if bombings take place and of course we have heard that said vis-á-vis ourselves and the Croats. The talk or threat may be empty and nothing might happen but we must now prepare for such action. On the other hand Serbia, being supplied by Greece, may attack on many fronts including Dubrovnik. Will Germany then stand and watch Croatia being attacked by a Greek backed Serbia ... and where does Italy stand in all this with troops being trained in the RSK ready to take over the northern Dalmatian coast?

Martin told me that the army in his area may prevent another convoy passing through their check-point at Gorni Vakuf. If they do they will be targeted tomorrow by NATO air strikes so it could be the Croats who will first feel the anger of NATO. This will surprise the Croats who always regard themselves as being whiter than white—a view held by few others.

That could make our life in Croatia very difficult/dangerous and may jazz things up a bit for us all.

In the mood for malicious gossip as the evening progressed we amusingly recalled that whenever there was confusion the Greeks were bound to be the cause of it. Indeed that very day had been a prime example. The next day that same confusion continued to reign over our involvement with the safe passage of the convoy for we could get no answer from our signals to ECMM Headquarters in Zagreb nor even an acknowledgement that they had been received. Fergus and I decided we should go ahead as planned for the headquarters seem to have a third-world inability to make decisions: unwilling to accept responsibility for doing anything while always having to seek authority from the next above which presumably, in HQ ECMM's case, meant all the way up to Brussels. The servicemen among us monitors were not used to this kind of shoulder-sloping and in the midst of this muddle Bryan Sparrow, British ambassador to Croatia, and Alexey Meković, British Honorary Consul in Split, called in to our office. The ambassador, himself an ex-ECMM monitor, stated that the convoy would proceed with or without permission from the United Nations—for which they were still waiting. As a side-line to his visit he told us he was in the hotel as the duchess of York was due to stay that night in connection with the charity Children in Crisis but that the cynical were saying that she was here to boost her image more than the charity. He felt that his presence might re-assure the cynics ...!

Then, as expected, nothing happened until Valentine's Day evening when Fergus and I searched, initially unsuccessfully, for the first tranche of vehicles in

Split's North Harbour. By chance we ended up in the main transit warehouse to the south-east of the port and found them being managed by good, well-meaning people but who were working in utter chaos through no fault of their own. Despite the confusion it was interesting and good for the morale to see Muslims around the same table as Croats but as the aid is for both factions this was perhaps not so surprising. Yet there was, indisputably, disarray with poorly-sealed, broken boxes spilling their contents all over the place and with no system for checking what was in, or what should have been be in, the containers, nor for which 'side' or faction each was destined.

With no organisation to insure that nothing 'nasty' got repacked Fergus, the professional logistician, by establishing a routine slowly produced order out of the chaos. The phlegmatic and charming Irish lieutenant-colonel, turned white-clad ECMM monitor gave the NGO volunteers leadership and through his example established an authority that, perhaps, even gave some transparent legitimacy that had, so far, been lacking. I watched the boxes being repacked and resealed under Fergus's direction despite knowing that the variety of the contents listed on the re-written manifests would be a nightmare at the border if they had to be re-opened for inspection. It was the pure naivety, the fairness and the sheer good intentions of this international mix of helpers that encouraged Fergus in his tireless efforts despite, as I was to note in my diary that evening:

The ECMM hierarchy showing less than a cursory interest.

Lorries will be driven ten at a time each day until the 400 have left Split for the Muslim and Croat enclaves beyond the border. There others will decide, on the spot, which lorry goes where so that each village should receive the same aid as any other on a random basis. We hope that they can convince all the various enemies along the way that there will be nothing nasty in any of the cargoes.

Apparently the ECMM does not consider that this is important work for us— or is it the Greek presidency that does not consider this is important monitoring? Judging by Vassilis's comments the latter may be closer to the truth. If by being a presence at a convoy of this magnitude is not positive, confidence-building monitoring then I do not know what is. As far as the Greeks are concerned their decisions are designed to make things easy for Greece and not the European Community nor, of more importance, the inhabitants of the Former Republic of Yugoslavia.

Back at 'home' and in a collective, subjective mood, we decided we were fed up with being the butt of the Greek-run, Forward Logistic Group and its crass decisions. Consequently, we four Team Split monitors unanimously agreed that we should seek alternative accommodation beyond Hotel Split's fifth floor. With the possibility of a 'new' and secure future we badly needed somewhere from where we would start afresh by being responsible, as was every other team across the Former

Republic of Yugoslavia, for our own administration, our own communications, our own transport and our own interpreters. We hatched a plan!

The next day, 15 February, the four of us, without an interpretress, drove beyond the lovely, old town of Trogir to the Villa Sandra where the ECMM's airfield monitors lived in style ... probably because their HQ was a retired bordello that had been frequented, without any doubt, by the officers of the former JNA air force and their paramours. Boasting its own secluded beach and with most walls and ceilings in the house, and even one or two of the floors, covered in mirrors it was not too difficult to visualise the villa's previous uses. Thoughts of moving Team Split there centred not only on a desire to escape the malign inefficiency of the FLG but, sad as we knew it was, we needed also to get away from visitors. Much as we enjoyed meeting our fellow monitors we were, unlike any other team, a meeting place, a choke point. There was seldom a night when we could relax for everybody who passed through expected to be entertained. We did not mind, indeed we revelled in the impromptu social events and the news from the interior that they brought ... but not every night!

It did not take us long, helped by the airfield monitors' shared enthusiasm, to assess that the villa's numerous and sometimes outlandish advantages far outweighed its few disadvantages and even the latter were not insuperable. There were spare bedrooms and unused rooms for our own communications centre and operations room and there was plenty of parking space. The two aviators victualled and cooked for themselves in a large kitchen and there was, undeniably, a fun atmosphere to the place which contrasted vividly with the communist-concrete of Hotel Split and its dreadful FLG inhabitants.

In buoyant mood we headed back to Split docks where we had been invited to lunch on board RFA *Resource* whose master, Captain John Wilkins, I had met before. On board we enjoyed a delightful meal of English food, decently cooked and appreciated without having to talk pidgin English for almost the first time. John very kindly photocopied pages of *Jane's Fighting Ships* for me which was useful for my understanding of the ex-JNA Navy. A tour of this 23,000 ton ship was more than instructive for she was being used as a floating and secure warehouse, holding food for 3,000 men for up to six months. This agreeable, three-hour oasis was very much valued before, too soon, we were back into the vagaries and uncertainties of the ECMM.

In Split's North Harbour, from where the *Roads of Peace* convoy was being administered, we found that Fergus's earlier practical help and suggestions were still holding; now working in gratifying harmony, were a Franciscan Monk, a Roman Catholic priest and a brace of Muslim mullahs. All, to a large extent, being encouraged by Kate Maughan, a lieutenant in the Royal Logistic Corps and 'Liz', a terrifyingly-efficient captain in the Adjutant General's Corps, along with representatives from UNPROFOR and the UN High Commission for Refugees. The only possible hiccup was that the convoy had yet to be accorded its final United

Nations accreditation: although the convoy organisers held a 'letter of approval' there were doubts that this would be enough to satisfy the warped authorities in Bosnia–Herzegovina.

The over-loaded lorries themselves were surrounded by an unlikely mix of Bosnians, Muslims and Croats all smiling and referring to this largely unrecognised project as being 'historic' while praising those who had had the imagination to make it happen: not the various feuding governments but honest and humble citizens. Because the day was now late and we had further meetings Fergus and I had to miss the inter-denominational prayers despite being convinced, judging by the state of some of the vehicles, that they would need every supplication and every ounce of divine intervention available if they were to make it to the border, let alone much further. Once Fergus and I had monitored the physical sealing of the lorries we returned to our hotel satisfied that we had taken part in a rarity: a day during which we had achieved something useful and positive.

Inevitably, the next day was the opposite and it began when Philipos, the 'nodding dog', quite literally stormed into Team Split's office screaming unintelligibly. Once he appreciated that neither Fergus or I would take any notice until he spoke calmly and in English he left to return with the long-suffering and mild-mannered Aris as his interpreter. For some inexplicable reason Philipos was demanding that only he should conduct the proposed interview for a new interpreter for Team Split. We had more important problems to consider especially as this extraordinary demand was pointless for the interpreter would not be working for him but for us. Anyway, as he could not speak English he was totally unsuited for the task of interviewer. This was not the first time that I failed to understand his problem and, sadly, it was not the last. Ever since his first day in the FLG he had believed Team Split to be under his personal command yet, as has been explained and no doubt will be emphasised again, this was, of course, nonsense.

> I am sorry to bang on in these notes about the Greeks in general and Philipos in detail but they blight just about every aspect of our life. This excitable little corporal just stands there screaming some new senseless demand while nodding his head like a brainless, wooden marionette. I asked him to stop nodding as I could not make out whether he was meaning yes or no, not that he would have known himself.

On 16 February Fergus, Hans and I left at 0520 to reach the forming up point for the convoy which, by 0715 and by some miracle, was ready to leave although we judged that at least one of the ten vehicles was not likely to make any destination, let alone one in the mountains of Bosnia–Herzegovina. Then, quite astonishingly and at the very last moment it was realised that they all needed fuel! At the time I blamed myself for not making this fundamental check the evening before although it was not really our responsibility and, thus, had not been foremost in our minds.

It was, though, a useful reminder to Team Split that, if we were to be involved, we had to be considerably more vigilant—and diligent.

Finally, with us escorting them from the rear so that we could assist any stragglers, this unlikely rag-tag of assorted heavy goods vehicles, not one of which was in the prime of its life, began limping towards the Bosnia–Herzegovina border beyond Imotski, forty or so miles from Split. It was close to midday and blowing a near-blizzard when all ten, rather miraculously, arrived. A signal was sent to the HQ ECMM in case anyone might have been interested but without an acknowledgement we assumed that still no one cared. Feeling slightly rebellious, we returned quite illegally—because the views were stunning and not to be missed—via circuitous country tracks through Bosnia before returning to Croatia via an unmanned crossing point.

The next morning Hans and I were ready to escort the second batch of ten lorries to the border only to find that the convoy had been cancelled for the day. Nevertheless we reconnoitred the route as far as the border on the road to Tomislavgrad with no hold-ups apart from deep snow drifts. Vinka, terrified of being once more in Bosnia forced us to return along a road she said that she knew was safe. How she could have known this was a puzzle, but it was a puzzle not for long. Soon we had snow-covered mine fields on either side of the rutted track until with a sense of false bravado designed to quieten the frightened interpretress I wandered off to have a much needed pee. Although she was as relieved as I had then become she still claimed she knew where we were until I told her that when we got stuck without snow chains it was her that would have to walk, in high heels, to get help as neither Hans nor I spoke the language nor 'knew the way'. Grudgingly admitting that she had no idea where we were or where we were heading, she let me take over the map reading.

I have to say when Vinka is on good form she is excellent value and good fun but when the smallest thing goes wrong then it is total doom, depression and 'I give up!' Not a person to take with you into the jungle …!

She was my predecessor's mistress and prudish as this sounds I do not condone this between monitors and interpretresses. Martin Garrod said that any of his monitors, of any nationality, he found with an interpretress in his room will be sent out of his Regional Centre. Considering who else the girls work for when they are not actually with us, and during their off days, this is sensible. But probably difficult to enforce particularly with those who are not British. And with our own HCC living with a Croat interpretress it would not be easy for me to act like that, not that with the four we now have here that would be likely. Hans is very happily married and having made it up from the ranks in the Dutch army and having already had more commands than most regular commissioned officers he is keen to do well. Fergus loves chatting up the girls but would not risk his marital happiness that way and Lennart—well I don't know about him but I think he has been married twice and may even be married again but I don't think he lives with a wife.

Inevitably, on our return we found more confusion. Zadar's Coordination Centre's Canadian Operations Officer, Steve Habbington, had ordered us to go to one hour's notice to carry out military-style foot-patrols along the physical border with the RSK but, as I explained, this was an impossibility because of the extensive minefields as well as the fact that the Croat Army considered us a legitimate target so close to the Confrontation Line, let alone actually on it—on foot! Then, just as I called a monitors' meeting to decide what, if anything, we should do at the expense of what we had already planned and agreed with the local Croat organisations, we received a counter-order from Knin.

I am becoming more suspicious that Habbington is doing things about which Vassilis knows nothing in an effort to discredit the Greek. Whenever I think Vassilis seems to be making dangerous decisions the more I believe that Steve Habbington is behind them in order to discredit his Greek boss. Why I wonder? I know Vassilis is tricky and does not have Croatia's best interests uppermost in his mind but all this to-ing and fro-ing is hindering our monitoring and that is not good for anyone.

Fergus and I left at five the next morning to check the convoy as it crossed the border. It should have departed Split at 0600 but we learned that it had actually left at 0530 so were in danger of missing it. However at the border there was no sign so we began our return along the reciprocal route only to have to pull into a ditch to let it pass. This time there were 14 not the agreed ten lorries but maybe, with some perverse practical thinking, this was on purpose as many appeared to have been on their last legs despite not yet having left Croatia's tarmacked roads for Bosnia–Herzegovina's snow-filled, deeply rutted lanes. There was great enthusiasm among the drivers and their crews but no experience so Fergus, ever the logistician, once again offered good advice and worked his Irish magic.

The news that evening was not so positive for Dino offered me what he considered to be a 'dire warning'. Apparently (and I mean apparently for although Dino had remarkable contacts for one so young he was prone to exaggeration) the Croat Army was planning to stop one of the convoys and would then conduct air strikes against whichever side supported the expected United Nations' response. If they decided to halt the convoy in Croatia itself then the ECMM and UNPROFOR would be, respectively, the preferred soft and hard targets. This seemed far-fetched to me and indeed I could not understand the rationale behind such provocative actions—but listened carefully. As we were living among civilians in a civilian hotel in a major city there had to be other ways of getting at us: when we were 'on the road' for instance. While the death of a couple of ECMM monitors would have been no big deal (apart, of course from the individuals and their relatives!) in the wider field of perverted Balkan politics our demise might take on a symbolism all of its own.

It was not the first time that the ECMM as a whole had received such warnings. Had Mike Rose's predecessor as Commander of the United Nations Protection Force, a Belgian (inevitably!) named Francis Briquemont, been stronger and supported the use of fire-power to get earlier convoys through then, frankly, a few drunk, dead Croat soldiers would have sent the appropriate message about the inadvisability of 'messing with the UN'. Apparently the Belgian lieutenant-general had stated that he would not support his junior commanders had they taken such aggressive action.

I have been told that the ECMM will be considered a legitimate target by the Croats, Serbs and/or Muslims. One part of me says, 'Good. Let's get going and sort out this thing once and for all.' But the other says, 'We are here to get the aid through, monitor ceasefires and help the helpless while preventing an extension of the Second World War still being waged by Italy, Germany, Greece and, possibly, the French.'

Not for the first time I considered what action the unarmed members of Team Split could take should we be targeted by Croat forces.

We must fine-tune our evacuation plan over dinner tonight.

I think we will take to the sea by night, hide in the islands before setting off the next day for Italy. We could of course, as I have mentioned before, seek asylum as it were, just up the coast at HQ UNPROFOR, but they may not welcome us with open arms. Which reminds me, the other day at Divulje we pulled into the side of the road to let a squad of French soldiers march past. They march with the palms of their hands open which made Lennart comment that a soldier's traditional symbol of fighting is a clenched fist, not an open palm, 'which is only used by women'. His view of the French military was rather revealing, coming from one such as Lennart whose country has seldom fought anybody in recent years.

Dinner in the Café Riva after drinking in the Foyer Bar, watching the girls arriving for a HDZ (political party) dance in the ECMM's dining room. There is obviously still much money and one has to remember that these are former communists who will have stashed away quite a bit. There is little income so there will be the usual problem of spending their savings now and suffering later. These are, for the most part, previously uneducated families but who made a killing out of the communist party. Anyone with 'old money' and old education has skedaddled, hence the appalling standard of the leaders that are left throughout the whole of former Yugoslavia and not just Croatia and the RSK. As I have noted before but am happy to do so again, the girls are remarkable for their very beautiful legs—and they are fun to watch.

As I had promised myself, that evening we discussed our escape plans. To start the proceedings I described the vessel I had already chosen and explained that I now knew where the keys were kept and had even been instructed how to start the engine by the harbour master himself, who knew exactly what I was up to. As the Croat owner had not been seen for three years the harbourmaster seemed unconcerned by my unspoken plans. *Eloise*, I confirmed, had easily enough fuel in her tanks to reach Ancona and, further positive news, by some strange prescience I had even brought the relevant charts with me from the UK.

Our deliberations were halted when, unexpectedly, an attractive Irish journalist stopped at our table to announce that she was called Samantha, before asking if she could join us. 'Delighted!' we all replied. Once we knew what her motives were I gave her quite a hard time which, being a reporter, she seemed to enjoy, showing good form when I suggested that to write in depth about the Bosnian conundrum after just two days was not a good idea: the whole problem was far too wide-spread and complicated for such superficial treatment. She took it in good heart (which is more than the BBC's reporter had done) and was probably delighted to find someone who was not fawning over her just because she was a pretty girl in a war zone. Anyway it all ended on the office veranda with a great deal of Fergus's out-of-date, draught Guinness.

On the Monday it was, once more and tediously, back to reality when Vassilis telephoned to read a formal report that had been sent about me to the ECMM headquarters by the 'nodding dog'. I countered that I was not used to being screamed at and ordered about by a Greek corporal who was nothing to do with Team Split. I think he got the point as well as the fact that if I wanted to use my transport to collect our interpretresses from their bus I would do so or we would never carry out any monitoring. Later I received a hard copy of the 'complaint' that the 'nodding dog' corporal had sent to HQ ECMM's Chief of Logistics and Personnel in Zagreb.

I send you the report of the FLG Chief of Transport (another corporal) which describes an incident that happened between the Team Leader of Team Split Mr Southby-Tailyour while I was away for a meeting in Zagreb. As it seems Mister Southby-Tailyour take your regulating at my command, which was not removed. [*I still have no idea what he meant.*] The vehicles to carry local personnel from their houses to Hotel Split and the opposite, said that these commands are silly and he also said that he had hasn't any obligation to obey them, while the Chief of Transport explained him that he didn't want to have a dispute, Mister Southby-Tailyour answered again that if there are these silly commands I will be in fight with you.

It not first time that the Team Split used there [*sic*] vehicle to carry interpreters. After my return from Zagreb I got informed about the incident, and despite that I ordered the Mister Southby-Tailyour to come to my office and have talk about it. He didn't appear. [*I have no idea what he was talking about.*]

So after that unprincipled behaviour of Mister Southby-Tailyour that he characterised the command of the FLG is silly and then he don't accept the position of head of FLG as his commander [*which he emphatically was not*] I consider that the operation with him is not possible. I will wait for you to make a decision.

Of course the whole point was that we were not in his command, they were Team Split vehicles and so, as there was no foundation to his complaint, I ignored it ... and what I wrote in my diary was:

In the evening the extraordinary smelly Greek Chief of Transport, who had taken over from a magnificently-efficient and comparatively more fragrant Belgian, asked me into his office only for him to be very rude about us misusing 'his' transport for the collection of 'his' interpreters from the bus station in the mornings. At least that is what I think he was trying to shout but his English is not much better than the 'nodding dog's' and so I told him (another Greek corporal) that we are all in the same business and that as we pool the girls for our daily work, when in the hotel, he should have had as much an interest in them getting to work as we did. Being a man of who could only see as far as 'his orders' were written I don't think he saw the point even when I told him that I would continue to collect the girls during the week and Sergio at the weekends.

It was now obvious that I needed a serious chat with the Head of the British Delegation. The Greeks—namely Vassilis and Philipos—were, frankly, buggering Team Split about: the former by countermanding Paul's orders and then, almost daily countermanding his own orders and the latter for his continual obstructions to our daily work under the impression that we were under his command and had to do his bidding. We were conducting no sensible monitoring of any 'nature', we had transport problems and because of the confusion surrounding Team Split's areas of concern we were quickly cultivating an air of incompetence and suspicion among the local Croats.

21 February. Decided not to go to the Melenica plateau as I deemed it sensible to telephone Godfrey Garratt in Hotel 'I' to sort everything out once and for all. Very glad I did. Although nothing positive has been gained in the short term I feel that at least someone in HQ ECMM is now aware of our situation. The rest of the team went on patrol which is where I would prefer to be but I feel strongly that I have to sort out our position and as Team Leader, I consider that is my job.

I explained to Godfrey the problems in general of the ECMM in the area and those of Team Split in particularly along with HCCZ's odd behaviour citing his lack of a uniform; visits with his girl to Dubrovnik; living with his 'illegal' interpretress; the confusion over our status, duties and future; his attempted prevention of our work with the convoys; the report to HQ ECMM from the nodding dog; his undeliverable promises to the Croats plus and, as if this list was not long enough, his declared hatred of the British as reported by Steve, and even by Dino.

During that afternoon we managed monitoring of a sort by visiting a Jordanian battalion billeted in a local ex-holiday camp where they were guarding a large number of refugees. It had been on this site, shortly after my arrival in Split, that Robert Lekeu had conducted some amusing and clever conjuring tricks for the enjoyment of the refugee children. Sadly, and this surprised both of us, his efforts to bring brief smiles to the young had been castigated by a number of older men who scolded him for not using his magic to make the dead reappear, 'That would be a much more useful application of your talents.'

I tried my fast-rusting Arabic, but with only a little success. I need considerable practice, possibly about six weeks-worth in order to progress from being able to say no more than, 'My soldiers are well. I hope yours are too,' and 'Point me in the direction of the enemy.'

Yet even more confusing signals in the evening. These seem to come in when Steve is on duty and Vassilis is away. Steve can then invent his own plans for our future in order to drop his Greek boss in the poo. Anyway, this latest batch state that Team Split is back to being one team with four monitors and just one Land Rover. As a result we are not to employ another girl despite having been ordered to do so just two days ago. We have already begun advertising by word of mouth. So, what on earth is going on? Steve says that there is a conspiracy against us and it is being orchestrated by Vassilis as he thinks (according to Steve) that we are becoming too powerful and could threaten his—Vassilis's—position as HCC. What utter nonsense. This whole business is now even more than laughable and extremely unprofessional.

The four of us went to the Split opera house to watch (me for the second time) the Splitska operatta—sat in the Royal Box again—excellent seats for the price of three beers each. I love this opera and the opera house, for it is all a far cry from the minefields on the ground and from those equally-dangerous hefalump-traps within the politics of our work.

Late night discussion in the Foyer Bar with a girl called Emma from some Scottish humanitarian organisation.

Events came to a head—in truth they always seemed to be coming to a head—on 23 February when Fergus, Hans, Lennart and I drove to Zadar for what we knew was going to be a long session with the impulsive Vassilis and his devious Operations Officer, Steve. It is best described direct from my diaries written that evening on our return to Room 519:

A difficult day. The four of us drove to Coordinating Centre Zadar for an awkward meeting. I was determined to hold our ground as ordained by Paul and so briefed my monitors that we had to sort out our status once and for all. We were not to allow Vassilis to alter Paul's ruling.

The start of this Vassilis-style meeting was normal and calm but, interestingly, was without the full military-style brief by Steve and his usual exhortation to patrol the borders and carry out what can only be called the gathering of military intelligence. And for whom do we collect this info? This is not, as far as I can make out, what we are here to do; it certainly is not in the ECMM overall terms of reference so there must be a reason why there is so much emphasis on gathering military intelligence within the CC Zadar sector. That is the UNMOs job—or part of it—backed up UNPROFOR.

Anyway, for once Steve began with an intelligent and useful overview of Dalmatia's economic and social problems before moving onto humanitarian matters, until suddenly … Vassilis was called out to speak on the telephone to, as I now know, the Chief of Staff in Zagreb shortly after I had made the point to him that we were not in the ECMM to be military intelligence officers. There are people in other organisations to do that. Vassilis had started to get agitated so it was probably just as well that he was called away.

When he returned Vassilis was in a mood that I had not seen before, inhaling even deeper from his huge cigar and very much without the veneer of false bonhomie that usually marks his performances.

We continued with the meeting. Having heard all sorts of things, that we never knew about, that were going on in our own 'patch', I managed to force Vassilis to agree that we should be kept informed on military matters in our area as we were made to look rather foolish when we did not know what was happening. Vassilis says he gets it all from the local military commanders which I find unlikely or implausible as they do not like or trust the ECMM (and even less so the Greeks) in any way, shape or form.

I raised, to no immediate avail, the strangeness of having Team Split as one team of four monitors but with just the one vehicle, despite having to cover one of the largest areas throughout the ECMM.

When the meeting was closed Vassilis demanded that Fergus and I stayed behind like naughty school boys and I steeled myself for the showdown I had been expecting all day. I was not going to be treated like this and I could see that Fergus felt the same. We were willing, and prepared, to take on the Greek face-to-face. Vassilis then started this extra session by declaring that he knew that we were talking about him behind his back to the Head of Mission in Zagreb. When he asked me a straight question I could say with a clear conscience that I had never approached the HOM as that would have been most improper but that I, Fergus, Hans and Lennart each of us discuss all manner of things with our own Heads of National Delegations, as was correct, and that his relationship with Team Split and his contradictory orders were some of the subjects raised. If those conversations were passed on to the HOM by the HODs then that was their affair. I explained that he was being particularly naive if he had not realised by now how unhappy we all were with the way we were required to run things— or not—in Team Split. Now was the time to stop giving us false and continually contradictory orders and time to get the whole thing moving for the sake of the ECMM.

I told him that he alone was behind our troubles and that there would be no problems if the orders he was giving us confirmed and supported those that we received from Knin. It would be better too, I explained, if they also matched the ECMM's Terms of Reference.

For good measure Fergus added, to his face, that Vassilis was, 'Making a bloody fool of yourself and of the ECMM.' I then agreed but in slightly more diplomatic terms. Fergus is a serving lieutenant-colonel in the Irish army and does not like being treated as a child by either Vassilis or the 'nodding dog'!

This extra 'meeting' then took a strange twist for Vassilis turned back to me and told me that he was removing me from Split and posting me, with immediate effect to Zadar—'Today!'—while he thought of my future. I was not sure why or with what authority he feels he can do this for the appointment of monitors within the Regional Centre is Paul's prerogative.

I put down my pen looked him squarely in the face and said very slowly, 'You needn't bother about my future, Vassilis, for if I leave Split under those circumstances, I will not stop at Zadar but pass on through to Zagreb and home to the UK. I have far better things to do with my life than to be buggered about by you especially as we have not done any serious monitoring for a long time. And while I am at it I am fed up with wasting my time working for incompetent and dishonest people such as yourself.' I think he got the message especially when I ended by saying that I would make quite sure that ECMM HQ knew precisely why I was leaving. He replied by saying 'This is blackmail.'

It was fun to watch his face as I think he expected me to be upset at such an accusation. 'Dead right,' I replied, 'Blackmail is exactly what it is. I am a volunteer out here and have a full time job back in England which I put on hold on the understanding that I would be doing something useful. So, I have no embarrassment at all in blackmailing you. I was sent to the coast by Paul to do a particular work for a particular length of time and with a particular team and that included the expansion of Team Split's area as agreed by Paul and DHOM Ops both of whom outrank you. I did not agree to be shuffled backwards and forwards every time I telephone you. So, Vassilis,' I ended, 'what are you going to do about my blackmail!'

Vassilis was, I am glad to record, speechless. In the silence I continued, admittedly with some arrogance, 'With my operational background I am not prepared to be messed about by the likes of you and if you want to play the seniority game, as you always say I should, I am more than willing and will tell you exactly what you could do in the way of running your CC properly, professionally and in accordance with the ECMM's Terms of Reference.'

As he remained dumfounded I ended with a flourish, 'You always say you think I am a 'super monitor' and a 'great friend' then bloody well act as though you mean it. For Christ's sake grow up, behave properly as a member of the ECMM and act responsibly as an adult and not like a spoilt child.'

He stayed silent allowing me to bring my monologue to a close. 'Now, let's get on with monitoring in accordance with our orders from Paul and not your immature whims. And while we are at it we should think very carefully about the breaking of the UN arms embargo.'

So far I had only rumours to support my concerns about the embargo but it had been worth a try.

Vassilis was more than a little surprised as I suspect that he is not often spoken to like this and I revelled in his discomfort. As he had no immediate answer he looked across the table at Fergus and told him he was off to Knin. 'Tomorrow!' Fergus's reply, although shorter than mine was very Irish, very direct, utterly polite and beautifully put.

Eventually, and I now know that his talk to the COS in Zagreb at the beginning of the meeting had something to do with it, he realised that we were probably more important and useful to his future (which is, in fact, what his behaviour is all about) if he kept us on his side.

Then, suddenly as though a wand had been waved, he offered us both a beer and returned to his old smooth self-confidant and rather smarmy self. All smiles and back slapping while Fergus and I emphasised that the only thing that is important is that Team Split is properly constituted, properly transported and properly briefed. With this Vassilis agreed.

On our way back to Split Vassilis telephoned us in the car, asking me to call my Head of Delegation right away but for what reason was not explained. Thinking that Godfrey might shed some light on Vassilis's behaviour changes I dialled his number. By coincidence he was, at that moment, in conversation with the HODs of Ireland, Denmark and Holland. Godfrey said they all thought that the COS wanted to fire a warning shot across the Vassilis bows and so had decided to act when he did for he knew that, this morning, we were all together at Zadar: hence the COS's telephone call. Godfrey confirmed that Vassilis now realises that his success depends on treating his CC teams correctly and not by messing us around or it will all backfire in his face. It was well that Fergus and I had stood firm. We certainly have the support of the British, Irish, Danish and Dutch HODs in Zagreb who are adamant that we are correct.

Awkward the meeting might have been but not only had the air been cleared, temporarily as it was to turn out, but at last formal confirmation had been received from Vassilis himself that, despite all the to-ing and fro-ing, I was now (not for the first time!) officially head of Team Split with our area of responsibility stretching from Šibenik in the north, under Fergus's direction, to Ploče in the south under mine. In other words, back to two teams and two interpretresses—but still with one Land Rover.

> At least, I think that that is what Vassilis finally agreed but we have been here so many times before I really don't know. Nevertheless, with Vassilis accepting Paul's earlier appointments perhaps we can actually now get on with monitoring Dalmatia's future.

Fat chance—as will be seen.

To balance all this confusion—order and counter order—on 25 February Fergus and I visited the Split Harbour Maintenance and Construction Company as the direct and positive result of my earlier visit to the Split Chamber of Commerce. To illustrate what a proper monitoring patrol on the coast should have achieved I quote here from part of the Special Report that I wrote on our return to Hotel Split.

> On Friday 25 February monitors Ewen Southby-Tailyour and Fergus Marshall called on Mr Jure Svetić, Director of the Harbour Maintenance and Construction Company.
> This is part of the continuing series of visits resulting from Team Split's meeting with the Split Chamber of Commerce on 4 January 1994. Present at the meeting was Mr Berislav Buselić of the Split Chamber of Commerce and Head of Foreign Relations and Promotion of Croat Industry whom the Team Leader had met at the previous meeting … In addition to being the Director of Maintenance and Construction Mr Svetić is also Director of the Luka Harbour Company. Both companies are interrelated but neither is directly responsible for the day-to-day running of the port ferries. Brodospas is responsible for these and will be visited as soon as possible.
> The two companies for which Mr Svetić is responsible are owned by the government, as is the company that runs the ferries. In reply to a question about ownership, there was clearly some confusion for they felt that as the government owned the land they did not quite see how a private company could then use 'government property' to run a private venture.
> There is clearly not a full understanding of the way private and capitalist enterprises works. We suggest that, apart from any financial help that will be urgently needed when regeneration begins in earnest, specialist economic advice will also be vital. Indeed, probably even more important than hard cash

to begin with. The Director stated that the ferry company, and indeed his own companies, would one day be sold into the private sector, but we were left with the impression that he was not actually quite sure what that really meant. He was, though, wise enough to acknowledge that 'all births are accompanied by pain and many by lack of knowledge'.

We began the meeting proper with an explanation of our duties as outlined by HRC Knin following which the director was grateful for the interest shown in his organisation by the ECMM and promised that he would give us all the cooperation that we might need.

We were then treated to the obligatory history lesson and listened patiently before continuing with our discussion. In accordance with Team Split's new principal of asking as few questions as possible, while allowing the interviewees to do most of the talking through gentle prompting, we were able to cover a wide range of subjects in a relaxed atmosphere ...

According to the director Brodosplit had been among the top five shipbuilding companies in the world and is a substantial concern with an excellent reputation. We hope to visit during the week of 7 March.

The end of the war with the Republic of Serbian Krajina was considered, correctly, to be the catalyst for regeneration, but on this point we offered no advice ...

The regeneration of all trade links and lines of communication are considered to be the top priority after the war ends, and that means the reintegration of the road, rail, air and sea links all of which will need massive funding. The rebuilding of the merchant fleet is seen as a high priority while a strong navy was not desirable. The point was made, often, that Croatia does not need anything other than the means to defend its own shores and its merchant fleet. It has no aspirations for territorial expansion ...

The current war damage to the infrastructure was estimated by the director to be in excess of $26 billion ... thus the regeneration of the economy must start with the rebuilding of communication links, links that include harbour facilities to meet the expected increased demands, these in turn will require a modern merchant navy and a fleet of new ferries for trade with Italy, linked to a modern railway network into the interior.

It is clear that the future of Croatia, as seen from Split (a view that is shared by the monitors) has to be based on a maritime economy. This includes tourists who by and large, arrive in Split by sea via Italy and spend their money on the coast.

It is appreciated by those whom we met that no foreign investor will put up capital during a war that prevents the movement of trade but, given a good business-like approach from within, Croat companies will probably fight among themselves to be part of a strong Dalmatia.

We finished the meeting with the feeling that we had conducted an open and honest dialogue containing a relevant amount of good humour mixed with seriousness. We issued an open invitation to continue our discussion in the more convivial atmosphere of Hotel Split at a future, but not too distant, date: this was accepted with alacrity.

Of course, as I have mentioned before and will mention again, we could offer Split Harbour nothing as, earlier, we had been able to offer the Chamber of Commerce nothing. But, and it was a significant 'but' throughout our discussions across Dalmatia and the islands, we promised to send our findings and recommendations, plus transcripts of our conversations 'up the line'. We expected, we assumed, that the outcome of meetings we had with the leaders of commerce and industry in Split—Croatia's second largest city—would find their way to HQ of the European Union in Brussels, as they should have done. This was, we always explained, in the hope, that 'come the peace' wiser men than us would know how and where to begin the regeneration of Dalmatia and thus Croatia. Tragically, I know now that these were forlorn hopes and that all we ever did was to waste our time and the patience of those whom we visited.

In effect the ECMM was involved in conducting a terrible con trick while we, its monitors in the field, offered only false hopes and promises. None of our Special Reports went further than Knin and often not even beyond Zadar if they conflicted with the xenophobic views of Vassilis, a Greek supporting Serbia, or (in due course) Jean-Pierre Thébault a Frenchman supporting Croatia.

9

Operas and Evictions

As expected the next day brought the now-mandatory repudiations from Vassilis Dertilis. By coincidence I was typing a detailed, formal briefing paper on Team Split and its new and proposed duties ... but ... this was to be a waste of time for it was a day punctuated continually by contradictory signals from Zadar.

A long day at the keyboard writing the formal staff paper that I have said I will send to Zagreb, Knin and Zadar explaining why Team Split must be properly and formally constituted, with confirmed boundaries plus Terms of Reference (TOR) that are relevant for the coast. If it can be phrased properly I hope the TORs can also refer to the monitoring of the UN Arms Embargo. In effect I hope to put on paper, perhaps with a little tweaking, what DHOM Ops agreed.

One signal from Vassilis says that, from today, we are to be one team with four members—which is NOT what we agreed yesterday but what Vassilis is currently proposing: a pro-tem measure around the problem. So not much has sunk in. Neither will he confirm our boundaries, the correct number of vehicles and interpreters now that we are aiming, as I thought we had agreed, eventually for three teams. The vehicle situation is a farce and I had hoped that Vassilis would have used the influence he always claims to have with HQ ECMM to sort it out.

One of the day's signals read:

You are not authorised to employ a third interpreter but are to take the two you have on to your formal strength in order to have more control over their employment.

[They had been on our 'formal' strength since before my arrival.]

Although the interpretresses work for us and are under our direction, in practice, we actually have to share them with the FLG on the very rare occasion that they need a translator.

I knew that this would not be approved by the Greek 'nodding dog' for he regarded us as being under his command and I guessed, too, that Vassilis had not considered that. The devil in me thought he might have done this on purpose to drive yet another wedge between me and Philipos who might then have cause for further complaints about my attitude towards the FLG … but, surely not? In an act of feigned innocence I did not argue and looked forward to the reaction I would get from the FLG. Not having the third girl was an unsatisfactory development but at least, as Fergus observed, we could now juggle the girls' duties entirely according to our own programme and the FLG, if they felt the need, could employ their own.

Although I was keen to send my 'Future of Split' paper as far and as wide as I could I felt that courtesy alone required me to send the initial draft for Vassilis's approval.

In the paper I argued that Split should become a Coordinating Centre in its own right with two, if not three teams covering the coast from Šibenik in the north to Dubrovnik in the south as well as the adjacent islands. Personally I did not mind if it was or was not a CC but what I did care about was the increase of teams to three or, preferably, four to monitor over 150 miles of coastline, the islands and two of Croatia's largest cities. Tourism, fishing, the white stone, the lavender, the olives and the wine added to its value as a core area vital for the whole of Croatia's regeneration … and yet it beggared my belief that it was so neglected by the ECMM. What was to happen next was no better!

My staff paper met with, I have to admit, some acclaim with copies sent by Vassilis on to HCC Zadar, HRC Knin, DHOM (Ops) and my own Head of Delegation as well as to the Eastern Adriatic Unit in King Charles Street. I was not to know until much later that a copy was also forwarded to the Dutch military academy where they trained their monitors. (They had formal training?) Thanks to Vassilis the Greek navy also had a copy to complement an earlier Daily Report I had compiled and which, he thought, set the bench mark for such documents.

How easily he is taken in!

Regardless of all that, the most important question to me was, would my paper be used to Team Split's advantage?

Yet another strange telephone call from Vassilis saying that he would discuss the interpretresses on Monday—but I thought the problem has been solved. I wish he would make up his mind and stick to it. I shall have to meet him head on again to remind him that this is a European commitment and not just a Greek benefit match. Meanwhile we continue to waste 'monitoring time'.

Keen for an oasis of civilisation Team Split decamped *en masse*—Hans, Lennart, Fergus and I—to the Split Opera house to listen to a Strauss concert. Knowing that I was ill-informed on classical music Lennart explained that were off to hear the 'waltz composer' and not 'the other one' apparently: whoever he might have been. We thought we had booked the Royal Box again but there was a problem and we were escorted to the Gods. Someone must have realised for we were then ushered down to the left side of the pits, overlooking the orchestra then, from here, we were finally moved to the middle of the stalls, seven rows back. It turned out to be an evening of Mozart not that I would have known the difference anyway but Lennart, the piano player, approved. During the long interval—the Croats like a good drink half-way through these evenings—a Croat woman came up to us and said in perfect English that she hoped we didn't like the scarlet-dressed mezzo-soprano 'as she was terrible'. She then walked away and we finished our beers. I could not comment for I thought she was rather good although what she had sang was not very inspiring. Our informant, also in flamboyant red, then returned to emphasise to Fergus that she thought the soloist was 'bloody awful too but as she was Italian that was hardly surprising'!

The Opera House was living up to its reputation as a social hub for John Watkins, the Master of RFA *Resource* was at the bar with the Master of RFA *Sir Geraint*, David Garrard, whom I had known 'down south' in 1982 when he had been the Chief Officer of RFA *Sir Lancelot*. David was accompanied by his ship's doctor who was obviously quite a character. I decided to invite them all to dinner in Hotel Split in the very near future.

By the time we returned to the hotel we had missed supper for it had been in the Café Riva which shut earlier but as the Opera House's 'refreshments' had been substantial I went to bed to watch David Frost interview David Owen on Sky TV.

I am not a fan of D. Owen's for two reasons. Despite having gone to the same prep school as my son he is a socialist and he gave the Royal Marines a hard time when he was a Plymouth MP and father was Commandant General, Royal Marines. Nevertheless he is probably the only politician, of any nation, who actually understands what the hell is going on out here—and he speaks the language which catches some of these local 'politicians' by surprise. He can be as rude as they and from all accounts as foul-mouthed! His observations seem to make sense and I hope he continues to be involved. If he is not, Heaven knows who will take over from him.

Sunday was a beautiful day, towards the end of which Fergus and I walked in the gloaming to the south and east for about two miles.

This is a fabulous coastline but one entirely spoilt by destitution because of the war. The sea is clear but I wouldn't trust the sewage system yet Fergus, being a military diver, swims regularly and he is still alive.

An immense amount of debris and rubbish covers this stretch of urban coastline—a sort of continual bomb-site. So much so that I doubt that the country will have enough money to re-build the tourist trap for a long time to come: which is of course behind one of the many reasons why we are here. To try and give them hope through our 'confidence building measures' and, less obvious to the locals, through our reports that should help the EU decide where its money will most gainfully be used when the war is over. But, and this is a big but, will Greece allow EU money be used in Croatia and will Germany allow EU money to help out in Serbia et al?

Quote from David Owen the other night: There is a great deal of difference between Air Strikes and Air Support! I agree.

Monitoring took on a different aspect the next day for, by appointment, I had arranged to meet a doctor whom I was only to know as Dr Nickolas. Surprisingly for one living in Croatia he turned out to be a Serb whose wife was half Croat and half Serbian and I understood that until Croat independence this was nothing unusual. Nickolas had, earlier, telephoned Team Split's office offering to bring in a large quantity of medicines that he had managed to 'hoard' with the specific purpose of somehow transporting them across the Confrontation Line into the Republic of Serbian Krajina.

If I can find some way of getting them across the border during the periodic crossings by HRC Knin's monitors I feel strongly that this is another way we can, and should, help with a clear conscience. The trouble is small parcels and even letters are often opened by the Croat border guards and much that makes the Krajina Serbs' lives better is often prevented. Whatever I arrange it will be considered illegal by someone but, in Fergus's words, 'Bugger the be-grudgers!'

Vassilis telephoned (not for the first time today) to tell me about a build-up of Serb forces beyond the southern port of Ploče and asked me to investigate. I told him that we are not spies for the ECMM at least, not overtly … Although we may, individually, gain intelligence for our own countries.

Apart from the illegality of his request we would always stand out, even without our whiter-than-white uniforms. If we could 'go covert' there were no northern European tourists we could have hidden among although, perhaps, we could have pretended to be a member of some obscure NGO despite the lack of 'civilian' transport soon giving the game away.

'What happens if we are caught?' I asked him. No answer. Quite happy to go and look quite openly and take a risk if that is what he wants. Of course many of us carry out military intelligence gathering but never in the ECMM's name.

Rather beautiful day but didn't get outside what with Vesna's humanitarian case and Vassilis's continual telephone calls about the build-up of troops. Anyway I am certain our telephone is bugged so it did not make much sense talking about these things on it but I guess the Croats all know what we are doing anyway!

The last day of February 1994 was an interesting one that started with the unexpected visit of Vassilis Dertilis to Hotel Split. Just prior to his arrival I was presented with the news that four Serb aircraft had been shot down while on a bombing run against the Muslim ammunition factory in Travnik in the centre of Bosnia–Herzegovina. In retaliation 1,600 shells (reportedly) were fired into a previously un-harassed village. This news came direct to me from an officer in BRITFOR and, although unconfirmed, subsequent reports indicated this bombardment might have been into Tuzla. The Serbs initially denied the aircraft losses despite Radovan Karadzic, the Serbian president, suggesting that they had been unarmed aircraft on a training flight and that retaliation would be swift.

Of course—even allowing for the lies—nobody is going to admit they were breaking the no-fly embargo. Personally I believe they deserved it but if one has to be critical it is about 18 months too late. However I think at last it may make the Serbs (and all the others) think rather harder about their actions … so, a good thing. The November Teams in the Knin area have all been recalled to base but two teams working out of Zadar were clapped by civilians as they left on patrol. They would not have been so applauded had they been Croat aircraft that had been 'splashed'.

For some unexplained reason Vassilis called in to the office and was rather contrite; as a Serb supporter he might have had something to be contrite about although I also felt that his remorse had nothing to do with events in Bosnia–Herzegovina. It was, though, satisfying to see a bombastic, over self-confident and sometimes likeable Greek (when he forgets to act the part) apologising. He was even wearing white uniform and Melisa his interpretress—and mistress—was not with him. I knew what she saw in him and he in her for she had the longest legs on the coast. She was equally self-assured while he had charisma in a Greek, moneyed sort of way.

I have no idea where he went during much of the day but he looked in occasionally and witnessed at first hand, and sympathised with, our frustration at having to cancel a planned visit to the mayor of Makarska. The previous day the FLG had hijacked our one vehicle for a supply shuttle into Bosnia, despite it being un-armoured, and when it returned in the evening not only was it too filthy inside and out to conduct a civilised patrol, when appearances matter, but it was in urgent need of a mechanic's close attention.

At tea-time Vassilis appeared once more, and once more surprised us with the first brief any of us could recall receiving from him, 'There are 7,500 Serbs in red berets on the other side of the border between Ploče and Dubrovnik which makes me think that the southern area around Dubrovnik could become another break-away, RSK-style problem as far as Croatia is concerned.' In which case, I presumed, it would be responsible for its own defence which, to me, did not make much sense.

I knew that Dubrovnik was agitating to become a 'state within a state', as it were, in the same mould as, for instance, Monte Carlo or Andorra. The town's elders were exasperated with the Croat government and, as with the Krajina Serbs, felt that it, too, deserved independence. Although no friends of the Serbs, following the siege of the city in 1991, the people of this most southern of Croat towns were cut off from the rest of the country by Bosnia–Herzegovina's miniscule stretch of coastline some 35 miles to the north-west and so felt that they had an arguable case. Naturally, Zagreb had other ideas for Dubrovnik's future as it and its associated coastline was, financially, vital to the country's welfare.

> While none of this is new to Team Split, indeed, we have mentioned it in a number of Daily Reports (and in my letters to Julian Metcalf) and I have even expanded this view in my staff paper on our future, it is good to hear Vassilis recognising the complexity of the task that lies ahead of us and in doing so—surprise, surprise—he even confirmed that Split should be a Coordinating Centre.

That evening, as Vassilis looked to be eating out of Team Split's collective hands, we felt it was a good moment to capitalise on such a rare situation. Although unstated it was obvious to us that he had come to realise that we were important to his long-term aims, whatever they might have been, and that it was better to keep us 'on side'. We were certainly of more use to him than he was to us for we were all northern Europeans and thus had less of a stake in Balkan politics. He knew that, should we really wish, and he had driven us pretty close to it and no doubt would do so again, we could ruin his reputation with his own government if he tried to use us for his own personal ends, or even his government's ends. It was a good time to strike and we planned the ambush with care.

'Vassilis,' I said over the post-dinner *Prošek* while my compatriots stared silently at the Greek, 'None of us in Team Split knows what lies behind your behaviour and in a way not one of us could care less. Promotion to Head of Regional Centre of a new coastal Regional Centre perhaps, or even a senior post in the ECMM's HQ. Either way none of us could give a damn providing we can continue monitoring in accordance with the ECMM's guidelines.'

The others took their turn, matching Vassilis's charm with their own individual versions of allure until we all decided that it was time to turn in.

'I do agree and now I have seen things at first hand I will do my very best for Team Split,' were the Greek's final remarks once we had reached the fifth floor's corridor.

'Which means the very best for Vassilis', Fergus whispered in my ear as we turned for our separate rooms. I knew he was right as he finished. 'Don't forget, we haven't actually got any details, only generalisations. Good night!'

Although Vassilis's private habits had been, and were to remain, an ECMM concern we felt that maybe, just maybe, we could start monitoring the coast in the manner that it deserved, including military monitoring but not military 'spying'. The former was within the ECMM's guidelines but not the latter although all— Croats, Serbs and monitors—appreciated that the dividing line was murky.

Earlier, I had been called to the telephone to talk to Vesna, a lovely, well-educated and professional Croat lady. Popular with Team Split, she spoke perfect English and was often in Café Riva with her partner and sister. Now what she had to say chilled me deeply and was about to occupy much of my time over the next few days. Her boyfriend had, the previous evening, been beaten up by Croat soldiers and thus she feared—correctly—that this was the prelude to something worse.

I knew that Team Split's diplomacy, tact and ability to face-down the worst that the Croat political and military 'establishment' could throw at us would yet struggle to see justice prevail. That might sound rather grandiose but the convention that allowed soldiers to march into a private flat, claiming it as their own, simply because they were back from the front and with nowhere to go, flew in the face of every known aspect of 'decent behaviour' that should have been central to a modern democracy: which Croatia aspired to be. The housing of Croatia's soldiers was an army, or government problem that should not have been solved by allowing individuals to barge their way into private property ... but, all too often, it was. Vesna was about to be evicted from her apartment and the perpetrator was an armed, apparently homeless soldier recently returned from the front line who was, he had explained, acting in accordance with what was considered acceptable behaviour for returning 'heroes'. In anticipation of this disgraceful threat her sister and mother had already de-camped to friends.

On the first day of March, thanks to Vesna's imminent expulsion, I was unexpectedly confined to the hotel waiting for the call. With no authority, other than humanitarian, I did not consider it politic for the ECMM to be involved until the deed had occurred; and so I waited. Lunch that day did not end with the preferred glass or two of *Prošek* on the Riva Bar's often-sun-drenched terrace as I was waiting for Vesna's call. When she did ring the Team Split office it was to explain that, as threatened, she had now been thrown out of her flat. All her furniture and personal effects had been tossed into the corridor and some, including a hamster in its cage, on to the street below from two stories up. Luckily she had friends in Trogir with whom she could spend the immediate future while I agreed to see if I could help sort things out that afternoon. Meanwhile, I promised her that I would contact the Chief of Humanitarian affairs in the ECMM's Zagreb headquarters as well as the Government Housing Officer. I was also happy to help her prepare her papers requesting asylum in Switzerland.

With Vinka I took a FLG minibus to Vesna's flat. Rather pathetic as the hamster's cage, lying on the pavement was empty. She had last seen the little fellow the night before it had been thrown out of the window. I tried to get the armed soldier to come to the apartment's door but it was locked. Vinka would not come near me for fear of being shot through it. Not sure why I took her as Vesna's English is rather better. We removed the furniture in two loads to Trogir. Vesna and her sister are very brave girls with both educated at Split University, Vesna graduating with a degree in civil engineering.

It was high time I visited the Chief of Military Police for I needed to know what the legal position was and what recourse to compensation was open to Vesna—and all the others to whom this was happening.

This is going to be tricky but Vesna's case, with ECMM involvement, should be the blue touch-paper that will bring an end to this obscene convention, except that, tragically, I doubt that it will be. With Vesna, Lennart and Vinka we called on Lieutenant-Colonel Michael Burdina the Chief of Military Police and found him particularly unsympathetic. He says he is powerless despite the fact that I got him to admit that the soldier had acted illegally. After much huffing and puffing he repeated over and over that he was merely following orders and could do no more. Burdina even tried to excuse the soldier by saying that Vesna was acting like an enemy of Croatia for not allowing this 'patriotic soldier', who had been 'fighting for his country', to have a well-deserved home. What a perverted society this is.

I explained that I would not be responsible for the story being carried by all the European papers as Fergus and I had already briefed Samantha Power, the Irish journalist, of the unfolding drama. Burdina did not like this and kept on repeating that he has no authority and was only following orders. 'So were Hitler's Nazi soldiers', I reminded him which may not have been very tactful of me bearing in mind Croatia's present stance vis-á-vis the Ustaše. He then asked Vesna why she had the moral right to be in the flat instead of the soldier. An odd question—but 'par for the course' among Croatia's warped military, government and civil servants. The flat was hers and had been bought by her father many years earlier.

10

Hvar for Punctures

The next day was yet one more filled with contradictory telephone calls. No sooner had our new monitor, the young and amusing Dutch army officer, Hans Spijker, settled in to the team, he was about to be taken back to Knin almost before he had unpacked. Exasperated, I had no idea what I was supposed to be doing and who I was supposed to be doing it with. Adding fuel to my anger Vassilis telephoned six times to tell me that he was, inexplicably, sending Hans to Gospić for two weeks whereas Tony in Knin was demanding, over yet more telephone calls, that Hans was required at the Regional Centre as the Operations Officer.

Bugger this, they have only just sent Hans to Split. So I said they would have to come and physically get him and until that moment he was part of my coastal monitoring team. That stopped the telephone calls from both Vassilis and Tony!

While I agreed that Hans, a really delightful, professional and charming Dutchman, would be superb as the HRC Knin's operations officer he had to learn more English and that, I argued, would happen quicker as the number two in Split where English was spoke by all in Team Split, even when off duty.

The other day Hans was trying to point something out and kept on saying 'upstairs the mountain'. It took us some time to discover that he was meaning 'the top of a small, earth mound.' So, you see, we have a bit of a problem with an otherwise superb monitor.

At last, on 2 March, Hans, Fergus and I were able to drive south down the coast to the beautiful village of Makarska with its stunning promenade along the sea front although Vinka's miserable and bossy mood removed some of the enjoyment. Further away from Split the coast becomes less spoilt by concrete and thus even more attractive. Using my developing technique of monitoring without questions I found the mayor rather more accommodating than most. He was, of course, some way from the phobias that swamped the Split society and, as the islands were close by, his views were much more in line with those offshore than with those of the mainland.

Lunch in a café where Croat soldiers spoke to us in German and were surprised, not a little put out and suddenly shifty, when we answered in English. They were escorting two anti-aircraft guns towards the northern Confrontation Line. On then to Ploče where we inspected the harbour which is of substantial quays but with no security worthy of the name and the dock manager evasive and shifty.

The build-up of troops, many speaking American or German, is becoming plain to see and now featuring regularly in our Daily Reports although who, further up the command chain, takes any notice God alone knows. And even He is probably being kept in the dark.

Thence to the island of Hvar via the ferry from Drvenik. The fifty mile drive down the spine of the island, through the stunning lavender fields to Hvar town took longer than planned and so we arrived well after sunset. This was a pity especially as Vinka became extremely difficult in the back of the Land Rover forcing me to wish, not for the first time, that we could have monitored without interpretresses. They wielded far too much power for we had no idea that what we said was being translated correctly and whether the answers they gave to us were the answers given to them. Nor was it unknown for the interpretresses to invent conversations we thought we were having for their own personal advantage. However … that evening Vinka thought she knew the way to the hotel but after we had driven round and round the town's outskirts for nearly an hour we ended up where we had started. We got out and walked straight there!

Hotel Shaia—on Hvar's quayside—is very beautiful and very old. After dinner Fergus and I walked round the harbour beneath a crystal clear sky and very bright stars. It really is a beautiful and unspoiled place with few cars and very old and stunning architecture. We passed many pubs with much singing and were about to enter one until we realised it was full of drunk soldiers on leave: all with their arms …

A small, inter-island ferry moored with much clamour outside my window at about 0500 the next morning and then sailed again with more wonderfully organised chaos. Fully awake by 7 o'clock I woke Hans so we could drive to a place with a telephone signal in order to receive the fine details for the day's programme from the local Croat liaison officer. As we rounded the corner at the head of the harbour and car park I commented that it was nice to see that the Land Rover's telephone aerial was still in place.

Hans replied, 'That is good but I see we have a puncture,' although he didn't say it quite like that! As we reached the vehicle it was clear that we had not one puncture but five for the spare tyre on the back door had also been slashed.

Walking away from the Land Rover, while puzzling our immediate future, a man appeared with a car jack and started to remove one of the wheels. 'Ah,' I said, 'now someone else is stealing them.'

At this moment a policeman came trotting towards us apologising profusely in passable English and certainly better than Hans's! He said he knew the perpetrators to be inebriated soldiers home on leave from 'the front'. He also explained that the mayor had already seen the problem and was trying to get the tyres repaired before we woke up. The man 'stealing' them was removing them, one by one, to be mended. We thanked him for this news and left them to it.

I told Fergus and Vinka the story over breakfast but, sadly, Vinka became terrified that 'they' would now 'get her' for being with us. However, as it turned out, 'they' once again thought we were from UNPROFOR for whom clearly 'they' had no time—similar to the Serb soldiers in the RSK.

We rearranged our programme over breakfast before meeting the mayor who turns out to be also the director of the local theatre company. He is clearly a nice, honest man and acutely embarrassed. I explained that I had forgotten the incident with the tyres and that I couldn't mind less and that these things happen anywhere to people in authority or uniform. I was not angry or upset which seemed to surprise him. However, Vinka thought that I should be furious with the mayor and his people but that is not how I felt and I trusted her to interpret correctly. Actually I think the mayor spoke enough English to know my feelings without Vinka's 'help'.

Called on the Local Red Cross for a most fruitful discussion about the present and future. After which we drove very slowly indeed back to the car ferry at Starigrad and thence to Split. The front axles must have been damaged when the tyres collapsed for the steering is very wobbly and, frankly, dangerous.

The next morning there was still confusion over Hans's future so I felt obliged to tell Vassilis that I was appalled that firm leadership and sensible man-management could be so lacking in such an international organisation. As a result I wrote a signal to RC Knin, copied to Vassilis at Zadar, saying that Hans could not write English and that as he has only spent one week in Knin he was hardly in a position to take over as Operations Officer.

As it stands we will be down to one monitor at times thanks to leave periods. As there is no sensible reason why Hans should go so soon after arrival I asked for a delay until wiser thoughts prevailed and a sensible and constructive assessment of our manpower problems has been made.

An angry Vassilis telephoned to tell me that I did not run Team Split. 'Oh,' I said, 'then who does? Because it is not you!' I then told him to, 'Sort the bloody problem out soon, Vassilis, as we are trying to get on with serious monitoring but at the moment we are wasting our time.'

By midday the problem had been back and forward twice more. As if to emphasise the points I made in my diary more stories of atrocities on both sides were reaching us almost on a daily basis.

The story has just been signalled of a man, somewhere in BiH, cut in half and stuck in the ground with a stake rammed up his backside to make it look as though he had been half buried. His hands were tied across his chest. When an ECMM patrol prised them apart he was found to be clutching his severed heart. The other story is of a couple who, while still alive, the wife had a foetus cut out of her womb and placed in her husband's stomach. His wound was then 'stapled up' and they were both left to die. Sometimes I wonder why we bother ... and then I remind myself that it is to stop that sort of thing happening is why we do bother.

On a more parochial matter I commented on how much we had to rely on the British military to keep our own show on the road—literally—as the Greek FLG was totally incapable of doing so.

Martin Sinclair is being extremely helpful over our replacement tyres and reckons he can get us some from BRITFOR and then we can pay them back when we get ours out from the UK. Surprisingly the ECMM holds no spares which I can either believe (in which case this is a disgrace for a serious organisation) or disbelieve (in which case the Greeks are lying to me).

On Saturday 5 March we were still stuck without transport thanks to the absence of tyres and the damaged axles so I spent the day writing a Special Report covering our visit to Hvar.

Still trying to get Hans to stay but as Tony Smith is being rather wet about it all I had to ask the question for the umpteenth time: 'Does the ECMM want this part of Croatia monitored?'

Rory Ormsby here waiting to fly to Tuzla with his quite ghastly 'ex-Hitler youth' HCC called Wolfgang someone or other. Possibly the only poor German that I've met out here and I must say he looked the part in every particular.

Last night Lennart, who knows Tony well, spoken to him in Knin but was told that despite our view that Hans is totally unqualified to act as Operations Officer in the HRC he was being appointed as such.

As if life could not have been more confusing, contradictory and muddled then worse was about to happen that would speed my decision to leave the ECMM. That afternoon we received a signal stating that the new HRC Knin, replacing the quite excellent Paul Ortholan, would be with us for a briefing in two days. This gave us a little time in which to prepare a formal presentation while being obliged, once more, to cancel a long standing visit to Brač for that day.

What a way to run a fucking railroad!

We did, though, manage to keep in place a second, lengthy patrol to Ploče the next day despite Vinka excelling herself by announcing, once we had reached Makarska, that she had to be back in Trogir by 1730 for a dental appointment.

On purpose? On balance I think not but we had to curtail our programme and work today which was a bloody pain. This sort of thing does not help.

Makarska is a rather lovely, very 'Mediterranean' village before the hoards of German and Italian tourists reappear. Saw various corvettes of the Kralj class— more than I have seen together before.

I do not like the Croats—the usual rubbish about their false view of their history which makes them out to always have been whiter than white and holier than thou down the centuries. I remember Clinton, during his inaugural speech, saying that he had been sworn in as president of the 'oldest democracy in the world' and if a leader says this and the population is simple and gullible, as so many third world countries are—including the Americans in this respect—then the people believe them!

Returned early from a slightly fruitless patrol to find that Vinka did not visit her dentist after all!

Šibenik Bridge and
a Mossad Infiltrator

On 8 March the new Head of Regional Centre Knin, Monsieur Jean-Pierre Thébault, arrived in Split to be briefed on coastal monitoring and our aspirations for the future. The extraordinary thing was that when I heard him coming down the corridor towards the office and stood ready to greet him at our door I quite unexpectedly smelt him even before I saw him. As he entered our office I offered my hand in welcome but he walked past into the room without saying a word while I pushed a red-spotted handkerchief to my nose.

I rather wish for VD and his cigars.

Sad to report but instantly neither Fergus, Lennart, Hans or I took to Jean-Pierre Thébault. We had prepared a seriously-professional, staff collage-style brief but once we had begun with an overview of our Area of Responsibility in front of the huge wall map and had just started to outline our priorities as laid down by Paul Ortholan and in accordance with ECMM guidelines Thébault began interrupting. His very first words to Fergus and myself were, precisely, 'I do not like this military style. You will continue in a different manner!'

So we began again in a more colloquial fashion but were soon silenced by a series of questions that bore no relation to the subjects that Fergus and I were trying to convey. At the back of the office I could see Hans and Lennart wide-eyed with astonishment while, alongside me, the ever-placid Irishman looked as though he would explode. I took a deep breath, 'Jean-Pierre, if you will allow myself and Fergus to complete our presentation we have allowed time for a question and answer session afterwards, based on what you will have heard.'

'No! That is not how I wish you to proceed ...' he declared before firing irrelevant demands to the four of us. So out of place were Thébault's queries that I saw no point in trying to record them in my diary.

He is a career diplomat with very much an I-know-it-all-attitude which had us all raising eyebrows at each other across the room.

I believe that we may have trouble with Thébault. But neither I nor Fergus are going to be lectured to by someone who has not yet had time to understand our area.

Much later I was to discover that even before he met me he was determined to have me sacked from Split—but of course I did not know this at the time of writing my diary.

After a very difficult lunch—Lennart suggested we should drink only water but neither Fergus or I were prepared to forgo our lunch-time wine for, of all people, a Frenchman!—he buggered off. Thank God! Without a word of thanks or farewell he just got up from the table and walked out of the room leaving us with the most clear understanding that all is about to change and that all we have been striving for is about to be destroyed.

With the departure of Jean-Pierre Thébault—and the return of sweet-smelling air—we were free to drive to the UN barracks at Divulje to pay for our Land Rover's spares and collect mail. Here, by chance, I met Major Simon Shadbolt, Royal Marines, with his general, Mike Rose, whose ADC he was. Also with Mike was the much admired General Sir John Wilsey and the brigadier who had appeared, so bizarrely, in well-worn 'camouflaged pyjamas' at the earlier Croat Independence cocktail party.

Interesting discussion in the evening with Nick Turnbull, Rory Ormsby and Fergus in my room over a whisky or two, the conversation mainly centred on what we all believe will be severe problems with Thébault. Although he was nothing to do with Nick or Rory they knew enough of his reputation to make Fergus and myself pessimistic for the future.

The following day I despatched the others to monitor the border in the Imotski area as I had been invited to a working dinner on board RFA *Resource* and the patrol would not have been back in time. However at about midday I was unamused to be telephoned with the message that I was now 'un-invited' to *Resource*. Having been asked to keep the date clear I had also delayed our two-day patrol of Vis so this was tedious.

Rather unimpressed with *Resource* as Hugo White, the Commander-in-Chief Fleet, had told Patricia he was looking forward to seeing me at the dinner. Indeed, he had specifically asked *Resource* for me to be there as he was particularly interested in hearing my views on the breaking of the UN Arms Embargo. So, spent the afternoon on a number of humanitarian matters dealing with a crowd of bloody, holier-than-thou Croatians.

I am now even more certain there is going to be a bloodbath between Croatia and the RSK before August.

[As it happened my prediction was exactly one year early.]

Nor do I believe that all is well in Bosnia (it never is!) as it is quite possible that if the Muslims, Croats and Bosnians agree to a ceasefire the United Nations will then leave and they can start it up all over again without, as it were, an umpire.

The final series of events that were to precipitate my resignation from the Mission began the next day, the 10 March.

Here we bloody well go again. Just when I thought we were finally in sight of getting Split under proper control I received a message today from Vassilis saying that there would not now be a team monitoring Šibenik. Then the final straw for the day was an evening call from Tony Smith in Knin to say that Jean-Pierre was posting me either to Knin, with immediate effect for some unspecified duty, or as the operations officer at Zadar with Vassilis. I told him that I would leave the Mission.

Simply couldn't believe my ears. I am furious with the poor ECMM, once again, being made to look extremely foolish. Bloody French this time which makes a change from the bloody Greeks!

The only bright spark in the day had been a patrol to the Bosnia–Herzegovina border with Lennart and Vinka. This was wild, rocky country overlooked by snow-capped mountains in the background and a stunning view of the Adriatic as we came over the coastal hills. A very delightful Serb met us at the border crossing plus a remarkably patient Slovenian policeman. In a funny sort of way our greeting and the subsequent brief restored, momentarily, my confidence that there could be a peaceful future.

With events beginning to alter swiftly I thought it high time that I updated Julian Metcalf back in the FCO and so wrote him a letter dated 10 March:

As you know I am now running Team Split, which seems to oscillate between two teams and one team with a movable number of monitors. The latest news is that we could now be divided up with one team based in Šibenik [*pace* the latest dictum] and the other team remaining here with responsibility for the area to the south-east. I am not sure that the ECMM quite realises the importance of the area for the future—but there we are.

I met Mike Rose yesterday who says he thinks he will be out of a job by August! My view that Croat troops can be released from Bosnia which will allow

Croatia to reclaim, by force and damn the consequences, the Krajinas. Another possibility is that if peace can be brokered and the United Nations presence is no longer needed, they will be at liberty to get at each other's throats without interference. An extreme view, perhaps, but you will know better than I that nothing is ever stabilised here, nor apparently, long-term.

There is more and more talk of Croatia being peace-loving (compared to everyone else) but that the Krajinas are 'altogether something different'. This argument, they say, should have the backing of the world as it has recognised the legality of the Croat state as a sovereign nation inferring, naturally, that the RSK are terrorists for conducting an illegal 'occupation' of a properly constituted territory. (Nothing new here). I think that the war will be like nothing we have seen yet in my view. Fighting is inevitable and could start before the summer.

[Again, I was early by almost exactly one year with my prediction.]

I notice almost every day an increasingly belligerent attitude towards the RSK and a rising anger at Europe's lack of support for its return to Croat rule. (Nothing new here either.)

We have an identity problem on the coast which we have been working hard to reverse. Team Split is seen as a holiday camp and quite openly referred to as such among many and not helped by last summer's monitors being reported in the local press for spending too much of their time by the pool. This seems to manifest itself currently in a real lack of interest in the work we are trying to achieve. My staff paper (you were sent a copy) on the future of Team Split was an attempt to explain to the ECMM that the coast is central to any financial recovery and will be one of the most important places as far as regeneration is concerned, let alone any war. We find it difficult to get anyone to take the Split area seriously and I fear it is almost all due to the image it has held in the past. We have explained that we are serious monitors here to do a serious job in the second-largest Croat city that will be at the hub of economic growth. Their only answer is to reduce us by one monitor in advance of a natural reduction due to leave ending with, on occasions, just one monitor.

The humanitarian problems are escalating with the lack of a dedicated humanitarian monitor in Split being badly felt. ECMM's policy towards, for example, the illegal occupation of private flats by the JNA oscillates considerably: the new HRC Knin, Jean-Pierre Thébault, has just reversed earlier appointments making steady monitoring a difficult task. This backing and filling, while accompanied by the quite unnecessary turn round of monitors, gives the Croat authorities here the impression of an unstable and unsteady organisation.

Godfrey is well aware of my views on these matters, and while they might give the impression of constructive criticisms they are merely points that we are working on.

If the sun didn't shine and the sea wasn't blue. We might be taken more seriously!

Julian was kind enough to reply on the 14th:

Thank you very much your letter of 10 March and the enclosed reports, which I read with interest. I have passed some onto the British embassy in Zagreb.

I was interested in your comment about the belligerent attitudes of local Croats towards the RSK. As I understand it Split has long had a reputation for being a centre of hard-line Croat nationalism. Given that it is the area most directly threatened—both militarily and economically—an uncompromising stance is, perhaps, to be expected. Nonetheless, I wonder whether the fervour to reclaim the RSK by force is shared by the mainstream politicians in Zagreb. The indications are that moderates are in the ascendancy within the Zagreb government.

Your letter raises the question whether the RSK could be taken by force. When I was in Zagreb, the consensus was that the Croats could achieve only limited military objectives of a priority nature, like recapturing the Zagreb–Belgrade highway. Talk of resolving the RSK crisis militarily was brushed aside as unrealistic. The coastal region, of course, has a large number of displaced personnel who can only talk tough about regaining their birthright but I wonder whether such sentiments run so deep elsewhere in Croatia.

You are absolutely right about the Dalmatian coast's economic importance. I therefore understand your frustration at the lack of priority accorded to the area by the ECMM. You are clearly doing everything possible to redress the image problem. Jean-Pierre Thébault is not the easiest of men to work with but he has a reputation for defending his patch vigorously. I hope this will help your efforts to convince the ECMM headquarters that they should not neglect the Split area.

Sadly Julian's assessments for any future conflict were not to be as the events of August 1995 were to demonstrate.

Support for my predicament came the next day from a source I had considered to be unsympathetic.

Spoke to Vassilis who is extremely angry at me being re-appointed without him knowing. He ended the short telephone call with the statement, 'The Frenchman is an arrogant tyrant!' A little later even Caroline in the United Kingdom's delegation office told me, once I had reported that I was being moved, 'Oh no! Not more complaints about that man.'

Knowing that I was, quite suddenly, at the crossroads of my career as an ECMM monitor yet not prepared to go down without a fight I managed to get a signal through to Tony Smith who telephoned me back accusing me of blackmailing the ECMM by stating that if I left Split I would leave the Mission. I explained that it was not blackmail so much but the breaking of a verbal contract that I had established with Paul that was forcing my hand. I had spent weeks trying to establish Team Split on a firm and permanent basis and all that was about to be ruined. I felt no compunction to keep my side of the bargain as I would now have to learn a new area while someone else who did not know Split would, too, have to start all over again.

'The trouble is, Ewen, Jean-Pierre regards you as being too important to be a simple monitor and so he wants you where the action is.'

For a start I did not believe this nor had I any idea what on earth was meant so I argued back: 'I came out here to be a monitor in the field and not a bloody staff officer.' I was not inclined to mention that I had unfinished SIS business on the coast and, if I ever got there, also in Dubrovnik. 'Anyway', I thought at the time, 'where is the action on the coast if it is not monitoring the arms embargo'.

Nevertheless encouraging news came from another quarter with an invitation to have dinner with Lynda Chalker[1] on the following Tuesday. In replying I promised Andrew Wells, the Vice Consul in Zagreb, that I would be on my best behaviour in the company of the newly-ennobled Baroness and, of more relevance perhaps, an ex-head girl of Roedean!

> Makes up for last night when I was removed from the list to have dinner with my old friend Hugo White—which I know will not have amused him especially as he asked to see me on board RFA *Resource*. I will now write to tell him what happened particularly as I am responsible, I think!—for the coast from Šibenik to the strategic port of Ploče and thus had much to talk to him about.
>
> Engaged a new interpretress called Dabilla: naturally a little hesitant but I'm sure she will be okay.

To continue my slide towards resignation one of the most significant events of my employment by the ECMM now took place. On 12 March I received an invitation—more like an order—to meet Vassilis Dertilis alone and in the middle of Šibenik bridge.[2]

> This is all rather melodramatic and 'cloak and daggerish' but both of us have no doubts that our various living quarters are 'bugged' while equally certain that the middle of the bridge is not!

I had no idea in advance what Vassilis wanted to discuss but it had to be important and sensitive. As this was to be the pivotal point in my employment by the ECMM the moment I returned to Hotel Split's Room 519 I recorded the occasion in my diary but I also typed a narrative of the event into my *Sinclair Cambridge Z88* laptop before the facts became too hazy and even corrupted.

The following narrative is what I tapped into my word processor.

'Ewen.' Turning his head, arms still resting on the concrete guardrail, Vassilis opened the impromptu meeting, 'Did you know that the Germans are importing Leopard tanks through the port of Pula in the north of Croatia.'

'Yes, Vassilis,' I concurred, 'I wrote it in yesterday's Daily Report that you will have received,' and then added for emphasis in the unlikely chance that he had forgotten what else had been in my signal, 'Along with the Americans sending fighter aircraft hidden in large shipping containers. I assume you, too, see the airfield monitors' reports from Pula?'

What is going on in Pula is almost certainly going on in 'my own' port of Ploče and the Pula team are anxious that I should be aware that these irregularities are taking place and that we should be forewarned. As it happens Ploče has been on my list of places to visit since my arrival on the coast but due to various internal shenanigans I have done so only once and that was really more of a reconnaissance for future visits. Now, of course, I have an imperative reason to institute a programme of in-depth monitoring of the port. While the monitoring of Ploče is at the head of my unwritten agenda there were one or two other factors that needed urgent discussion far from prying or electronic ears—and where better than the middle of a bridge!

'Vassilis, I have already begun to establish a monitoring programme to include the port of Ploče. There seems to be an Irishman who I believe is responsible for port operations. The one time I have met him he was most friendly and keen to help. I'm damn certain that whether hidden in containers or not little will escape his notice.'

'That is fine,' Vassilis argued, 'but, as you know, Jean-Pierre has told us not to conduct such monitoring…' Vassilis was relaying nothing new, other that I was about to receive contradictory orders from both the Greek naval officer and the French diplomat.

'… Which is, of course, precisely why we are all out here in Croatia.' Vassilis knew this only too well.

'And that is why you must continue with your plans.'

'Jean-Pierre has already told me not to continue with my plans!'

'I know… so I have a proposition to suggest.'

'Which is?'

Knowing Vassilis, I was more than half prepared for his answer.

'You must continue to monitor any illegal imports through Ploče but Jean-Pierre must not know that you have even visited the place and he must certainly never know what you find there. So, I want you to continue monitoring as planned but now you will need to falsify your daily reports by saying that you have been somewhere else. When you do go to Ploče, I want you to tell me, and me alone, what you have found.'

I needed no time to prepare an answer. 'Vassilis, you know my background well enough to know that that is an impossible request for me to meet. Not only is it immoral but it goes against everything that the ECMM is supposed to represent.'

Vassilis continued staring down at the river so I elaborated. 'There has to be a reason why the Frenchman does not want us to discover any embargo breaking and there has to be a reason why you, a Greek, need to know … and I don't like either of them.'

'I'll see if I can get Jean-Pierre to change his mind,' was his unconvincing response. I know Vassilis will not try and I also know that Jean-Pierre will not change his mind.

There was a long silence and then Vassilis rather abruptly changed the subject.

'I am worried about my standing with your Foreign and Commonwealth Office in London and indeed with your Head of Department in Zagreb.' I have no idea why my London office should be his concern but I have many ideas why my Head of Department in Zagreb should be.

'Oh really!' I feigned surprise, 'And what precisely do you want me to do about it especially as you have just asked me to falsify my Daily Reports?'

Vassilis now presented a side of him that he had clearly been anxious to hide from me ever since we had first met in Knin. I will not go so far as to say that I feel sorry for him, for much of his probably-feigned unhappiness is entirely of his own making. Nevertheless I do not, at the moment anyway, wish to make an enemy of him as we have work to do over the illegal importing of tanks and aircraft.

'I'll square things away with my Head of Delegation, Vassilis, but in return you must abide by the original promises made to me by Jean-Pierre's predecessor … and just to remind you what those were they include me staying at Split so that I can divide my current monitoring team into two while also establishing a third monitoring mission in Dubrovnik.'

'I'll do what I can, and that is a promise.'

He also said that the Deputy Head of Mission (Operations) and the Chief of Logistics and Personnel have told Jean-Pierre that I was a 'known personality' and not a simple monitor (whatever that may mean) and that I was to stay in Split until the end of my mission. We'll see if that actually happens but at least the ground rules are being laid down—or should I say that the status quo is being maintained—by HQ ECMM. Sadly, though, I have my doubts that Jean-Pierre—a Frenchman—will take any notice of the Greeks in Zagreb. I sense trouble.

Ending this strange meeting we walked back to our Land Rovers to drive off in opposite directions leaving me, perhaps naïvely, with no clue that any promise would be kept and that I would still be required to falsify my Daily Reports.

Then it was back to reality on my return to the hotel.

Met again Andrew Wells—Vice Consul British Embassy—with his girlfriend Julia Swain and Tamsin (?) who I think is a secretary in Lynda Chalker's press office. Amusing drinks before dinner, then we had the ECMM dining room to ourselves as the Greeks eat so early. Thank goodness!

I knew then that one of the reason why the Greeks and French, including Vassilis and now Jean-Pierre, wanted to clip my wings. Alone among all the monitors within the Knin HRC it must have looked odd, if not suspicious—for these things always got reported backwards and forwards within the ECMM—that I had the ear not only of the British Ambassador to Croatia, the British Vice-Consul in Zagreb as well as the British and Italian Consuls in Split but now the British Secretary of State for Overseas Development. My friendship with the Commander-in-Chief Fleet and the Masters of RFAs *Resource* and *Sir Geraint* had not gone un-noticed either and my 'private' visit to Captain Dragan was also well known. As I have mentioned before, my room was certainly bugged as were, without much doubt, the telephones not only in my room for local calls but the one in Team Split's office which was connected to the international telephone network. It was not possible to keep anything secret—unless discussed in the very middle of Šibenik bridge!

On 13 March Jean-Pierre excelled himself by demanding that all monitors within his Regional Centre on both sides of the Confrontation Line be confined to their quarters with immediate effect and until further notice. This was apparently because of 'trouble' in Gospić and the Bihać 'pocket' although we in Split and, I had little doubt, those teams based in Zadar, had no idea why 'trouble' in the Bihać 'pocket' was likely to affect our monitoring on the coast.

This is ridiculous as we are a long way from Bihać but apparently the Serbs shot up the French again yesterday so NATO called in an airstrike although this was, strangely, cancelled just before the aircraft became airborne as the Serbs had stopped their shooting. Rather wet of NATO in my view.

Additional, but amusing, confusions appeared with the arrival in Hotel Split of Zariah Stein: almost certainly not her real names. I had noticed this attractive, long-dark-haired girl a few days earlier for she was alone and, I guessed, in her late twenties to mid-thirties. For a couple of days Fergus and I had watched her in and around the hotel's lobby and bars for she looked out of place: judging, by the stylishness of her clothes, she was not a refugee. I doubted, too, that she was a Croat. As it happened, her arrival in Split had coincided with a message from my SIS contact in London warning me that a female member of Mossad was in the area and believed to be intent on infiltrating a monitoring team. The name he gave me was ... Zariah Stein! Sharing this news (although not its source) with Fergus, on a strictly confidential basis, we guessed that not only was she 'the one' but we deduced that her presence was in order for Israel to keep an eye on the possibility of disruptive Muslim influences on the coast. We decided that, to keep an eye on this enigmatic lady—assuming that she was 'the one'—we should make the first move on the principle that attack is the best form of defence. While we prevaricated she beat us to it by offering to buy us drinks in the Riva Terrace Bar to where Fergus and I, now in civilian clothes, had retired to discuss our latest set of contradictory orders. We had seen her again, late that afternoon, watching us as we were dropped off from an ECMM, white Land Rover. In our white uniforms it would not have been difficult for her to have gauged our business.

'You look like a couple of interesting people. Let me buy you both a drink. I am new here and need some advice about hotels on the islands.' She then explained that she was working for an international company—no name or nationality was mentioned—planning to advertise and sell holidays on the offshore islands while they were still cheap.

Her excuse for being so forward was pretty lame especially in the charged atmosphere among Hotel Split's eclectic assortment of 'clients' that ranged from refugees to transient politicians and journalists representing most European countries along with, no doubt whatsoever, carpetbaggers manipulating the black market, self-employed 'spooks', crooks, con-men, hired hitmen, drunk American mercenaries and heavens knew who else. Pretending that we did not know her real background we willingly accepted her offer and, in return, invited her to join us for dinner in Café Riva and not the ECMM restaurant.

> Clearly an intelligent girl, she is humorous and attractive—probably ideal for the job. But we have the measure of her and avoided any talk of ECMM business while she, naturally, did not mention her nationality or her real job. I am certain she does not know that we know! This may be useful to us if she stays much longer. Anyway, an amusing if not instructive evening. Sent a message to 'London' detailing all I have gleaned which wasn't much other than her *modus operandi*.

Then, extraordinarily, on 15 March I read the following in the consolidated Daily Report from CC Zadar to RC Knin:

Other matters: … Journalist Ms Zariah Stein joined Team Zadar for the whole day.

Zariah was obviously getting around the ECMM in her own professional manner! And while Team Split, thanks to the SIS, had been forewarned Team Zadar had not had this advantage so I wondered how much they had given away. Earlier I had considered warning the other coastal teams of her presence and her background but had decided against doing so for fear of exposing my reasons (and my source) for knowing so much about her.

Late this evening we received another ridiculous signal, this one relayed by Vassilis from Jean-Pierre, saying that we were to cancel all patrols except those involved in military monitoring. But ... at the moment we are under the impression that we have been 'confined to our quarters' so God knows what, in reality, we are supposed to be doing.

A touch of light relief came with the arrival of Matt Burford for the night while a British army, lady officer, Captain Vicky Fifield, also called in. A lively and most plucky girl she had witnessed, at first hand, some of the very worst atrocities although perhaps nothing to compare with once having been a girlfriend of a Royal Marines officer that I knew!

Ignoring Jean-Pierre's ruling, for we had fought for many weeks to secure the visit, the next day Fergus and I drove to Brodosplit shipyard. This visit did much for my own morale and that of my colleague for it was precisely what we were in Croatia to achieve. It was, too, a visit that showed me that there were a few—a very few—serious and mature business people who appreciated what we were trying to do to help them in the long term. Once again it is best told in a narrative that I tapped into my laptop on my return to Hotel Split.

In the early afternoon Brodosplit's Chief Executive Officer greeted us at the entrance to his boardroom. Once seated around the table with cups of bitter, black coffee and the obligatory glasses of raquia I felt that I should start with an apology.

'I'm very sorry for the late setting up of this visit,' I began, 'especially as you were visited by our predecessors only recently.'

Vinka effortlessly translated my words while Fergus and I studied the Chief Executive Officer's face.

Looking at me the CEO held up both hands in mock despair, 'We have not had a visit from the ECMM for many months. And although we don't welcome them we know they are necessary so we were a little surprised that you were no longer taking any interest in us. Especially as we will be one of the major factors in the regeneration of Dalmatia's economy.'

Despite being conscious that I was in danger of making Team Split look foolish I repeated my apologies. 'I was under the impression that monitors had visited you just before Christmas.'

'No,' the CEO replied then, anxious to move on, continued, 'Let me explain what we do and then I will hand you over to my Operations Manager for a tour of the shipyard. He will be happy to answer any further questions.'

'We used to build warships. Mostly of the corvette size and we have an acknowledged expertise in small submarines. Especially the Mala class of swimmer delivery vehicles. We don't build any military or civilian vessels now. But we try to maintain our expertise for the day when we can.'

'I believe you once built an 800 ton landing craft.'

'First of the Silba class. We launched it earlier this year but since then nothing, although we would like to finish two more.'

The CEO passed round a list of civilian ships, mostly passenger ferries, they were currently refitting. 'These jobs help us to retain our skills but obtaining raw materials is not easy.'

'And where do those materials come from,' asked Fergus.

Vinka translated.

'Before the war we imported steel plate through Split so it was delivered direct to our doorstep but Split docks are now taken over mostly by ferries transferring refugees along the coast and the few general-cargo ships that are prepared to run the gauntlet.'

'Gauntlet?'

'The embargo. NATO navies, yours included,' the CEO looked carefully at both of us in turn, 'put many civilian shipping companies off from accepting cargoes for Croat ports even if they are not carrying weapons. They get delayed and they get hassled.' [The Irish navy was not involved but the CEO may not have known that Fergus was not British.]

'That's not right.' Fergus watched Vinka as she translated.

'It happens. The British and Dutch navies are the most diligent. American and German warships are not so fussy. Sometimes their inspections are over very quickly.'

Vinka paused in her translation to glance at Fergus but the CEO had not finished his résumé.

'Maybe if any good comes out of your monitoring you can get the message to whoever needs to hear it that enforcing the embargo may be working too well. And I for one, even if the United Nations doesn't,' he laughed briefly, 'would be prepared to accept the import of a few weapons if it means that we can get the thousands of tons of the steel we need to keep my business going. Right now it comes in insignificant packets overland from Ploče.'

'You make the point well,' Fergus said, 'We will certainly emphasise that.'

The CEO looked at his watch, pressed a buzzer on the table and spoke to Vinka. 'The Chief Executive,' she translated, 'will hand you over to his Operations Manager. He says that you will not see any ships under refit as that happens in the main sheds. Then they are finished out in the open but currently we only have one vessel at that stage. A passenger ferry which you will be at liberty to inspect.'

A short, jovial tubby man in a light grey suit that he had bought long before he put on weight, entered the room. Once introduced to Team Split he moved to the door, stopped and looked back. 'Come,' he eventually said in passable English, 'I show you.'

Outside, he stopped. 'We do not allow visitors to enter the sheds,' he explained implausibly, 'in case you breathe dangerous dust. But,' he continued with a smile, 'as we walk past the buildings you will be able to look beyond me. I have ordered that the doors be left open this afternoon to let in some of this warm, fresh air.'

As good as his word the Operations Manager, with a theatrical choreography each time we changed direction, allowed myself and Fergus to look past him and into each building without making it obvious to a casual observer.

That evening, having compiled a most positive Daily Report, we went out to dinner with the airfield monitors in Trogir during which they confirmed the illegal importing of main battle tanks and aircraft that was occurring at Pula.

As the result of my meeting with Vassilis on Šibenik bridge and my subsequent decision I knew that the only way Team Split was going to properly monitor the quite obvious breaking of the arms embargo was to ignore Vassilis's order to 'falsify our Daily Reports' and to carry on as normal and report, as normal. What he did with my reports was going to be up to him for I now, courtesy of the airfield monitors, had first hand confirmation that aircraft were being imported through the northern port of Pula in unmarked crates and 'sure as hell' the same was happening in Ploče. We just had not spotted them—yet.

I say, and have said often, that the breaking of the arms embargo was obvious although I personally had no first hand facts to back up my views. But, on the other hand the irregular convoys of heavily-tarpaulined army lorries coming north from Ploče were suspicious in themselves as was the almost total lack of any security at the port's gates. The increase of mercenary soldiers in American army uniforms, some also sporting swastika arms bands, was another sign that re-manning was rife and there could be only be one purpose behind this unavoidable fact: the invasion of the RSK.

Relaxing evening with Roger Sugden and Günter in a Trogir fish restaurant during which Fergus and I learned much. Also having dinner by sheer coincidence were Professor Eric Grove the maritime historian and author and Jonathan Worthington a naval 'schoolie', both stationed on board HMS *Ark Royal*. They wanted me to go back on board to sign copies of my book *Reasons in Writing*. Giles Penfold (a photographer) was also there with Lindsay (?) the Head of British Public Information. So, quite a delayed departure back to Hotel Split. All in all a pleasant evening away from all the petty and unprofessional stupidities of the French and Greeks.

However on our return to the hotel I found more buggering about by Jean-Pierre Thébault and a second signal from Vassilis telling me, formally, to '*cook your patrol reports*' until the old programme had worked its way out of the system.

I feel this may be the beginning of the end of my involvement. The fact that it was all due to the discovery of tanks and aircraft being imported into Croatia by Germany through the northern ports and as result of that my desire, indeed my duty, to monitor the port of Split and the port of Ploče to report if this is happening here. The French do not want to know and therefore do not want me to monitor the ports or they would have to do something about it, whereas the Greeks do want to know and thus insist that I monitor the southern ports. The net result being that I have been ordered to continue monitoring by the Greeks to whom I shall report what I find while also reporting to the French that I have not been anywhere near the ports and thus have never seen anything. This is now an illegal farce.

Once more I cleared my mind with a letter, this time to another first cousin, William Tailyour in Connecticut, USA.[3]

I think I have a quiet moment to bring you up-to-date with life in this desperate part of the world …

I am now in Split.… In practice Croatia has committed some of the worst atrocities and is capable of carrying out the most horrific acts, even to my eyes. I will not describe some of the things they are capable of doing to each other—just the simple act of killing women and children in a village is almost tame compared with what they then do and how they do it.

In Split I am responsible for a vast area. Much too large for two monitors and with the very real probability of the war between Croatia and the Republic of Serbian Krajina taking off in a big way, that will eclipse much of what has been going on in Bosnia, This coastal conflict has been simmering away with the taking and losing of little strips of land for nearly three years although Sarajevo has, I suppose understandably, taken the limelight (if that is the correct expression for such terror).

So until the war starts again in earnest much of my time is spent just keeping a low profile, military eye on the illegal build-up of arms and disposition of troops and ships while I meet and discuss with industrial and political leaders, the areas where European money will most be needed to help regenerate growth once a full overall peace is sustainable. I, as you know only too well, am and not a political, diplomatic or economically minded animal so these new disciplines, in such a place, are really fascinating.

The only sadness is the internal bickering and squabbling within the European Community itself, based in Zagreb. I won't bore you with the details until we meet over a gin or six except to say that the internal 'complications' take up much of our time—far more than the actual monitoring. I'll be glad to leave.

12

Split Yacht Club and Minefields

15th March 1994 The Ides of March—how appropriate!

Yet another blank day as far as monitoring is concerned. I had no time to go on patrol—again—as I was 'forced' to deal with the problems following on from Jean-Pierre's instant and continual changing of our programme.

Had a very long talk in the evening with Martin Garrod on his way through to Zagreb from Mostar. Hugh Wilson [not his real name either] also called in on his way from the 'interior' to leave in the UK but he has been bedding—rather ill-advised to do so I would have thought—the Mossad agent Zariah Stein which is interesting. Although I had warned my own team about Zariah's status I did not think to spread this across the Mission! Had I done so maybe Hugh would have been a little more selective in whom he beds! It might even have saved his marriage.

I learned on this day that Martin, had, too, been buggered about by Jean-Pierre when he, the Frenchman, had been HRC Zenica and Martin had been HCC Mostar. It was quite clear from the studiously-correct and always-polite Martin that Jean-Pierre was a very difficult character.

Following the cancelling of our long-planned visit to Vis I felt it time I spelt out one or two 'home truths' in a signal to both Vassilis in Zadar and Jean-Pierre in Knin:

From: Team Split
To: HRC Knin, HCC Zadar
DTG: xxxx

We are in receipt of HRC Knin's recent guidelines for ECMM monitoring in Team Split's Area of Responsibility.

As I warned in yesterday's Daily Report, the proposed cancellation of our forthcoming monitoring of the island of Vis is already causing anger with our Croat liaison officer and the island's authorities. The CLO (a pro-ECMM official) has asked me to say, quite clearly, that the cancellation of the visit following his lengthy efforts to obtain clearance has demonstrated that the ECMM lacks respect for Croat feelings and that cancellations of this nature, destroy Croat confidence in us. He has further asked me to say that future requests to meet political leaders may be refused on the basis that they will not know whether or not we will actually attend.

A number of aspects are relevant: this visit to Vis was set up under the earlier RCK's guidelines for monitoring issued this month thus it would be more sensible and more courteous (and perhaps less suspicious) to conduct a smooth change of policy rather than a sudden one; according to Standard Operating Procedures monitoring of the economic infrastructure will remain a constant objective and while there are political and economic reasons for visiting the islands the overriding reason is military. This is not intelligence gathering but a straightforward look at what is—publically—happening.

My experience of maritime and military matters, coupled with what I know of Croatia's warship building programme, (plus snippets of related military news) indicate that in any forthcoming conflict the island of Vis will, once again, become a major naval and military base out of range of Republic of Serbian Krajina ground forces and defendable against any (Serb ex-Yugoslav National Army navy) pre-emptive strikes.

This makes a visit to Vis obligatory as part of our overall need to assess future military intentions and I recommend, with respect, that you take my advice in this matter.

You should also be aware that in accordance with our new guidelines I have initiated meetings next week with the HS, LS, HDZ, [local political parties] the editor of the *Dalmatia Tribune* and am hoping to fix further visits to the HSLS, HMS, HSP, DA, SDP, SSG and the SENS [local trade unions] (if they exist in Split). In addition, I intend to meet the commanders of the 113, 142 and 126 brigades and the commander of the 15th Artillery Regiment.

Signed, Ewen Southby-Tailyour

During the early evening I had a serious, and I mean serious, sense of humour failure over the telephone with Tony in Knin about the re-appointing of myself and all my monitors away from Split. This outburst was witnessed by the long-suffering Matt Burnford, late of the Royal Tank Regiment and HCC Zadar prior to Vassilis, and who had had his own troubles with the Greeks. Quite rightly, Matt tried to calm me down and succeeded—eventually. We went off to have a glass of wine or two and to talk quietly about the problem while puzzling over how we were expected to carry out our duties without the tools: including the correct number of monitors, the correct orders, the correct number of interpretresses and the correct number of vehicles.

I appreciated that I was involved in what I could only describe in my diary as 'a bloody farce'. I knew, too, that I was wasting my time for I was certainly not achieving anything that could, in the slightest way, be considered useful for the refugees and displaced persons: as I had—we all had—expected to be doing. At Zagreb we had been led to believe that our work—even on the coast—would be largely humanitarian but our already-paltry humanitarian efforts were being stopped by Jean-Pierre. Quite suddenly and since his arrival, no longer were the monitors on either side of the Confrontation Line allowed to offer telephone calls, nor were we allowed to carry letters or parcels across the border in either direction. In many ways this was the most important, morale-boosting task of all to which blind eyes were turned by both the Serbs (always, when parcels were coming in) and the Croats (sometimes, when parcels were going out).

> Of course we will all try to carry letters and parcels (and teddy bears) as the border guards of both sides are, by-and-large, tolerant for they see it as a two way traffic and if one side was to stop so would the other side. Sadly, tragically I should say, Jean-Pierre does not see that, yet without these tiny rays of hope we can now offer these distraught people even less than before and that was pretty minimal. All our promises are empty for a future that does not, in reality, exist.

The good, personal, news was that, as mentioned earlier, I had been asked to a Foreign Office reception in the Split Yacht Club to welcome Baroness Chalker as she passed through the town. Fergus and I had visited the yacht club before to find that not only was it still active notwithstanding no 'yachting' ever taking place throughout my time on the coast. Nevertheless, on the rare occasion we had turned up for dinner with no notice, we had eaten extremely well despite, often, being the only clients. As anticipated this FCO-sponsored evening for BRITFOR and local diplomats turned out to be a thoroughly civilised affair made even more enjoyable for me by the presence of Aleksi Mejković, the honorary British Consul in Split. Inevitably this extracurricular activity only enhanced the view within the Reginal Centre at Knin that I was on the coast for 'other reasons'. When he heard of my presence at the dinner Jean-Pierre was particularly scathing but his comments were now just more water off this particular duck's back.

I had been warned the day before the dinner that Lynda Chalker would be asking me for a comprehensive résumé of the ECMM's problems. Fortunately, I had also been asked by the Embassy if there was any other British monitor in Split who should be invited, giving me just enough time to persuade Martin Garrod to be in town; he, too, was sent an invitation. This was a good—indeed an excellent—move as he could speak with such authority and feeling unlike the brigadier, of camouflaged-pyjamas notoriety, who appeared to annoy the lieutenant-general by telling him that he, the brigadier, was going to hand over 'peace in his time'! If he had been able to look just one year into the future this hapless British army officer would have witnessed the worst case of ethnic cleansing since the holocaust and certainly unlike anything that was experienced throughout the Balkans since the beginning of that dreadful period.

The dinner involved a number of tables during which Lady Chalker moved from one to another while seeking a myriad of opinions from among the British military and the local 'civilian establishment'. From the ECMM's perspective she heard, luckily, the same views from Martin and myself in turn.

Simon Wilson, Head of the Political Section in the Zagreb Embassy, and I were on the same table thus he was able to brief me on the Croat special forces based on the island of Vis—which I knew—while adding information on a number of associated facilities that I did not know and that the Croats would rather were kept secret. He further explained that all the locals knew what was going because the military were opening up certain parts of Vis to the non-existent tourists in an attempt to put the islanders off the scent. We both knew of the ex-wartime airfield in a valley which could not be overlooked by public land and knew, too, that the islanders often talked of the ground 'rumbling under their feet'. From this last snippet we guessed that the old communist, underground silos were still being used for something nefarious.

Worryingly, but perhaps not surprisingly, towards the end of the evening Simon took me aside to pass a message from an 'un-named' Foreign Office source suggesting that my life was in danger: I had been seen taking too much interest in the arms embargo. In mitigation I explained that all I knew came from unsolicited sources such as the Croats themselves and our airfield monitors, as well as my own overt observations. One source of these rumours about my safety might have been, we assumed, the interpretresses for it was not beyond the possibility that they, the rumours, were 'plants' to see what action I would take if I knew I was being 'targeted'. I told Simon I was not falling for that ruse and would continue to 'play the innocent' with very wide open ears and eyes and no questions asked.

'Be very careful, Ewen. Very careful,' he said as we left the yacht club, followed by the assurance that he would speak privately tomorrow about this and associated topics.

The next morning, as promised, Simon called into Room 519 to talk about our work as monitors plus one or two more intelligence topics revolving around what was and what was not happening on the island of Vis. I expressed a personal view based on my own casual observations that somehow UN Arms Embargo 713 was being broken or it was, 'pretty certainly' being circumvented but that, as yet, I could offer no concrete evidence. I did, though, mention the 'secret' military airfield on Brač.

Team Split's subsequent Daily Report was fairly typical, except, perhaps, for paragraph 4, and read as follows:

FM   Team Split
To   CC Zadar
            RC Knin

DAILY REPORT 16 Mar 1994

1. GENERAL SITUATION: Unchanged
    a. Political Situation. The team has been informed by the Croat Liaison Officer
    that an official protest letter will be forwarded to Zagreb complaining about
    the cancellation of the arranged meetings at the island of Vis.
    b. Military Situation. The team today patrolled along the Confrontation Line (CFL)
    without escort. At a joint military/police checkpoint at road-T (XJ1639) it was made
    clear that they did not have restrictions to impose on us beyond 10 km WNW from
    the village of Kjlake (XJ0648). The team therefore patrolled the villages of Crivac
    (XJ0846)—Pribude (XJ1247)—Milesina (XJ1646)—G.Ogorge (XJ1843)—Bidnici
    (XJ1640) area. All was peaceful, soldiers in uniform (probably on leave but not
    sure) were seen in many places and a manned Croat Army Observation Post was
    observed at hilltop Veliki (grid point 964) at (XJ1048). The UNMOs in Šibenik
    patrolled their sector of the CFL but as always with CALO escort.
2. CEASEFIRE VIOLATIONS: Sinj UNMOs reported a few rounds incoming
    last night.
3. HUMANITARIAN ISSUES: In *Slobodna Dalmacija* today a letter was
    quoted from the state lawyer to the Croat Helsinki Watch Committee which
    in part indicated that there are no reasons for mistrust towards Croat legal
    authorities over humanitarian matters. He ended his letter stating 'Therefore
    I ask you to submit data—if any—on the violation of human rights in Croatia'.
    (COMMENT: As this team has submitted much data to HQ ECMM this
    statement has to be treated with the utmost scepticism.)
4. PEOPLE MET: The Rt Hon Baroness Chalker (British Minister of State for
    Overseas Development) HE The Ambassador of Great Britain to the Republic
    of Croatia, Mr Simon Wilson (Head of the Political Department, British
    Embassy). Team Leader attended UK national reception.
5. TOMORROW'S PROGRAMME: Patrolling Confrontation Line.

Regards: Lennart Leschly, Fergus Marshall, Ewen Southby-Tailyour

Following Lynda Chalker's visit I held a long telephone conversation with
Godfrey Garratt, in Zagreb, about our problems with Jean-Pierre during which
I learned that he, J-P, had asked for a meeting with Godfrey to debate my
'predicament'. A little later in the day Godfrey reported back on the discussion he
had just concluded.

'Ewen, I must start by telling you that we are not fans of Jean-Pierre in this headquarters but I must also say that he is accusing you of disobeying orders and so I was required to listen.'

I explained to Godfrey that this was an odd accusation since I had yet to receive an order to disobey and those instructions that we did receive in Team Split from Jean-Pierre were not only via a third party but always immediately countermanded by Vassilis Dertilis. It was not an easy position to maintain nor, I elaborated, were any of the so-called orders given by Jean-Pierre in line with the ECMM's Terms of Reference and thus, to my mind, were illegal anyway.

'Godfrey, all we are trying to do in Team Split is to question the wisdom of splitting up a newly formed and growingly efficient team that has made an excellent base within the local community. We are simply intent on preventing the beleaguered ECMM in Split from making an even greater fool of itself in the eyes of the Croatians for when that happens we will not be allowed to move out of our five-star hotel without the stars!'

Although aware that I was pushing at an open door I reminded Godfrey that Jean-Pierre had been treating my team with the utmost disdain.

'He refuses to speak directly to us but passes vague messages through the long-suffering Tony who of course does not know what is in Jean-Pierre's mind only that he is determined to transfer every single monitor in the whole of RC Knin. His predecessor—Paul Ortholan—is popular within the Quay D'Orsay and, we are told, has been promoted and sent to Riyadh as the French ambassador. We understand that Jean-Pierre is, thus, so incensed that he has set out to undermine and destroy all that Paul has achieved. Any decision that Paul made is being reversed as a matter of spite. All this we know. It really is very strange.'

Unexpectedly, a short time later, Godfrey opened his ECMM and diplomatic heart in a 'private' signal:

'I have to say that Jean-Pierre knows that he has made a great cock-up by his treatment of you all in Team Split, as well as the other teams in his Regional Centre and now does not know how to get out of it without losing face. I have no idea how the problem will be solved as Jean-Pierre told me, quite categorically, that he will refuse to apologise or rescind any of his decisions. I reminded him that he had an experienced military team under his command in Split and in many respects one that is tailor-made for the coastal monitoring you are required to undertake. Sadly he seems unable to grasp this significance and so we are at a form of stalemate.'

It was not music to my ears but at least I knew where we, as a team, stood. I also knew that not much was likely to change in the immediate future. To wrap up this episode in my life as a monitor I wrote a letter to Lynda Chalker.

I must thank you very much for including me in your reception and dinner at the Split Yacht Club … It was fascinating to hear of events out here from an entirely different (and British) source—putting into proper perspective so many ideas and conceptions …

I hope Martin Garrod and I were not <u>too</u> outspoken—we both feel very strongly about the work we do and what we are trying, against considerable odds, to achieve …

The [public] news of the Krajinas and Croatia seems to be good but, being a little cynical (and having listened to so many down-to-earth people on both sides of the Confrontation Line) I hope it remains good but the hatred and distrust is so great that some of us wonder whether the signing of the [latest] political and military agreement is enough to satisfy those who have been dispossessed and suffered such extreme cruelty on both sides …

Then it was back to what passed for a normal day in the life of a monitor in Split.

Another day trying to un-scramble our programme as I am not prepared to lie to satisfy the Greek/French problem. We should have been in Vis today seeing, as part of their subterfuge, what is publically on show while saying that there is nothing else to see. This is to put the locals off the scent. I know this and they do not know that I know. I expect our visit will have been conducted utterly properly and openly and that we would have been shown all there is to see on the island without showing us what I/we know surrounds the island: the mined sea approaches. So, we would have pretended to come away happy that they are not using the place other than for tourists and all would have been satisfied. I agreed that the Croat authorities had every right to be angry and so when Dino told me that they would be putting in a formal complaint about our last minute change of plan I told him that that would be a good thing and that I have already warned Jean-Pierre in Knin. Dino understands our problem and is indiscreetly amusing about it.

He also says that he will find it difficult now to fix new meetings as people will be wary of us not turning up and failing to keep to our schedules which they probably did not want to fix in the first place as they are heartily sick of the same old questions. Of course and paradoxically Dino and the rest forget the many, many times that we are turned away at the last minute from long-scheduled meetings when all we are trying to do is to smooth the passage for the introduction of funds when the peace comes. I suppose, to a local with no sign of a peace anyway, ours are empty promises and only an excuse for us to gain intelligence whether that be political, economic or military

I have also learnt that we do not now have permission to call on any of the three Croat army brigades in our area 113, 126, 142 or, for that matter the 15 Artillery Regiment so Jean-Pierre's stupidity is now reaping the non-benefit of his quite extraordinary decisions. What a bloody fool. We are now prevented from any 'legal' military monitoring (rather than the less-legal military intelligence gathering) despite his view that it is our priority!

There were, though sunnier moments to lighten our continual tussles. On 17 March, St Patrick's Day, I prophesied that I was not expecting to see too much of Fergus! And I was right, to a certain degree.

Apparently John Major is in town. Simon hinted as much last night but was sufficiently devious and diplomatic to let us think the British visitor was 'female' and so us non-FCO types all assume that it is Princess Anne working for her Save the Children Fund. Sadly it isn't.

After lunch, and deciding that celebrations were in order, Fergus and I changed into civilian clothes so that we would not be thrown out of the British forces' NAAFI shop located in a warehouse close to RFA *Resource's* berth in the dockyard. This was now a necessity for the NAAFI no longer allowed the ECMM to use its facilities and the sad reason was understandable. The FLG Greeks had been caught buying up all the luxury goodies on offer before having them packaged up and sent to their families in Greece. Now, for each visit, Fergus and I pretended that we were UNMOs by brandishing our service ID cards. Fergus was still a serving lieutenant-colonel in the Irish army so his was extant. On the other hand mine had 'expired' when I retired and so was, in practice, an illegally-held document. Not that it would have mattered much to the pragmatic team running the 'shop' who were not taken in, indeed they appreciated our efforts to avoid being seen, by the Greeks, entering the building in ECMM uniform. Not for the first time a delightful Royal Logistics Corps captain gave Fergus four cases of Murphy's Irish Stout without asking for payment as it was well past its sell-by date: which Fergus considered to be a very good thing anyway! We did, though, pay for the 'genuinely-duty-free' Irish whiskey and London gin.

At tea time Fergus hosted his real-Irish-coffee party—at least, it started at 'tea time'—and was open to all in Team Split plus Sandra, Vinka and the various ECMM visitors who just happened to be passing through: one of whom, Swedish monitor John Volgers, was delivering a more-than-welcome replacement Land Rover.

So we can begin to monitor again in some comfort—but it is, typically, badly in need of a service and some repairs so we shall see.

Fergus's tea party 'went on a bit' so I left them still celebrating over dinner to join Simon Wilson, and a female FCO colleague of his, in the Riva Terrace Bar.

Here we held an interesting discussion during which we covered just about every topical subject including the reasons why Malcolm Rifkind, John Major and Lynda Chalker were all passing through Split at the same time. They were on their way to, and back from, Sarajevo but apparently the British press was not giving Major any credit by saying that he should have been in Sarajevo one-and-a-half years earlier. That was fine for the press to comment but we could not remember them pushing him then. At least he was here supporting his army general on the ground unlike other nations and especially the USA which was shouting from the side-lines but had nobody on the ground. As Simon declared, 'If you are not a shareholder then you should not run the company or tell it how to be run.'

The press seemed desperate and I, and the others, wondered what their real motive was. I recounted the story of how one of the BBC's reporters had tried, outrageously, to get Richard Perry to admit that the Coldstream Guards deserved the nickname 'cold feet guards'. We agreed that the 'bloody press' should all leave the Balkans and let the locals and the military sit it out without always having to mind what the media might see, do, say or mis-report. Not for the first time in an operational setting had I felt the desire to see the back of all journalists!

> Major is prepared to lead the way with more troops and a further 15 million pounds in aid on top of his morale boosting visit. Now perhaps the rest of Europe will follow but the Germans, Italians and French do not want peace for that would spoil their chances of licking over the pieces once their individual sides have won.
>
> Where is the common European Foreign policy? Non-existent!
> Where is the common European Defence policy? Non-existent!
> It is good to see the British taking charge of this area—at least we have the balls to do so—good leadership at military levels (bar one exception!) being backed up by good positive leadership (plus practical results) at political level. Thank God for a first world power using its experience to good effect rather than wringing its hands in the background like America and of course we are strictly observing and enforcing the international arms embargo unlike France, Germany, Russia, the USA and Greece. I am not sure about the Italians. Maybe training in Serbia does not count as 'embargo busting'.

While we were discussing all these matters Lynda Chalker joined us briefly. Encouragingly she was 'anxious for me to know that she had taken in and noted everything that I had said at the yacht club'. This was particularly thoughtful of her and I thanked her profusely and then again in a subsequent letter.

The next day, 18 March, Martin Garrod came to Room 519. He had been talking to Godfrey Garratt about me and, as a result, asked me if I was on the coast 'for other reasons' connected with the SIS. Knowing that Godfrey was, or had been, with the SIS himself, although I was not sure that Martin knew that, I was pretty certain that Godfrey did not know that I had been asked to carry out various tasks. While not wishing to lie to my former Commandant General I could, with a clear conscience, say that there had been a vacancy on the coast, caused by Noppeneau's sudden departure, and that Paul Ortholan had decided that I, with my nautical background, was best placed to fill it … and I left it at that and refused to be drawn further even by my old general. On a slightly different tack the SIS and the people to whom I sent my 'coastal reports'—DI4—were not the same so there was no reason for the one to know what I had sent to the other.

After an early lunch I drove to HQ 126 Brigade to see Major Bandelo, the brigade staff officer: or was it 142 Brigade for surprisingly it was never easy to know in advance quite who one was meeting or from which military formation and I assumed that there had to be a reason for this. Despite having been told that I would never receive clearance to meet him a direct call through to the major indicated that there was no problem at his level. So, off we set on the twenty-mile journey but when we arrived at the army garrison we were told that Bandelo's two year old nephew had been killed in a house fire a few days earlier and was being buried that same afternoon. As so often we were never to know if this type of sad excuse was true or false. As compensation Marco, the brigade's liaison officer, conducted us to the Peruća Dam, another seven miles further north.

> It was last shelled eight days ago but usually it is every other day which is not helping the reconstruction which of course is why the RSK is shelling. One round landed between the caterpillar bulldozer and its truck which scared the workers but with no casualties they carried on, rather grudgingly we were told. I'm surprised they are working at all as they get bugger-all money.

The Croat Army captain did not want us to walk too far across the dam as we were being watched by RSK soldiers who would, of course, have noticed our white uniforms and probably considered us to be fair game, particularly as the ECMM was, for some never-revealed reason, forbidden from patrolling their area.

The visit to the dam had been, as always, impressive. The Serbs watching me watching them through my binoculars as I tried to spot any ECMM monitors on the other side. There were none but the gun positions were clearly identifiable.

Naturally the guards had not been keen for us to walk across the top of the dam: not for our own safety for which, in practice, they cared little but to avoid bringing down fire onto the dam itself. The guards would not have minded if we had been hurt for it might have put us off patrolling which I knew they regarded as a 'bloody nuisance' but our presence is to show the RSK that we are in evidence.

> On, then, to the village of Beare (at least, that is my anglicised pronunciation of the place as I never saw it written down or on a roadside sign), in the foothills close by the Confrontation Line and to the west of the Peruća dam. Once, it had

been inhabited by about five hundred people but now every house has been destroyed except two, one with only one room remaining habitable. Three people live here, one old woman who has quite clearly gone mad—not surprisingly—and one fascinating couple who gave us very passable red wine and revolting cheese but absolutely delicious bread—probably the finest I have ever eaten as it really was that good. I was worried that we were eating their meagre ration but they insisted so vigorously that it would have been worse not to have accepted.

These three people are Serbs who refused to leave when their own countrymen, Krajina Serbs, had taken the area during the early part of the break-away of the RSK from Croatia and then destroyed it in their wake as they left the area. So now they are Serbs living in the recently-independent Croatia. All the other Serbs fled to the RSK side of the Confrontation Line to avoid living among their enemies. Subsequently this couple and the other old woman refused to leave even when the Serbs clandestinely crossed the Confrontation Line one night to evict them. The memories of the terror were too much for the couple who broke down, clutching each other for support and comfort. I asked if there was anyway we could help but they were too proud to ask apart from....

...Vinka knew their daughter who had originally been married to a Serb but who had since run away with a German. Vinka told the couple that she could get in touch with their daughter in Germany but at this they both broke down again. Despite all their hardships they said they did not want to see their daughter as she had broken her vows of marriage. I would have thought that under the present circumstances they might have liked to have had the contact but their moral view of marriage was stronger than their desire to see their daughter again.

I came away very, very sad indeed for a number of reasons.

While I was photographing the water catchment area there was sudden shelling close by from the west and much Heavy Machine Gun fire—probably 0.5 inch stuff but I could not work out where it was coming from nor what the target was ... other than it was too close for comfort!

19 March brought the sun but, sadly, more unsolvable humanitarian problems very much along the lines of those that had attended the noble Vesna when she was evicted from her family home. A Mr Marić, whom I had met before, came yet again to Team Split's office and this time to say that the threat he had first aired to us had now been actioned. The previous night a bunch of 'black-shirted, swastika-arm-band wearing' Croat soldiers, probably high on *raquia* or some other 'substance' had forcibly evicted him from his flat. This premeditated action took place despite the publically-known fact that he had been a popular naval captain heading the Croat navy's marching band. If I did not understand the rationale of evicting a civilian lady such as Vesna, even less could I comprehend the eviction of an elderly, retired senior naval officer and a military bandsmen who, during his

years of service, would have given so much exceptional pleasure to soldiers and civilians alike.

The Chief of Military police, who I telephoned without much optimism of a positive outcome, refused, yet again, to help. I did not expect him to. What a bloody unpleasant people these Croat officials are. I shall arrange to call on him as soon as possible and hope to give him a difficult time as these evictions are totally contrary to the Croat Government's own code of conduct and official agreement with the 'International Community'.

There were though, if rare indeed, some professionally—and socially-satisfying moments, most of which involved patrolling well off the beaten track, as we had done the day before, despite the tragedy that lay behind Beare village's current state and its three inhabitants.

Today, Sunday lunchtime, was an all-too-infrequent moment of proper peace. Sitting on the Riva Bar's terrace with Lennart, Hans and Fergus planning our escape routes for when push comes to shove. We enjoyed a warm south-easterly breeze while admiring the deep blue Adriatic and the island of Brač over glasses of local wine.

A few windsurfers—even fewer yachts (both as infrequent as a smile on the Chief of Police's face)—white Dalmatian wine—much amusement—most relaxed. Yet all the while the three of us are aware of so much tragedy and sadness that is, perhaps, reaching its climax inland and around us here on this otherwise peaceful-seeming coast. Of course it is not peaceful and the seething resentment and hatreds beneath the surface are all around us. But we did luxuriate, very briefly, in our surroundings and genuinely-formed friendships between an Irishman, a Dane, a Dutchman and a Scot ... so maybe that is not so unusual.

An interesting thought: suppose there was to be a war then would not the Croats need the Serbs in their traditional role as the buffer between them and the Muslims (which is why they were here in the first place, 500 hundred years or so ago) who must be the common enemy despite present talks that there might be some form of agreement between the Croats and the Muslims against the Serbs. If Croatia actually 'buttered up' the RSK instead of refusing to understand their quite understandable (if illegal) views as a buffer then that might be interesting. Croatia should think carefully about life in a generation's time and how their current actions might then be viewed. I will put this to one or two Croats and the FCO and see what comes out of the thought.

Writing this on 20 March before going to the Opera to watch/listen to Verdi—I think. Later: it was Lombardi (or something like that) and beautifully done. As always a night at the Opera House is well worth it—regardless of what we see or listen to.

On our return from this rare, but thoroughly enjoyable oasis, I found two signals waiting for me from Knin. The first ordered us to revive our weekly programme: a programme that we had just expended a great deal of time, effort and local goodwill cancelling, as ordered by Jean-Pierre. Among other contradictory instructions the second signal informed me that, with immediate notice, I was 'sacked' as the leader of Team Split and being sent to Team Gospić to cover the Bihać Pocket as the fourth monitor. Oddly (or, in fact, not at all oddly!) nobody in Knin had discussed this move with me nor even with our 'intermediary', Vassilis, in Zadar. This unwelcome news came in an open signal with no preamble or warning.

The next morning I managed to get through to Tony Smith in Knin who confirmed that I had, indeed, been removed as Team Leader and so I decided to execute my threat to resign. At this stage it was still only a 'threat' in the naïve belief that calmer judgements might have prevailed. Notwithstanding that vain hope my resolution to quit was forced partly because of all the buggering about but largely for being ordered to falsify my Daily Reports in order to hide the probability that the UN Arms Embargo 713 was being broken. In practice there was no doubt that Croatia, courtesy of Germany and the US, was re-arming in preparation for, we were all certain, the eventual destruction of the Republic of Serbian Krajina.

> Again, Tony accused me of blackmail and I told him he can call it what he bloody well likes but I have had enough of being buggered about.

The telephone lines must have been zinging for about fifteen minutes later Vassilis called from Zadar to tell me that he would have failed in his duties if I went home for good. I countered by explaining that that was his problem. He then suggested that I went on leave early while he fought my case in my absence but I was not swayed for the good reason that due to the 'Apex rules' I could not alter my flight dates and, anyway, a change of timings would rot up my plans for leave which were already firm. Apart from that I did not believe he would actually do anything. I suggested to Vassilis that the most useful action he could take would be to persuade his Greek colleagues in Zagreb to be rid of Jean-Pierre Thébault for only then would some sense of purpose be re-injected into the ECMM and particularly into the perception, within the Croat authorities in Split, of its effectiveness. 'Vassilis,' I began with a blunt statement, 'Jean-Pierre has caused much disruption and unhappiness in the Regional Centre and, on a wider stage, with the locals on both sides of the Confrontation Line.' As he remained silent I drove the point further home, 'I am just one of the many monitors that are being moved and buggered about throughout the whole of Jean-Pierre's area of responsibility. Coupled with that the people of Dalmatia have lost all confidence in the ECMM and the sooner that he goes and the sooner we can return to normal the better.' Vassilis remained mute so I ended, 'Surely, you are not so stupid that you do not see that yourself. It is all a seriously-bloody mess and utterly unnecessary.'

My view of the Croat loss of confidence in the ECMM in the Split area was due, I believed, to the quite extraordinary behaviour of a French diplomat. Nor did I think that the EU, as a whole, was covering itself with glory when it allowed Germany, Italy, France, Greece, Russia, Iran, Algeria and God knows who else to break international agreements on embargoes or, at least to connive in the 'embargo busting'. I had been prevented from entering my suspicions of these illegalities in my reports and those incidents that Fergus and I did actually witness and report, such as the obvious increase in foreign military personnel and new, modern 'fighting vehicles' suddenly appearing on the streets and in the skies, were removed in Zadar and then in Knin prior to onward transmission. Thus the truth was hidden from those, further up the 'food chain', who should have known. This was hardly surprising as our daily reports went, first, to a Greek who re-wrote them from a Greek perspective before being sent to a Frenchman who, I had no doubt, then re-wrote them again to accord with his own xenophobic satisfaction. In my and Fergus's views the ECMM was morally bankrupt under the then Greek presidency and would remain so while it connived at these illegal acts.

Following my rather one-sided telephone conversation with Vassilis I sent him a signal stating my intentions. Buried in the text I explained the reasons behind my threat to resign. Then, having despatched this signal I tried to continue with my afternoon … but Philipos—the nodding dog head of the Forward Logistics Group—stormed into Team Split's office. As he was dragging the unfortunate Aris with him as interpreter I instantly realised that this was 'serious'! In a shouting fit, translated quietly by the equable Aris, I was ordered to pay for the new interpretress, Dabilla, out of my own pocket. He would not, I learned, sanction her employment and thus would never use her. This suited Team Split perfectly although hearing this news did nothing for his temper. As I have already remarked, he had wanted to carry out the interview himself but as he spoke about three words of English (three more than when he arrived) and not one word of Croat this had not seemed like a good plan. He also ignored the fact that I had been instructed by HQ ECMM to employ a third girl to give us cover for when the others were on leave or sick: both of which came up rather often.

To halt his childish screaming fit I told Philipos, quietly and calmly, that I would listen to him if he could, just this once, behave like a grown up in a responsible position. Later I was to learn that this episode was the subject of yet another signal to Zagreb complaining that I had, once more, 'impugned his dignity'.

During this awkward period in Team Split's history and while news of Jean-Pierre's weird behaviour in Knin was spreading across the Mission, Michael Shuttleworth telephoned from Belgrade to tell me that the Head of Mission himself, during a recent visit to Mike's area, had tried to 'fire' Jean-Pierre but that the French would not send a replacement. Neither of us was quite sure why the ECMM had to have a French replacement but supposed it may have had something to do with Brussels and quotas spread across the participating countries. I gathered, too, that the Head of Mission himself was not amused by Jean-Pierre for, in his own words, he believed that a *coup d'état* was being staged by the Knin monitors—and he was right! Lennart was demanding a transfer to 'anywhere providing it was out of Jean-Pierre's Regional Centre'; Jack (the French marine, Yvon Graff) was refusing to come to Split and, instead, had volunteered to go to Gospić in my place while Hans was fighting his return to Knin, as was Fergus. I had no idea about what other monitors across the Knin Regional Centre were doing other than that rumours indicated that we, on the coast, were not alone.

This confusing day ended with another evening at the opera:

Tosca, not as impressive as Verdi the other night but a good break nevertheless which took all our minds off 'the subject'. Sadly this was short-lived for on our return at ten 'o'clock in the evening we have now discovered that Jean-Pierre has ordered Fergus to Knin and Hans to Gospić. We think—but it is not easy to keep up. With all the monitors in Split being re-appointed we might have expected replacements but none have been mentioned. If Jean-Pierre has his way there will be no monitors in Split. I wonder if he has realised this. The Head of Mission certainly has.

On 23 March we were actually able to execute a pre-planned patrol and so took off for the Confrontation Line in a minibus as our Land Rover was once more unserviceable due to the lack of spares. Leaving very early on purpose we hoped to pre-empt any last minute cancellation by Knin. The minibus, although comfortable and with plenty of room, was not the ideal vehicle for off-road motoring, alone and among the haphazardly-marked minefields: but we 'got away with it' yet not without the attendant dramas. In a perverse manner I was rather sorry that we did not experience 'a drama' for in the most theatrical way possible we could have proved to Jean-Pierre that his 'off-on-off orders' for military monitoring, without first seeking clearance, were a dangerous nonsense.

Today we became stuck up a steep, rocky dirt track as our Belgian driver tried to be too clever by half despite my ordering him to turn back. As instructed by Jean-Pierre we were monitoring in an area for which we had no military permission and while Jean-Pierre says we need no permission as it is within the ECMM's mandate he is right in law but totally wrong in practice. I could have refused but thought the best way to prove Jean-Pierre wrong is for one of our patrols to meet with a serious problem. It was a risk but one I calculated to be worthwhile if the end result stops this crass business. We do indeed have such a mandate but common sense, courtesy and experience have shown that we are not going to win too many prizes by swanning through a war zone (even in our official capacity) without clearance. Without escorts, we do not know which roads are actually mined and which are not; which are covered by enemy fire, or indeed friendly fire, and which are not and so on. This is a typical politician's/diplomat's view of life which so often means that the poor bloody military have then to step in and sort out their self-generated mess. It happens across the globe.

The border guards showed me their building which had been shelled by the RSK last Sunday—with no casualties although the roof will no longer keep out the rain! They looked like mortar remains and not shells so must have been fired quite close.

Anyway today Sandra refused to get out of the minibus as she was convinced that we were in a minefield. I wasn't so sure as it did not seem a particularly sensible place to mine so I did my usual trick of getting out to have a pee to reassure her. If we had had an incident then we could finally have proved Jean-Pierre's orders to be dangerous which is what I have told him. Sadly no mines have exploded and so no proof of that!

24 March was what I called in my diary the 'deadline day', the day on which I would make the decision whether to resign—or not. Nevertheless life, such as it was, had to continue.

Called on the Chief of Police. None of my team accept the fact that I am no longer the Team Leader and for our collective parts we are continuing as close as we can to 'normal' in the hope that sense will, one day, prevail. The Chief was in a rather better mood and even smiled occasionally although I was not going to be fooled into being conciliatory back. He also seemed quite positive and even agreed that we were 'doing good works on behalf of his people!'—but I suppose that like most others he is entirely ruled by Zagreb despite what he privately might think and want to do.

On our return we found Martin Garrod and Patrick Brook 'in transit' and, during a long discussion, both advised me to send a signal to Jean-Pierre at Knin asking for a meeting. I did but the result was a lengthy signal refusing a consultation while giving a completely new set of orders for the disposition of every one of RC Knin's monitors. This was now beyond the pale for the twenty or so of us but we had no answer unless we had the support, not of the tricky Vassilis, but of the Head of Mission himself.

Patrolled to the north of Trogir where we drove rather foolishly (but in accordance with Jean-Pierre's dangerous rules) to the border through a marked minefield. On our return from this fruitless exercise we 'enjoyed' a raquia and much wine and food with the local home guard on the border. As they had informed their HQ in Ulisec of our unannounced presence we were obliged to call in there as well where the commander was very definitely not amused by our unescorted patrolling. At least I can now report this to Jean-Pierre and hope that this lever will make him change his mind. It is either that or false reporting—which I will not do.

Jack (the French marine) now joined Team Split having failed to be sent to Gospić despite Split being very definitely his last choice of all. Then at last, on 24 March, Team Split received the signal that was to be the last straw to be placed on this particular Scottish camel's back! This was not a message passed via a third or even fourth party—as was often the case—but direct orders to us from Jean-Pierre that set out his warped vision for Team Split's future. Some of the English is, shall I say, quaint and I have annotated in brackets our collective views scribbled at the time onto the signal.

From: HRC KNIN
To: HCC ZADAR
Info: HQ ECMM for DCOS Logistics and Personnel, Team Split, Heads of
         Delegations of United Kingdom, Denmark, Ireland, Sweden, France.
This message is an occasion to put on paper the definitive intentions of this Regional Centre as they have yet been widely discussed *(not with Team Split nor DCOS (Logistics and Personnel) nor with HCC Zadar)*, and as it is now required for the overall information of the team.

Until recently the deployment of Team Split was depending from a decision of HQ ECMM on the interest/possibility to deploy there 2 teams. This is now clearly considered not relevant. *(Why? HQ ECMM's own Deputy Chief of Staff has ordered me to execute Paul Ortholan's orders to form two teams, if not three: one each for the Šibenik region, Split and the adjacent islands and, in the near future, Dubrovnik.)*

Since two weeks Team Split is so clearly overstaffed *(3 monitors, 1 driver for two teams)*. Decisions had to be taken in order to ensure the best redeployment suitable with the interests of the Mission, in particular the need to implement the precise guidelines issued for the Team Split by the Regional Centre as to meet the needs of the Regional Centre in all its components. *(Guidelines which cannot be more imprecise and changeable by the day—and often only issued second or third hand over the telephone as Jean-Pierre refused to speak directly with anyone in Split. Because we have no humanitarian monitor one of the three of us often remains behind to deal with such problems. Jean-Pierre never takes this into consideration nor the fact that we are not only responsible for 80 nautical miles of coastline ['straight line measurement] plus all the vital offshore islands but of Split itself, the second largest Croat city of nearly a quarter of a million people, civilian and naval dockyards, a major airfield, ship-builders, ferry ports, numerous yacht marinas, an army division, Chambers of Commerce, consulates of the major European countries.)*

In this context, taking into consideration the respective End of Mission dates and leave dates it has been decided:

To appoint Mr Southby-Tailyour for the next week in Team Gospić which has to face for one week a dramatic decrease of its establishment due to, from long time ahead, bad managed leave … *(Totally against the instructions given to me in person by DCOS [Logs and Pers].)*

To appoint Mr Southby-Tailyour as Ops Officer Zadar after his return from leave (around 23 April) until his End of Mission (midth [*sic*] of June). In so about 2 months he will be able to provide his deep knowledge of Split area and experience of Gospić area for the benefit of all Coordinating Centre Zadar and so of the Regional Centre Knin and the Mission. *(Claptrap. I am hardly likely to gain any significant experience in one week, confined to our quarters in Gospić while my knowledge of the Split area is hardly 'deep' as we have been prevented, so often, from gaining that experience.)*

Other moves are:

Mr Leschly to Zadar … .

Mr Marshall to Team Leader Split … and then to Knin after his leave.

Mr Spijker to Knin as Ops Officer … *(His English is extremely limited.)*

Mr Graff [*Jack*] to Team Split … *(He is refusing as he wants to go to Gospić. Anyway the silly bugger Jean-Pierre is overlooking the fact that both Fergus and Jack have the same leave dates!)*

The strict respect of this planning will provide Coordinating Centre Zadar and so Regional Centre Knin and the Mission not only with the best use at key posting of the experience of its monitors but will solve the problem mentioned in para 1 of Team Split redeployment as a smooth running until May. *(None of us have the slightest idea what he means. By buggering about with the well-knit team, by reducing the team to an unworkable size when balanced against the vast area and disparate functions required of Team Split and by having the only two proposed monitors going on leave at the same time is unlikely to engender 'smoothness'!)*

Signed: Jean-Pierre Thébault

(We are all aghast at the muddle now made formal in this unintelligent, unintelligible and ill-thought-out signal.)

13

Resignation

Decision made: on 25 March I compiled a draft signal stating my intention to resign from the European Community Monitoring Mission. In practice I said that I would not now be taking up the agreed offer of an extra three months and then tidied up the draft while being driven to Škradin and the Confrontation Line to the east of Šibenik.

Well away from any pretence of a vehicle track we were met by Tony Marsh, a Canadian-born Croat, acting as the local Liaison Officer. By prior agreement he then led us to a different section of the Confrontation Line from our usual 'patch' and one that, he assured Sandra—with a wink over his shoulder to Fergus and myself—was safe. Nevertheless as soon as we left the vehicle to make our way towards a tiny, stone observation hut on the top of a small rise, the firing started from across the border.

Fergus, Tony and I stood and watched the fall of shot which was, I suspect, to make the point rather than hit us as the shots were landing a few yards to our right and yet they were being fired from just 200 yards away. Either the Serbs were not good shots or, as I guessed, aiming to miss on purpose. Just showing us who is 'in charge'.

Sandra had a sense of humour failure as I took a photo of the border when, quite suddenly, she screamed at me.

'You're a spy. I always knew you were. The sooner you leave my country the better.'

I replied quietly, 'If the outside world knew the truth about Croatia the sooner your country will enjoy peace and if you are not prepared to help me achieve that, as is your duty, I will sack you the moment we get back to Split.'

It is not her duty to help us monitor, merely to interpret, but I had made the point. Being kicked out of the ECMM will cramp her social style and, anyway, she needs to save money. She was nice as pie after this little—but by no means unusual—exchange. Really quite charming. Too charming but I thought no more of it!

Thence to the Pačovo Selo crossing on the plateau and lunch (unplanned) in the house that belongs to Sandra's mother, right alongside the current Confrontation Line but that is now requisitioned by Home Guard soldiers. They gave us much red wine and a delicious form of stew made from dried fish—a delicacy but not to my liking although I ate as much as they offered.

One English speaking platoon commander from Drniš told me that he forbad his men to drink on the border (which is the first time I have heard of such discipline). He owns—or owned—a small video shop in Drniš. 'When the war is over I will kill everyone that I have watched through my binoculars going into my shop and taking stuff away'. He was serious and calm while making this declaration which I have no doubt he will carry out for he knows the family that have commandeered his shop and belongings. He expects to spend the rest of his life behind bars but feels that that is his duty. This is a common feeling throughout the country on both sides and thus the coming of peace will certainly not bring about any rapprochement. Passed a ruined T55 tank and armoured personnel carrier on the road plus the normal detritus of battle from when the border had been further into Croatia.

As it was to turn out there would be no Serbs left in Drniš once the Croat invasion began in August 1995. On our return to Hotel Split and after some hours of mulling my future over and over in my head as we drove back from the Confrontation Line I decided that I really had no option but to send my formal signal of resignation direct to the Greek Head of Mission, copied to Jean-Pierre, Vassilis and Godfrey. At least I was able to do so but poor Fergus, Jack, Lennart and Hans, as serving officers who had been sent as part of their military duty, were stuck here. There was not one shred of doubt that everyone across Knin's Regional Centre would have done the same as I, had they been free to do so. I was, though, still an ECMM monitor and work had to continue.

And now yet another fax from Philipos complaining about me to HQ ECMM. This latest one concerns the head of the UN War Crimes Committee. I gave this wonderful lady, whom I had met on a number of occasions, permission to use Team Split's telephone to fix up a meeting with the ECMM to our mutual benefit. While she was talking Philipos burst into our office and there was a major screaming fit (and I mean 'screaming') as I have seen him do so often. Sadly, as the direct result of his appalling manners in someone else's office, the UN's War Crimes Committee will not now be meeting the ECMM and the team have left saying they want nothing more to do with the ECMM if this is the way we behave.

Following this latest infantile episode the Forward Logistic Group 'boss' decided to lock the communal communications office at the end of their working day thus on our return from monitoring we could no longer send or receive our evening signals including our mandatory Daily Reports. With all humanitarian matters, for which we were responsible 24 hours a day, we needed to be in touch with the outside world even if the FLG did not.

Acting on a hunch based on what I had seen from my bedroom window, after lunch on 26 March I drove Fergus and Hans to the top of Marjan Hill which overlooks Split from the south. I already knew that the view was lovely but the added bonus, as always, was that I could see clearly into the naval base. Using my binoculars I read out to Hans the types and pennant numbers of the moored craft plus a few pithy but relevant comments for the record. Because of the angle, many of the vessels were head- or stern-on; identification was not as easy as I had first thought but … 'never mind'.

One 210 ton *OSA* class fast attack craft. Pennant number 41 which confirms that it is HRM *Dubrovnik*. One of only two of ten that did not escape to Yugoslavia following independence.

One unidentified, elderly 'motor torpedo boat'. This puzzles me as Croatia does not, 'officially', own any such craft unless it is the one remaining *Končar* class fast attack craft. But it is so clapped-out it could be one of the river patrol boats built in 1952—difficult to tell at this distance.

Two motor gun boats of the *Mirna* class of fast attack craft.

Two very old landing craft of a non-descript type that I do not recognise but probably Type 21 LCUs.

No *Silba* class, 'roll on-roll' off tank landing craft which also puzzles me as I know from our visit to Brodosplit shipyard that the first of class is already in commission and not expected to have gone far from Split while still under trials.

Nor the first of the *Kralj* class corvettes which I see occasionally from my bedroom. It must be on patrol.

These notes were logged into our Daily Report while I sent a separate report back to my SIS contact.

Returned for tea after a pleasant drink on the Split boulevard, known as The Riva, beneath the British Consulate balcony. We watched a 'memorable drunk' zigzagging along The Riva reciting in pidgin English what could have been Hamlet, surprisingly convincingly. As he reeled theatrically along the promenade it was really very funny and caused much welcome laughter from all around us.

In the evening I received a sympathetic signal from Martin Garrod in Mostar. Despite never having elicited his support it was clear that the plight of Team Split was becoming recognised beyond the Dalmatian coast. His words were a tonic for our hard-pressed moral.

Can I say how extremely sorry I am that it has come to this ... particularly as I am aware of all the effort you have put into the Mission in Split. I am quite sure that your message to the Head of Mission (HOM) will indeed by a catalyst for action [it wasn't!] and I only hope that it does lead to a meeting with Jean-Pierre [vulgarly declined] so that at the very least you can get your views about the future of Team Split, and its value to the future of Dalmatia, across face-to-face. Please let me know how matters develop. I am glad that Godfrey Garrett is able to talk to HOM. I have, as you know, had a number of conversations with Godfrey on this subject and expressed my views to him but if there is anything further I can do please do not hesitate to let me know ... In the meantime my very best wishes, Martin.

While I was, realistically, not expecting any reply to my resignation signal an associated snippet reached my ears the next day direct from HQ ECMM.

DHOM (Ops) has told Vassilis that he has known all along that Jean-Pierre, before he met me, wanted me removed from Split to a position of no authority at all. Apparently even before he took over as HRC for he had seen me as some sort of threat. The reason for this odd behaviour was nothing to do with me, *per se*, but because I had been posted to Split by his hated predecessor, Paul, and was, apparently (not my words) 'making a success of it'. According to DHOM (Ops) Jean-Pierre did not want any limelight to reflect on his predecessor and his decision making. In his view the sooner I was out of the way the better.

The next morning a call from Vassilis informed me that the moment I left the Mission Jean-Pierre would be focusing on Fergus's removal from Split ... and then another call from Tony Smith in Knin who told me that this whole mess was my fault since I had refused an order

'What order will that be?' I argued, 'I have received no direct orders until Jean-Pierre's latest effort. And if any order has been refused it was Fergus's original and quite understandable refusal to return to Knin as the Operations Officer. Almost as soon as he had reached the coast.'

Jack, who had, most reluctantly, arrived in Split now joined in with considerable Gallic glee, by announcing that Jean-Pierre regarded me as a 'mere nobody'—'Monitor Tailyour is nothing,' Jack parodied ... so we walked to the Riva Terrace Bar to celebrate my new-found notoriety! Jack even bought the drinks while I agreed that I was a thorn in Jean-Pierre's side and happy to be so as various fundamental principles were at stake. Not least of all my determination to uncover real evidence of the embargo busting, the monitoring of which—or, rather, the non-monitoring of which—had to be at the heart of Jean-Pierre's behaviour.

With still no news from HOM three days after my signal I sent a polite 'hastener'. I was certainly not frightened at upsetting a Greek 'ambassador' so was not embarrassed by despatching this second, 'studiously correct', message. In reply I heard from Godfrey that the Head of Mission was so embarrassed that his weakness had led to this impasse that he didn't know what to do—and so he was doing nothing.

> Drank in the evening with Matt Burnford. Talking to him I have realised how little I have achieved in six months out here compared with other monitors and of course how much I could have done if I had been allowed to get on with it. Ever since arriving in Knin I was number three in the back of a Land Rover and not allowed nor encouraged to take part then, since arriving in Split we—all of us in Split and not just me—have been buggered about from the moment I arrived to now. It is difficult even with hindsight, to know how else to have played it.

The next morning, 29 March:

> Caught naked by a cleaning lady in my room which is the most exciting thing to have happened to me for a long time—and to her, too, judging by the look on her face!
>
> Spoke to Lennart on the telephone who was in HQ ECMM on his way back from a short leave. He says that he has just spoken to the French Head of Delegation who confirmed (a) that the French consider that they have won as the Head of Mission could not alter any decisions that Jean-Pierre has made even though he did not agree with them and (b) the French have no replacement for Jean-Pierre anyway and (c) the French do not want Jean-Pierre back! I knew this already but it was good to have it confirmed.
>
> Message in saying that Martin Garrod is being medevac'd to the UK due to high blood pressure which will be very sad indeed if it is permanent. I hope he recovers quickly as he is invaluable to the ECMM.

On 30 March I completed my handover report for the Team Split area then spoke again to Lennart, still in Zagreb, to hear that he had had a good break in Budapest. He had gone there and not home as he would still receive danger money from his Danish government. Despite being broke the silly bugger admitted that he then spent all he had saved over the months on a few hours with a 'young lady'!

> Must have been some gal but I don't know how much Danish danger money is per day. We don't get any.

During the morning I worked on the case of Mr Marić who had been dispossessed finally of his flat. His wife, quite understandably, was in floods of tears in the office but without an interpretress I could do very little except, in my very best and only Croat (about five words!) explain that they should come back at 0900 on the morrow by when I would have someone who could translate.

On the last day of March I spoke on the telephone to my cousin, Brigadier Robert Tailyour then Director of Royal Marines Operations, to tell him about Martin Garrod. I felt that the Corps should know about one of our former Commandant Generals in the hope that they could help with the reception of Martin's 'medevac flight'. In the course of the conversation I also spoke to Robin Ross, who was just taking over as Commandant General. Apparently my 'relationship' with Jean-Pierre was known in Whitehall although I thought, at the time, 'God knows why or even how!' Both Robert and Robin expressed amusement that 'I had been a victim of my own success'—although that is not how I saw it, nor was I quite sure that 'success' was the correct expression.

The 420 Million Dinar Hotel Bill

Also on the last day of March Fergus and I met Doctor Dick and Lady Rozelle Raynes for drinks in the Riva Terrace Bar, followed by dinner in the Split Yacht Club. This was another civilised, delicious and most amusing evening during which I enjoyed, for the second time, a beautifully prepared steak tartare. But also for the second time I pondered how the under-used yacht club could afford—or even acquire—such good food. I knew, but not well, Dick and Rozelle from membership of the Royal Cruising Club but now they were in Croatia to distribute presents and food to various displaced friends living in temporary accommodation on the islands, which is why my room was suddenly choc-a-bloc with heavy suitcases and bulging boxes that they had brought out in a mini-van.

Although unconnected with the Raynes's arrival, but just as welcome, I received a telephone call from Swan Hunter Shipbuilders asking me to discuss an MOD contract for the design and build of new vehicle and personnel landing craft (LCVP in naval parlance) and the possibility of them bidding for a new style of roll on–roll off medium-sized landing craft (or LCU). Suddenly an embarrassment of riches in the consultancy business for Charles Curnock of Vickers Shipbuilding and Engineering Limited also telephoned to tell me that they needed help assessing the contract for the replacement of HMS *Fearless* and HMS *Intrepid*. Charles also needed to 'unscramble some of the appalling work' done by YARD and the consortium of British Aerospace and the French company Sema.

This was becoming a busy non-ECMM day for I also received a letter from my publisher, Leo Cooper, telling me to re-write the synopsis for my book *Amphibious Assault Falklands*[1] while complaining that he could not read my writing anyway, which is odd since I had typed it!

He's just keeping me on my toes.

As if these were not enough 'private' events for one day, an upright and most decent, ex-'special forces' contact, Sam Waters, who had resigned a fortnight before from a 'security organisation' with which we had both worked now felt able to warn me about them for they were, again, seeking my services. As they still owed me the VAT for a previous task I had become a little suspicious of the company but could never pinpoint why. Now I knew: it was not difficult to cut all my ties with them.

'They are a crowd of cowboys,' Sam explained over the telephone, 'that would best be left with plenty of sea-room. They could be dealing in drugs and guns. I have learned that the MD was arrested for commissioning a murder and that the other partner was a con man who had once robbed a bank, nor had he ever been in the SAS—in any of his many aliases.'

All Fools' Day saw the Raynes's head back to Hvar with more suitcases full of goodies. They were two remarkable people but their stories of how various Serb refugees were treated and reviled in the UK were nearly as disturbing as how they were treated by their kith and kin in Croatia. Their friends did not want to be refugees nor 'sponge' off anyone which is what those in the UK were accused of doing. Rozelle was writing about her Balkan experiences in a book she was calling *27 Kisses. The Last Coach from Croatia* and I looked forward to reading it when it was published; which it was in 1995, the month after Operation Storm. Sadly, with their departure for Hvar, life was back to normal.

Mr Marić has had all his furniture smashed in his home so he has nothing left to take away: no possessions except what he and his wife were carrying on them at the time. Now he is being followed night and day by Croat army soldiers making continual threats AND he is a bloody Croat himself and retired naval captain for God's sake.

Having digested the more-than-welcome fact that the expected work was waiting for me at home—'right on cue' I noted 'and perfectly timed'—the question of my resignation was becoming less an ECMM affair and more a personal one. I had, after all, left the UK for six months on the understanding that once the MOD had assessed the several 'invitations to tender' for the UK's next generation of amphibious ships I might be required to help with the next phase in the more-than-convoluted business of warship procurement. Quite suddenly I would be required to help two interested shipbuilders process their individual contracts further. I had no more reason to be in the Balkans. Life was looking up.

The best thing I could now do was as to ensure that I had as smooth and un-acrimonious departure as possible from the ECMM, but particularly from Jean-Pierre and Vassilis. There was, therefore, unfinished work to be completed and now that a new ceasefire had been in force since 29 March—effective from 0900 on 2 April—I revised my notes on this latest 'interruption' of hostilities between the RSK and Croatia. While doing so I thought it ironic that just as the opportunity was arising to carry out monitoring duties as we should have been carrying them out—throughout a rare period of 'peace'—I was being moved (or I would have been had I not resigned) to run an office that a lance-corporal would not find taxing and I meant no disrespect to lance-corporals. I could, of course, have cancelled my resignation but useful work now beckoned alluringly from home.

The devil in me persuaded me to send a copy of my handover notes to Jean-Pierre in the vain hope that he might learn something about real-time monitoring on the coast—but I knew, full well, that that was indeed a forlorn hope!

A drinks party in the Riva Terrace Bar that evening celebrated Danielle's twenty-first birthday; a petite, pretty and intelligent Croat girl whom I had once earmarked as an interpretress. She was the girlfriend of François, a French ECMM administrator in the area who always understood that she would be returning to France with him when he left the Mission. They often discussed their future together and in public, for they were a highly amusing, vivacious couple enjoying what seemed to be a genuine and deep love affair. Indeed Danielle once went to Paris with François for a holiday and only had to return when her visa ran out. The only way she could have left Croatia permanently to live in France was if she was to marry and he had promised her that future. We were very fond of Danielle for her presence in the evenings would often offset the boorish behaviour of the Greek members of the Forward Logistic Group. Tragically, and I only heard this once I was back in the United kingdom, when François did leave for France he just walked out through Hotel Split's foyer saying that he never wanted to see her again. She tried to commit suicide—although I believe she was saved but it had been a real attempt—and then I heard no more.

Before Danielle's party Dino called in to say goodbye and in doing so offered a final piece of news that, as so often, surprised me for he always seemed to know more about what was happening within the ECMM than we did. 'Ewen I have heard that Knin may be downgraded from a Regional Centre to a Coordinating Centre and that Zadar will become the new RC. If that happens I think that Jean-Pierre will have to stay in Knin as a simple monitor as we may not accept him running a RC from Zadar.'

> Good heavens the Croats know this and make their own decision over who should serve where—not that the ECMM will necessarily listen but if the Croats decide they do not want someone I suppose the ECMM may have to take note. Supposing the RSK's Serbs do not want Jean-Pierre in their capital either then they may decide to cancel all ECMM work if they see that their capital is downgraded in the ECMM's eyes as being only worthy of holding a CC while Zadar becomes responsible for the whole cross-border area.

On 2 April I was handed my 'mess bill' by the hotel staff. At first glance the invoice for 420 million dinars (420,000,000!) might have seemed just a touch excessive but in practice it worked out at about £450 or £8 a day, including meals in the main dining room, laundry and my many bar bills, over the 55 days. Having stifled a gulp or two I then smiled for this was the second time that I had made a 'profit' from my hotel bills! Hotel Split seemed more than happy with this 'extortionate' figure and so was I!

> Various signals received including an Operation Order from UNPROFOR detailing actions to be taken in light of the latest ceasefire from which it is clear that the UN clearly regards us as getting in the way but we shall be needed if (or more likely when) the UN leaves and we are left to get on with our original mandate. As long as we are forced to play 'second fiddle' to the UN then we have no constructive role especially as the various European nations are jostling (not all that covertly) for position while some are breaking the embargoes left right and centre. If the UN pulls out of the Former Yugoslavia then the European nations that are bickering may be forced to pull together. I refer to the Greeks, Italians, French, Germans and, possibly, the Russians. Although the Russians have no monitors they have a vested interest in the Serbs as, of course, do the Greeks while the Germans have an equally vested interest in the future of a united Croatia. In other words there will be no 'pulling together'.

My last night in Split was spent quietly at dinner in the hotel with Fergus and Jack. We had planned to dine in the Split Yacht Club but they arrived late back from a fruitless visit to Knin and then had to work on an entirely new set of orders from Jean-Pierre for closer cooperation with the UN. This was, inevitably, a pointless exercise for they both knew that when they returned to Knin on the morrow Jean-Pierre would have changed everything. And he did.

> It will be interesting to see how Jean-Pierre handles this—as a diplomat he should really concentrate on the diplomatic/political side of things and let the UN/UNMOS get on with the military aspects of the ceasefire. Actually I believe that the ECMM is a bankrupt organisation now which has way outlived its usefulness—unless it changes its mandate which has not been altered since it was formed before the UN arrived. Surely someone must have seen that, with the arrival of the UN, the ECMM's role had to change but nobody did and it has been muddling along while getting in the way so often. We certainly have nothing left to offer as Martin Garrod used to say so often and so emphatically.

On the morning of my departure from Split I was up early as the Greeks wanted the baggage loaded by 0730 for an 8 o'clock start—with just me in the mini-bus. I commented at the time that this 'hurry up and wait' attitude was even worse than RAF 'movements'—and that takes some doing! Sadly I missed saying goodbye to Fergus as he and Jack had departed even earlier to visit the UNMOS at Sinj but

Fergus left a delightful note on my desk and a present of an Irish army book about the Former Yugoslavia. When I got round to reading it, back in the UK, I found it to be wonderfully clear and detailed. I had wished that I had seen it before I arrived in the Balkans for it was infinitely better than anything that the FCO or ECMM gave us at their briefings. In return I left Fergus a number of 'goodies' including a world atlas and a bottle of Irish whiskey.

> It will be sad not to be working with Fergus as he has been a thoroughly enjoyable companion and colleague. I believe we made an excellent team—when we were allowed to get on with monitoring—which is something that Jean-Pierre simply never understood.

As I settled into the back of the mini-bus, preparing myself mentally and physically for the looming journey to Zagreb, I noticed the 'nodding dog' sometimes known to me as Corporal Philipos, standing in the hotel's entrance making sure that I was on my way out of 'his' self-declared purview. Wickedly, a childish urge came over me. Telling the driver to 'wait' I slid open the door and walked across the forecourt.

'Ah Philipos,' I said, 'How nice of you to come and say goodbye.' He had not of course and remained staring straight ahead not able to believe that I was actually talking to him. His head began nodding controllably. 'How kind,' I continued, 'but there really is no need as I am only going on my two weeks mid-tour leave. I'll be back in a fortnight for another four months.'

Whether or not he understood I had no idea but the look of real, unqualified horror on his face as it lost its colour and began perspiring was worth all the weeks of his farcical screaming fits and his unlawful and often disruptive orders to me and my team. I hoped, earnestly, that he would remain in his muck sweat for two weeks— and so I left Split with that maliciously-pleasant thought uppermost in my mind!

Equally memorable, and touchingly so, P. G. Wilks and, surprisingly, Vassilis had arranged a small reception for me as the mini-bus staged through Zadar. I was offered wine and delicious small eats while the vehicle was refuelled and re-packed with baggage and passengers from the Coordinating Centre: none of whom I knew. More than adequately 'refreshed' we set off in the now-laden mini-bus for the Pag ferry crossing where, on the mainland side, I was met by a Belgian monitor who introduced himself as the leader of Team Gospić.

'Here, let me help you with your luggage,' he said and started to load my bags into his Land Rover.

'Thanks but I'm going on to Zagreb.'

'You are coming with me.'

'No, I'm going to Zagreb.'

Suddenly the mood changed, 'You, monitor Tailyour, are bad news and a disgrace to the Mission.'

I cut him short. 'And you are mistaken for I am not a member of the Mission and have not been one since I resigned some days ago.'

'Jean-Pierre told me only yesterday that you were joining us in Gospić and I was to collect you from today's ferry. Which is why I am here.'

'Then I suggest you talk to him.'

I clarified the situation and he claimed to have understood but whether or not he really did I no longer cared. The Mission was about to be behind me and I could move forwards again. I did, though, discover that Team Gospić had been expecting, in turn, just about every other monitor to join it from across the Regional Centre but none had ever done so. I was simply the latest name to which the Team Leader was looking forward to 'employing'. Jean-Pierre had never expounded his plans to this Belgian monitor but, instead, continued to make promises without once contacting the monitors concerned until the last moment.

Jean-Pierre really does seem to have caused a great deal of confusion. Gospić is the area covering the Bihac pocket and I had in fact actually agreed to go there for a week to stand in; and possibly then to Zagreb as another temporary measure before returning to Split. But, as I have written, I heard no more and as by then I had resigned I had stayed at Split.

On arrival in Hotel 'I' there was not a soul to be seen so following a welcome cold shower I sat at a table in the bar for an hour or so scribbling a few paragraphs of the book that I was then contracted to produce for Leo Cooper. A hot bath then back to a still-empty bar to find, as expected, that almost everybody had eaten by six in the evening. I went in search of whatever was left for dinner.

Interestingly I am sitting by myself at dinner—compiling this log/diary—and have just received a written message asking my reasons for writing at the table. I am the only one in the huge dining room apart from an unseen table of people behind a pillar at the very opposite end.

A waiter has come to my table with a card that tells me that the sender is John Georgiadis (DCOS Logistics and Personnel) and he is demanding to know why I am writing at the dinner table. I have scribbled on the reverse that I am working on a new book. I can see no one in the room but handed the card back to the waiter who disappeared with it at which John G came across ten minutes ago and was very definitely not in an amusing mood. He refused my offer of a seat and a glass of wine then just stood staring down at me while taking some obvious pleasure in telling me that he had received numerous faxes from Philipos over the weeks all of which painted Team Split in a very bad light. I asked him what on earth he meant. He then explained that there had been a steady stream of faxes, sometimes many a day, detailing every single conversation I had ever had and presenting a remarkably false and unpleasant picture of Fergus, Lennart, Hans and myself.

Having listened in dis-believing silence I finally cut him short to state that twice I had cause to tell Philipos that I was unsatisfied with the unprofessional service he gave and if that was abusing his honour 'good', I was happy to repeat my accusations here and now. I stood by my words and explained that I was not used to such non-existent events being reported to a major HQ three or four times a day. Georgiadis then surprised me by saying that they had not received the faxes directly in the HQ but all had been sent via Vassilis in Zadar who had then passed them on. So Vassilis has been behind much of this 'substantially embellished' unpleasantness, probably because I refused to falsify my Daily Reports.

I swallowed a large gulp of red wine then calmly and slowly gave Georgiadis a potted but hard-hitting view of my side of the whole unsavoury saga of Team Split since Paul Ortholan's departure. I took some delight in including the Šibenik bridge incident with Vassilis plus Jean-Pierre's equally crass behaviour. Whether or not he believed anything I said I no longer cared for I was angry and made damned sure he knew I was angry and that he knew the reasons why I was angry. Unable to leave until I had finished, the Greek major-general was clearly uncomfortable and the more uncomfortable he clearly became the more I piled on my condemnations. When I finished I dismissed him rather more imperially than I intended with a flippant wave and a further slug of wine. With nothing to say he turned sharply and, shaking his head, walked away. I doubt he had been spoken to in such direct language before and I was pleased that, quite unexpectedly, I had managed to get my message across.

Thankfully, I never saw him again.

During my last day in Croatia, 5 March 1994, I called in to the movements office to find that my flight had been delayed to midday on the morrow and so I would not get to Heathrow until late in the day which meant that Patricia would be unable to meet me with my six pieces of luggage. I would have to struggle by bus to Reading and a train.

Just been told that neither the Head of Mission or Georgiadis or the Head of Humanitarian Affairs wish to say good bye to me as 'they are not interested'. Frankly I could not give a damn.

Went for a very long walk of about six miles along the river bank on the outskirts of Zagreb and did not meet one soul—pouring rain, all very refreshing after Split. Back for a late lunch by myself which was equally peaceful and welcome as I really don't know what to say to the Greeks even if they talk to me which they don't, thank goodness!

Later Godfrey and I met for dinner after which we were joined by Claus Cramer, bearing a full decanter of port. Claus, a most experienced German monitor, had just returned from a long day drinking *slivovitz* at meetings and so was amusingly expansive on Jean-Pierre's character. Clearly no love was lost between them either.

Claus was revealing as one of the things that had alienated me from Jean-Pierre was my insistence on carrying out monitoring of the ports and thus the embargoes after the Germans had been caught importing three Leopard Tanks into Croatia via Pula. Claus was full of sympathy and then—what a surprise— asked me to return once the Germans take over the presidency in the summer! To which I replied that the German breaking of the embargo, to which French blind eyes were being turned, was the core reason—the camel's final straw— behind my resignation. He laughed and told me that it was precisely because I was so diligent that he wanted me back. He then said that he had been following my case—as had many in the rest of the HQ ECMM. Chillingly he knew that Jean-Pierre had long decided that he did not want me on the coast, even before he met me, and so purposefully appointed me to a place that he knew I would find unacceptable. Apparently the HQ Greeks wanted to take my side but felt that that would be a loss of face as they had appointed Jean-Pierre to be the HRC Knin and they could not afford to back down. Instead they acted shamefully and weakly and in his, Clause's, view lost much more than 'face'. Now I know! Godfrey described the clash as that between two strong-willed people. He even used the word Titans but I would never describe myself as a Titan and even less so would I consider Jean-Pierre to be one! I'm not even sure that 'strong-willed' described Jean-Pierre either. Unpredictable might be more accurate.

Godfrey also told me that he had argued with Jean-Pierre, believing that economic monitoring for the future was the most important aspect of ECMM work—especially on the coast. Eventually Jean-Pierre was forced to agree and apologised to GG. At least I feel vindicated especially when Godfrey remarked that that justified my stance in both his and the FCO's eyes.

And now it has dawned on me. Perhaps Jean-Pierre knew that the only way he could stop me monitoring any breaking of the embargo was to appoint me as far away from the coast as possible. He knows what I was up to and therefore probably knows, too, what Vassilis was up to. I wonder if he bugged Šibenik Bridge! Mind you, there are dozens of other monitors who know far more than I do (and first hand) about UN embargo 713, but they are not in Jean-Pierre's bailiwick.

6 April; last day as a monitor; end of Mission. Following a breakfast of olive-and garlic-stuffed pita-bread I met Caroline Scott-Barker. She was a delightful, gutsy, attractive and very efficient girl married to Peter, an ex-Gurkha officer whom she had met and worked with in Angola. Caroline, among other duties, was responsible for transport so, having fixed a lift to the airport I sought Godfrey in order to say goodbye and to thank him for his efforts on my behalf. As I was leaving his office

he, rather hesitantly, presented me with my ECMM medal. This has a strangely-colourful ribbon which the Queen had recently given us permission to wear. While I may not have been a success as a monitor I decided to wear it as a reminder of one of the less forgettable experiences in my 'military career'. At least, I mused, as I studied the optimistically-chosen 'dove of peace' on the medal's reverse, I had heard more gunfire and shelling in the Former Republic of Yugoslavia than throughout the 32 years of my more conventional military employment; even if, this time, the shots had not necessarily been aimed at anyone in particular. I describe Godfrey as being 'hesitant' for he had only one medal left and this he had earmarked for another monitor leaving 'on cue' as it were, but now after me.

Following breakfast and surrounded by my luggage I sat in Hotel 'I's' lobby for an hour writing a chapter of 'the next book' until Caroline drove me to Pleso Airport and an Austrian Airlines Fokker 50 flight to Vienna. As I gazed out of the airliner's window at the sun-burnt islands of the northern Adriatic I could not help but regret that General Aidid had never been caught. It might have been a more dangerous assignment and certainly a perfidious one *vis-á-vis* the United Nations and the United States but nothing was more dishonest, underhand and downright despicable than many of the incidents involving the European Community's Monitoring Mission in Croatia and the Republic of Serbian Krajina.

A pâté sandwich later we landed into a deathly quiet Vienna air terminal with, quite literally, not a soul about apart from the cleaning teams. The Austrian Airlines business class lounge, where I savoured decent wine and—another luxury—cashew nuts, was equally empty. I had no idea what had happened to the other passengers.

No sadness at all at leaving the ECMM, but some sadness at leaving a job unfinished while never having had the opportunity to get to know *Eloise* better!

15

Aftermath

Returning home it was obvious that a certain amount of debriefing was necessary. On 20 April I called on Julian Metcalf in his King Charles Street office where he sympathised with the impossible dilemma in which I had been placed by Jean-Pierre and Vassilis. For various other reasons too he now believed that the ECMM had 'outlived its usefulness' and thus he would not be recruiting British monitors for longer than nine months, with a view to running down the British participation completely.

On 28 April Ian Richardson and Ralph Rochester of the Ministry of Defence's Defence Debriefing Team visited me at home where, having been given plenty of warning, I was prepared with a comprehensive debrief. Ian and Ralph were particularly interested in my 'relationship' with the Greeks: I spared them no details. Nor did I pull any punches on what might or might not have been happening underground on Vis island and at the 'then secret' airport on Brač. On one hand there had been no doubt that the Greeks were keeping the Serbs well-informed on naval movements and, on the other, the Croats had mined some of the sea approaches to Vis. Following copious drams of my private supply of *raquia* kept for just such opportunities, Team Split's 'weekend interpreter', Sergio, had once passed across hand-drawn diagrams of the mined sea areas that he had, on my suggestion, coerced out of an unsuspecting naval 'friend' of his. At the end of a long day the MOD team took away these and various maps and charts I had annotated during my time on both sides of the border. They returned to Whitehall happy!

Later in the year, on 27 July, the delightful Swedish monitor and some-time Operations Officer of the Zadar Coordinating Centre, John Volgers, also called at my south Devon farmhouse from his Plymouth-berthed yacht as he made his way up-channel while on leave from Zadar. He brought snippets of news from the ECMM after I had left.

Vassilis, John explained, had had further problems with his women and felt obliged to marry an Austrian girl he had met at the Hotel Esplanade in Zagreb.

There was a reception in Zadar with all his 'previous' ladies present as well as the Zupan of Zadar and General Gotovina the local army commander.

John continued with his brief. One Malay and two Canadians had been killed at one of 'our' border crossings. Consequently Jean-Pierre cancelled all unescorted patrolling along the Confrontation Line with economic and political monitoring becoming the top two priorities: as they had been in Split until he arrived. Then he moved all of the Regional Centre's monitors into Croatia in anticipation of some un-specified 'trouble' in Gorazde following which the Serbs, rather naturally, would not let them return to Knin. Finally, in April, Jean-Pierre went on leave, never to be seen or heard of again apart from a short spell as a 'counsellor' in the French Embassy in Zagreb.

'So,' John Volgers finished his résumé, 'the ECMM finally sacked the ghastly man! Ewen you can come back now, we miss you!'

Later, between 2014 and 2017, Jean-Pierre was appointed the French ambassador to the Republic of Ireland and I wondered whether or not he had, by then, taken a shower!

As a final act I needed to honour a promise I had made to the Split Chamber of Commerce on 4 January 1994 so, in the April 1996 edition of *Yachting World*— nearly a year after Operation Storm—I wrote an article under the title *Is it safe to go back?* The journal's editor added the strapline: *As bitter fighting tore Yugoslavia apart, yachts ran for cover from one of the loveliest parts of the Mediterranean. Ewen Southby-Tailyour finds it safe to return but says go soon, for strife may break out again.*

The bulk of the text contained a summary of the relationship between Croatia and the Republic of Serbian Krajina and ended with the suggestion that it was now safe again to sail the Dalmatian coast but with the caveat that one day it may all flare up as the Serbs have long memories. I also warned that it might still have been inadvisable to sail too close to certain sections of the south coast of Hvar and Vis. Inevitably, as he was the Croat Ambassador to the United Kingdom and expectedly, as he was also a yachtsman, Dr Ante Cičin-Sain refuted much of what I had written and ended his letter:

> British yachtsmen and tourists are most welcome to come and enjoy, as the author himself has stated, the 'magnificent, charming and unspoilt' Croat coast.

Two or three letters followed both supporting and objecting to, my views—which was fair. One of the latter, judging by his name and address, was from a Croat living in Italy, gave the game away by stating:

> Thanks to help from Germany and the USA, military balance in the area and therefore stability has been achieved. Serbian terrorism of this area has been halted and normal life and navigation have resumed.

Although not the final words, for *Yachting World* kindly allowed me to reply, I will end with another quote, this from an English-sounding correspondent to the magazine, living in Dubai:

> Two of the three letters of protest regarding Ewen Southby-Tailyour's Croat article are from [those] with dutiful axes to grind by virtue of their positions as Croat ambassador and Director of Information in the Croat tourism office … There may be some truth that the coastline is free from hostilities—at the moment … But one wonders why it has taken an article from an unbiased and objective author to stimulate these claims … Personally I am not inclined to return to the area until the residents have had more time to prove that history is unlikely to repeat itself.

The Serbs do indeed have long memories but now, 27 year later, these waters are as safe and as beautiful as they ever were and long may this last. At least this correspondence highlight the Dalmatian coast in what turned out to be a positive manner, despite my being obliged to offer a few extant, but now, hopefully extinct, cautions.

.   .   .   .   .

When packing my white 'uniform' for the last time I knew that it had been a risk joining what had sounded like an efficiently-managed organisation, conducting quasi-military operations. After 32 extremely satisfying and professionally sustaining years as a Royal Marine it was, perhaps, a mistake to have thought that such well-commanded organisations existed in the multi-national, civilian world. It was clear, almost from my first day in Zagreb, that the cause for such inadequacy and internecine skulduggery was the mix of disparate European nations, each with its own agenda and each fighting for some form of supremacy. One has to remember too, that the United Kingdom was an integral part of that mix and, itself, operated in what might have been considered an underhand manner as my involvement with the Secret Intelligence Service proved: I am certain I was not the only British monitor reporting back along 'covert' lines. Every nation was at it! My final diary entry reads:

> Britain should not become involved with any more joint European Union commitments. Common European defence and common European foreign policies are unworkable and it would be naive to think otherwise for there simply can never be significant cooperation among such dishonest, duplicitous, deceitful, and perfidious European 'allies'.
>
> The roles, too, of the United States and Germany in Balkan affairs should be regarded with deep cynicism.

There was a reason for America's nefarious actions in blatant support of Croatia even if others found them deceitful. The United States' Congress never made any secret of its opposition to the UN's Arms Embargo while Serbia was backed, equally wrongly, by (*inter alia*) Russia and, to Clinton, that would never do! But, the USA signed up to the embargo and thus not to stick with it was at best hypocritical and at worse dishonest. The story at the beginning of this account, regarding the UN, America and condoms, remains apt!

Finally, and as I have stated or indicated throughout, 'they' were all as bad as each other and, as far as the United Kingdom was concerned perhaps Perfidious Albion indeed but, I suggest, marginally less so than Perfidious Europa!

.   .   .   .   .

In summary I was, frankly, out of my depth: not with the genuine, monitoring work required by the Foreign and Commonwealth Office and the European Community Monitoring Mission—which I thoroughly enjoyed—but when dealing with a cabal of Machiavellian strangers (from every nation, the UK included) the like of which I had never come across before and hope never to come across again! The ECMM was brought to a close in December 2006.

.   .   .   .   .

However, there were, too, a good many superb, honest, decent, straightforward, transparent and professional monitors, from across the constituent nations, with whom it was a real pleasure and privilege to work—and play! Each of these successful monitors and colleagues, despite their own problems of dealing with their less scrupulous contemporaries, were employed for a least a year by the ECMM, and some for many more, during which time they made a significant and beneficial difference to the present and the, then, future of the Former Republic of Yugoslavia. Many monitors escaped unscathed yet others had, too, their tribulations with which to contend. It was Team Split's misfortune to be caught between a Frenchman and a Greek each with opposing views on how monitoring should have been conducted on the coast and each with opposing views on whether or not the breaking of UN Arms Embargo 713 should have been ignored, denied or made public.

Those with whom I enjoyed working—or who were 'useful' in Team Split's attempts to carry out coastal monitoring in accordance with the ECMM's mandate—are included here in (rough) order of their appearance and with the ranks and titles held at the time:

Julian Metcalf (UK), highly regarded and perceptive acting Head of the British Delegation and head of the FCO's Eastern Adriatic Unit. Quote 'With your help I am being paid to predict!'

Cath Baker (UK), of the FCO's Eastern Adriatic Unit. Superbly helpful in my early days with the FCO.

Eric Elstob (UK but with a Swedish mother), financier, conservationist and social historian of the Foreign and Colonial Management Limited whose briefing, *en route* to Zagreb, was invaluable and never forgotten. In his book *Travels in a Europe Restored 1989–1995* (published in 1997), he wrote of statesmen and populations facing the uncertainties of the new economies. It was my great good fortune to have been placed next to him on the aeroplane. Sadly he died of cancer in 2003.

Roddy de Norman (UK), monitor, lately of the 9/12 lancers and an amusing dinner companion.

Lennart Leschly (Denmark), laid back monitor whose presence was always welcome. Member of Team Split who suffered at the hands of J-P. Thébault.

Paul Ortholan (France), remarkably calm and intelligent Head of Regional Centre Knin whose well-crafted, deeply thought-out plans for the future of monitoring Dalmatia were countermanded by his successor J-P. Thébault.

Roger Vincent (UK), amusing Zagreb monitor and *inter alia* responsible for the FCO's logistics. Lately of the Royal Navy.

Godfrey Garrett (UK), head of the British Delegation. Patience, experience and diligence were his prime characteristics yet they were impotent when ranged against the intransigence of J-P. Thébault.

Captain Dragan Vasiljković (Serbia), although kept at arm's length he offered a useful insight into Serbia's military aspirations within the RSK.

Mike Shuttleworth (UK), lately of the Royal Marines. Belgrade monitor, life-long, highly valued friend and confidante.

Sir Martin Garrod (UK), lately Commandant General of the Royal Marines. Head of monitoring in Mostar and staunch supporter. Suffered at the hands of Thébault.

Peter Strauss (Germany), amusing and civilised monitor in Knin whose early advice and friendship were vital.

Patrick Brook (UK), lately of the Royal Horse Guards. Highly regarded Deputy Head of RC Knin and thus served with J-P. Thébault.

Lieutenant Kevin Brown (Canada), once 'on-side' he facilitated my visit to 'Captain Dragan'.

Sandra (Croatia), despite her private problems, and when it suited her, a great interpretress.

Vinka (Croatia), when on 'good form' an invaluable interpretress and reliable fount of knowledge—historical and current.

Bryan Sparrow (UK), lately of the ECMM. British Ambassador in Zagreb. A source of 'wise counsel'.

Roger Castle (UK), monitor and retired Territorial SAS officer.

The Italian Vice-Consul in Split, an intelligent and balanced gentleman. Most supportive of the ECMM's work.

Major P. G. Wiik (Sweden), monitor and major in the Swedish Air Force.

Captain Aleksey Mekjavič (Croatia), British Honorary Consul in Split and helpful 'ally'.

Walter de Keyser (Belgium), superbly organised and calmly-efficient head of the Forward Logistic Group who was much missed once the Greeks took over.

Rory Ormsby (UK), monitor, lately a Gurkha officer and amusing colleague.

Dino Genda (Croatia), Croatian Liaison Officer in Split who smoothed Team Split's way.

Lieutenant-Colonel Richard Perry (UK), BRITFOR's phlegmatic and sensible Head of UK Public Relations. An unenviable task under the circumstances but one carried out impeccably and with balance.

Captain Maroje Moroević (Croatia), Split Marina's harbour master and, fortuitously, the Foreign Port Representative in Croatia for the Royal Cruising Club and thus a useful ally with Team Split's 'escape' plans in a yacht.

Zariah Stein (Israel), almost certainly not her real name. A member of Mossad but one who kept Team Split not only entertained but on the alert.

Roger Sugden (UK), calm, experienced airfield monitor lately of the Royal Navy who suffered at the hands of J-P. Thébault.

Günter (Germany), calm, experienced, no-nonsense airfield monitor who suffered at the hands of J-P. Thébault.

Philip Watkins (UK) Monitor, retired Royal Artillery officer and head of Mostar Coordinating centre.

Lieutenant-Commander John Pentreath (UK), Senior Pilot of 845 Naval (Commando) Air Squadron.

Geoff Beaumont (UK), monitor and retired officer in the Prince of Wales Own Regiment.

Squadron Leader Martin Sinclair (UK), RAF and amusing dinner companion. Good for morale!

Lieutenant-Colonel Fergus Marshall (Ireland), monitor, logistics specialist in the Irish army with a calmly devastating, no-nonsense approach to monitoring. An invaluable companion throughout the good times and the bad. Member of Team Split who suffered at the hands of J-P. Thébault.

Hans Spijker (The Netherlands), monitor and amusing, professional Dutch army officer whose English caused endless amusement—to himself as well as the rest of us. Member of Team Split who suffered at the hands of J-P. Thébault.

Nick Turnbull (UK), monitor and retired Queens Own Hussars officer.

Vesna (Croatia), unfortunate flat owner whose unflappable attitude to her illegal eviction was a lesson to all.

Baroness (Lynda) Chalker (UK), Secretary of State for International Development and a helpful 'sounding board'.

Andrew Wells (UK), Vice Consul Zagreb and a source of wise advice.

Simon Wilson (UK), Head of the PR section, British Embassy. Another source of wise advice.

Matt Burnford (UK), monitor, lately of the Royal Tank Regiment. Good for morale during his visits to Split.

Tony Marsh (Croatia), Canadian-born Croat who acted as Team Split's Liaison Officer for visits to some sections of the 'front-line'.

Brigadier Robert Tailyour (UK), Director of Royal Marines' Operations. A steady, conscientious foil for his cousin's problems!

Lieutenant-General Robin Ross (UK), Commandant General Royal Marines and another much appreciated adviser.

Lady Rozelle Raynes (UK), quite remarkable entrepreneur and member of the Royal Cruising Club.

Claus Cramer (Germany), charming, senior German monitor, un-tainted by his country's dubious involvement with the circumventing of UN Arms Embargo 713.

Caroline Scott-Baker (UK), a welcome breath of fresh air in the ECMM HQ who, among other duties, was responsible for transport.

John Volgers (Sweden), monitor and delightful fellow yachtsman who, too, suffered at the hands of Vassilis Dertilis and J-P. Thébault.

… and, of course, there were a few remarkable oases of 'local' appreciation for what we, in Team Split and the ECMM as a whole, were trying to achieve. The executives of the Split Chamber of Commerce were one such example as was the management of Brodosplit Shipyard. Visits to the mayors on the offshore islands of Hvar and Brač were always worthwhile for their enthusiasm and 'can do' attitude towards their individual futures. Throughout, Mr Šifko in Knin and the Croatian staff of Hotel Split did their utmost to ensure our well-being.

16

Operation Storm

Following the breaking of United Nations Arms Embargo 713 by, among others, Germany and the United States, Croatia was, in early summer 1995, strong enough to launch its long-planned assault on the Republic of Serbian Krajina during what it called *Operation Storm*. Although I had had well-founded suspicions I was never quite privy to the events involving the re-armament of the Croat armed forces. During 1993 and the early months of 1994 it was clear from the increase in the numbers of troops walking the streets and travelling the coastal roads, that manpower was increasing, mainly as the result of mercenary conscripts, most of whom wore American-style uniforms: a few sported swastika armbands—an anathema to the Serbs. Sightings of main battle tanks and heavy artillery plus German fighter aircraft arriving at the northern port of Pula in crates could not be ignored by the monitors in the field but would seem to have been dismissed by those further up the reporting chain. It may be remembered, too, that in my letters to Julian Metcalf in his King Charles Street office I mentioned the certainty of a war against the RSK 'probably next year'. My covert reconnaissance of the Brač airfield was not a coincidence although at the time I could not work out what it was about to be used for, but I was mightily suspicious. Likewise my visits to the port of Ploče.

I became even more suspicious that something nefarious was going on behind our backs when ordered to falsify my daily reports in order that only the Greeks knew where I had been and what I had seen while the French, had the Greeks had their way, were to be kept in the dark. Supporting my fears was the knowledge that Greece, among others, supported the Republic of Serbian Krajina and that France, among others, supported Croatia.

As I did not witness *Operation Storm* I have compiled a précis culled from issues of *Time Magazine*, *Jane's Information Group's Foreign Reports*, *Jane's Defence Weekly*, and *Amnesty International* reports plus, inevitably but with caution, the internet; especially an article written by a 'freelance scholar' on Yugoslavian affairs, Mr Elich.

To begin with, a very brief glance at the chronology of Croatia and the Republic of Serbian Krajina that led to *Operation Storm* will help:

April 1990	Franjo Tudman elected president of Croatia.
May 1990	The modern national flag of Croatia with the red and white chequerboard board symbol is a near duplicate of the original Ustaše flag.
July 1990	Krajina Serbs establish a Serbian National Council to coordinate opposition to Croat independence. 'If Croatia can secede from Yugoslavia then the Serbs can secede from Croatia'. Milan Babić elected 'president'. Serbs establish paramilitary militia units under the leadership of Milan Martić, the chief of police in Knin.
1990	Serbs wage the 'Log Revolution' to express their secession from Croatia. By blocking the roads with trees they effectively cut the country in two.
December 1990	The Constitution of Croatia reduces the status of the Serbs from 'constituent' to a 'national minority'. The Serbian Autonomous Oblast of Krajina (SAO Krajina) established. In a referendum 99.8 per cent of Krajina Serbs vote to join the Republic of Serbia and to stay within Yugoslavia along with Serbia, Montenegro and others.
April 1991	The SAO Krajina declares its succession from Croatia and stops paying taxes to Zagreb then implements its own currency, army regiments and postal service.
June 1991	Croatia declares independence from Yugoslavia. Yugoslav National Army 'defects' from Croatia leaving the country all-but bereft of a navy, army and air force.
July 1991	War escalates between Croats and Croat Serbs. Yugoslav National Army supports Serbs. Croats lose about one third of their territory as the Serbs, goaded into action by Nazi symbols, cleanse Krajina of Croats. First group of 20 ECMM monitors arrive in Slovenia.
September 1991	ECMM monitors increasing to 700 with the focus now on Croatia.
December 1991	SAO Krajina declares itself the Republic of Serbian Krajina (RSK)
January 1992	Cease-fire brokered by UN's Cyrus Vance takes effect. Germany pressures European Community to recognise Croatia.

| February 1992 | UN Security Council sends 14,000 peacekeeping troops (UNPROFOR) to supervise the withdrawal of Yugoslavian federal troops and the demilitarisation of Serb-held enclaves.

Milan Babić deposed and replaced by Goran Hadžič as president of the RSK.

Re-armament of Croatia underway. |
|---|---|
| May 1992 | UN pressures European Community to recognise Croatia. The old Ustaše kuna adopted as the Croat national currency. |
| August 1994 | Nazi swastikas and *Ustaše* 'U's appear daubed on walls and roads in Croatia: not to be removed. |
| Throughout 1994 | Against the terms of the UN Arms Embargo 713, the USA establishes a base on Brač airfield deploying *Predator* UAVs to gather real-time intelligence in support of future Croat invasion plans against the RSK. |
| May 1995 | Croatia recaptures area around Okučani, astride the Zagreb–Belgrade motorway in western Slavonia from the RSK during *Operation Flash*. 42 Croats and about 200 Serbs killed. 15,000 Serbs made homeless. |
| July 1995 | With Bihać under attack Croat troops enter Bosnia and capture strategic area north of Knin. |
| July 1995 | Four US *Predator* UAVs flown to Albania in USAF C-130 Hercules.

The USA Secretary of State Warren Christopher and the German Foreign Minister meet the Croat diplomat Miomir Zuzul. Christopher approves Croat plans for military action against the Serbs in Krajina and Bosnia. Subsequently the US ambassador to Croatia Peter Galbraith confirms the approval. The Croat assembly deputy Maté Mestrovič claims the 'US gave us the green light to do what had to be done.' |
| August 1995 | Croatia invades Republic of Serbian Krajina during Operation Storm. |

By August 1995 re-armed, re-manned and with American-supplied intelligence from *Predator* UAVs operating out of Brač and Albania, Tuđman was ready to attack the Republic of Serbian Krajina in what was to be the worst case of ethnic cleansing throughout the entire Yugoslav civil war.

With the final American presidential approval received by Tuđman on 4 August 1995, via the US military attaché in Zagreb, the Croat army launched 130,000 ground troops supported by armour and aircraft, against 30,000 Serbs along a 750 mile front.

The Croat ground attack began at 0500 but prior to that, between midnight and 0400, American EA-6B *Prowler* electronic counter-measures aircraft destroyed, electronically, all Serb communications while US Grumman F-14A *Tomcat* fighters engaged the anti-aircraft batteries defending Knin. The Croat Army had then exactly one hour to coordinate its final radio instructions for the attack by the 4th and 7th Guards Brigades against Knin. Within hours the Croat flag was flying from the castle.

So much for United Nations Arms Embargo 713 and the shameless contempt in which it was regarded and thus circumvented by the Clinton presidency.

Once the Serb anti-aircraft defences had been destroyed Croat fighters strafed and bombed refugee columns. As they passed through Sisak Croat extremists attacked the fleeing Serbs with rocks and lumps of concrete. One UN Spokesman stated that 'The windows of almost every vehicle were smashed and almost every person was bleeding from being hit by hurled rubble.' Some were pulled from their vehicles and beaten. Similar scenes were enacted across Krajina.

While Croat and Muslim troops burned Serb houses and daubed *Ustaše* signs and swastikas on their remains President Clinton expressed his satisfaction with *Operation Storm*.

While it cannot be denied that the Serbs had, too, committed ghastly atrocities across the Former Republic of Yugoslavia it might be considered that they had done nothing that compared with the ethnic cleansing, murder, rape and torture to which the Croats subjected them in August 1995. The end result was the complete destruction of a 500-year old society.

Following the fall of Krajina, Tuđman undertook a train journey through the area where, at each stop, he addressed the crowds with the words, 'There can be no return to the past, to the times when Serbs were spreading cancer in the heart of Croatia, a cancer that was destroying the Croat national being. The ignominious disappearance of the Serbs is as though they have never lived here. They didn't even have time to take with them their filthy money or their filthy underwear.' While that may be so, the Serbs have long, very long, memories.

Peter Galbraith, the US Ambassador to Croatia dismissed claims that Croatia had engaged in ethnic cleansing since he defined this term 'as something only Serbs do'... and I have to say that I found this statement to be about as repugnant as it is possible to get.

It remains beyond comprehension that the Clinton administration has never been held to account for breaking the arms embargo and for politically and militarily supporting such well-documented atrocities.

.   .   .   .   .

In the wake of this ethnic cleansing of an estimated 200,000 Serb civilians from the Krajina region during *Operation Storm* in August 1995, of whom upwards of 2,000—and possibly as many as 20,000—were murdered as they fled east, a United Nations official commented that: 'Almost the only [Serb] people remaining [in Krajina] were the dead and the dying', notwithstanding the fact that Krajina had been their homeland for over 500 years. Despite these cruel statistics the number of prosecutions and permanent convictions for war crimes has been, and remains, lamentably low.

Mladen Markač, the Croat Commander of Police Special Forces during *Operation Storm*, was indicted by the International Criminal Tribunal for the Former Yugoslavia (ICTY) for war crimes in the Republic of Serbian Krajina. In April 2011, he was found guilty and sentenced to 18 years imprisonment. On 16 November 2012, the ICTY Appeals Panel found him not guilty on all charges. On his return to Croatia he received a hero's welcome.

Anté Gotovina, also of the French Foreign Legion, served during *Operation Storm* as a major-general commanding the Croat forces that attacked Knin. In 2001, the ICTY indicted him on war crimes and crimes against humanity in connection with that operation and its aftermath, from which time he spent four years on the run until captured in the Canary Islands in December 2005. Gotovina's convictions were overturned by the ICTY Appeals Panel on 16 November 2012 and he was released from custody. The author, as part of his ECMM monitoring duties, met him in Split.

Ivan Čermak, Croatia's one-time Assistant Defence Minister, commanded the Croat Army's Knin Corps during *Operation Storm*. In February 2004 he was indicted by the ICTY on charges of conducting criminal operations to remove permanently, and by force, the civilian Serb population from the Krajina region. In April 2011 he was acquitted of all charges and released.

Gojko Šušak, was the Croat Defence Minister in 1995 and a prime architect of *Operation Storm*. Croat judges declared that he, too, had been implicit in the same 'joint criminal enterprise' as Gotovina but he was never charged and died in 1998.

In September 2002, the ICTY indicted the former Croat Chief of the General Staff, Janko Bobetko, with war crimes following *Operation Storm*: he refused to surrender to the court and died in 2003 before a decision could be reached regarding his extradition.

Emilio Bungur, who was convicted of war crimes against Serb civilian prisoners, was arrested on 22 August 2015 near Sibenik after ten years on the run. The Croat supreme court had, in 2007, sentenced Bungur to six years in prison, *in absentia*, for crimes against Serb civilians at the Lora military prison camp in Split between March and September 1992.

In 2014 Croatia sentenced Bozo Bacelić to seven years for killing two civilians and one prisoner of war in Prokljan, near Šibenik.

Radovan Karadžić, a former Serbian President, was arrested in Belgrade on 21 July 2008 and extradited to the ICTY while Ratko Mladić, a former Bosnia Serb general, was extradited to the ICTY on 31 May 2011 after nearly sixteen years on the run. By 2015, both Karadžić and Mladić remained on trial for charges of genocide, crimes against humanity and war crimes committed in Srebrenica, Prijedor, Ključ, and other districts of Bosnia. On 24 March 2016 Karadžić was found guilty of ten out of eleven counts of genocide, war crimes and crimes against humanity. He was sentenced to 40 years imprisonment. In October 2016 Mladić awaited trial while in March 2016 Vojislav Šešelj, a former deputy Serbian prime minister was cleared of all charges of crimes against humanity, causing the current (2016) Croat prime minister, Tihomir Orešković, to describe the acquittal as 'shameful'.

Dragan Vasiljković, nicknamed Captain Dragan and known to the Secret Intelligence Service as Daniel Sneddon, was the founder of a Serbian paramilitary unit, *Knindže* (*Knin ninjas* or Red Berets). Accused by Croatia of war crimes a warrant for his arrest was issued by Interpol. It was not until January 2006 that he was detained in Australia and imprisoned on the orders of the High Court of Australia in anticipation of extradition to Croatia. He was extradited on 8 July 2015 after losing his thirteenth appeal and, in December 2017, was sentenced to 15 years (later reduced to 13 and a half) in prison from which he was released in March 2020. The author, as part of his ECMM monitoring duties, met him twice in his training camp in the RSK.

Milan Babić was elected the first president of the Republic of Serbian Krajina. In 2004 he was indicted for war crimes by the ICTY and became the first to admit guilt and make a plea bargain with the prosecution. He was sentenced to 13 years in prison but was found dead in his prison cell in The Hague in March 2006. The author, as part of his monitoring duties, met him in Knin in 1993.

Milan Martić is a former president of the Republic of Serbian Krajina and a senior commander of RSK forces during the Croat War of Independence. Martić was convicted of war crimes by the ICTY on 12 June 2007 and sentenced to 35 years in prison.

Goran Hadžić, also a former RSK president was, in 1995 and *in absentia* sentenced to 20 years for launching rocket attacks on Šibenik and Vodice. In 1999 he was sentenced to an additional 20 years for war crimes, then in 2002 Croatia accused him of the murder of almost 1,300 Croats in Vukovar, Osijek, Vinkovci, Županja and elsewhere. On 4 June 2004, the ICTY indicted him on 14 counts of war crimes and crimes against humanity. In 2011 he was arrested and extradited to The Hague. In November 2014 Hadžić was diagnosed with terminal brain cancer. His trial was delayed until April 2015 when the court ordered his release. He died in July 2016.

Four further war crime cases came before the Zagreb courts in 2014, including that of a former Croat soldier, Rajko Kricković. His was the first case relating to *Operation Storm* in which Serbia and Croatia worked together on the basis of a war crimes cooperation protocol. Subsequently, some 40 other war crimes, involving 200 victims connected to *Operation Storm*, were investigated by Serbian and Croat prosecutors. Several former Croat troops were convicted of aggravated murder during *Operation Storm* rather than war crimes. Jelena Djokić Jović, a war crime trials monitor with the Zagreb-based, Non-Government Organisation *Documenta*, described this as: 'A poor criminal proceedings statistic [for crimes that were undoubtedly committed].'

While Croat President FranjoTuđman was still alive the ICTY's chief prosecutors decided against indicting him for war crimes. However, in 2002 a new chief prosecutor, Carla del Ponte, indicated that she would have indicted him had he not died in 1999. Graham Blewitt, a senior ICTY prosecutor, was also quoted by the AFP wire service as saying that: 'There would have been sufficient evidence to indict President Tuđman had he still been alive'.

It is of note that, in 1995, Germany and the United States refused to condemn *Operation Storm*. The US President, Clinton, allegedly stated that he was:

> … hopeful that Croatia's (August 1995) offensive will turn out to be something that will give us an avenue to a quick diplomatic solution.

The US Secretary of State, Warren Christopher, also stated that events of summer 1995 'could work to our advantage'. Bearing in mind, *inter alia*, the breaking of United Nations Arms Embargo 713 by both Germany and the United States, coupled with the air and intelligence support provided by the US during *Operation Storm* these might be considered duplicitous statements. Tuđman's forces were partially armed and supported by the US thus making it obligatory for him to receive the 'green light' from the Clinton Administration before embarking on *Operation Storm*. Therefore a question must be asked: why were no indictments considered for those Americans responsible for approving, ordering and supporting with intelligence and *materiel* these illegal actions?

For the Russian part it is useful to quote *Time Magazine* of 14 August 1995: 'The Russians, who have close ties with the Serbs, expressed particular anger at the German and US responses. The Russian Foreign Ministry declared that "unnamed" western governments (Germany and the United States) showed solidarity with the military action of the Croat side.'

On the 20th Anniversary of *Operation* Storm—in 2015—the then Croat Prime Minister, Zoran Milanović, described *Operation Storm* as: 'just, defensive and humane' while, conversely and unsurprisingly, the Serbian Prime Minister, Aleksandar Vučić, described the US-supported and US-approved *Operation Storm* as: 'the biggest [example of] ethnic cleansing since World War Two.'

A report by the Croat Helsinki Committee for Human Rights is worth reading for further information on events that led up to *Operation Storm* and its aftermath. One passage from 1993 states: 'Since 1991 the Croat authorities have blown up or razed ten thousand houses mostly of Serbs but also houses of Croats. In some cases they dynamited homes with the families inside.'

A later Wikipedia report states:

The International Criminal Tribunal for the Former Yugoslavia later tried three Croat generals charged with war crimes and partaking in a joint criminal enterprise designed to force the Serb population out of Croatia, although all three were ultimately acquitted and the tribunal refuted charges of a criminal enterprise. In 2010, Serbia sued Croatia before the International Court of Justice claiming that the offensive was an example of genocide. In 2015, the court ruled that it was not genocidal, though it affirmed that the Serb population fled as a direct result of the offensive and that serious crimes against civilians had been committed by Croat forces. Up to November 2012, the Croat judiciary had convicted 2,380 persons for various crimes committed during *Operation Storm*.

A report titled *US Role in Operation Storm* by Ivo Pukanić dated 24 May 2005 will be of interest and can be found on the internet at <http://www.nacional.hr/index3e.php?broj=2005-05-24&kat=english&id=516>.

Janes Information Group's Foreign Report dated 21 September 1995 is headed: 'Croats try ethnic cleansing … But their recent victories will cause nightmares for years….' The article begins:

Once it was a defiant assertion of Serb power in Croatia: a large slab of Serb-controlled land protected—up to a point—by the UN. Now the Krajina is a wasteland. By one reckoning, man's inhumanity to man has left 95% of the houses there in ruins, burnt and looted….

A penultimate note: as early as 20 November 1991 Lord Carrington, presiding over negotiations to ensure independence for individual nations following the break-up of Yugoslavia, posed the question:

Does the Serbian population in Croatia and Bosnia-Herzegovina, as one of the constituent peoples of Yugoslavia, have the right to self-determination?

Then, on 11 January 1992—just two months later—it was concluded by the commission:

> ... that the Serbian population in Bosnia–Herzegovina and Croatia is entitled to all the rights concerned to minorities and ethnic groups ... and ... that the Republics must afford the members of those minorities and ethnic groups all the human rights and fundamental freedoms recognised in international law, including, where appropriate, the right to choose their nationality.

Several of the major players in the 1995 Balkans conflict are still involved in world politics having suffered little damage to their reputations ... and yet there is no Statute of Limitations for War Crimes.

After Note

On 3 February 2015 both Serbia and Croatia were 'cleared of genocide during the Balkan Wars'. According to a factual report published in *The Daily Telegraph* by its Chief Foreign Correspondent, David Blair:

> The ruling from the International Court of Justice (ICJ) in the Hague settled an outstanding claim arising from the civil wars that tore apart Yugoslavia and forced millions to flee their homes.

Blair goes on to report, in part:

> Croatia argued that the 'Serb attacks on Vukovar were directed not simply on an opposing military force but also against the civilian population'. The onslaught amounted to an act of genocide because the 'aim' was the 'destruction of the Croats of Vukovar', it claimed. But the ICJ rejected Croatia's case, concluding that the crucial element of an intention to destroy a specific ethnic group had not been proved.
>
> Serbia accused Croatia of committing genocide via *Operation Storm* in 1995. During this offensive Croatia recaptured a Serb-inhabited region of its territory known as Krajina. About 200,000 Serbs were driven from their homes.
>
> Serbia claimed the aim of *Operation Storm* was the elimination of the Serbs of Krajina. But the ICJ rejected this interpretation. The 'specific intent to destroy which characterises genocide' was missing from the Krajina offensive, it found.

... and you can read into that what you like!

In a separate comment in the same issue of *The Daily Telegraph* by David Blair and headed 'Serbia and Croatia were cleared of the ultimate sin, but their actions were still horrifying' he wrote:

The reason why both countries were cleared was, in the words of the ruling, the absence of the 'specific intent which characterises genocide'. As he read out the judgement, Peter Tomka, the Slovakian president of the ICJ, made clear that Croatia and Serbia had carried out 'ethnic cleansing'—but that was not the same as genocide.

So the crime of genocide does not depend on the specific horror of violence but on the intention of the perpetrator. If the aim of the violence was to wipe out a given ethnic group, even if few died, then it would pass the threshold; if the goal was to force the victims from their homes and kill any who resisted, then it would not ...

The problem with our attitude is that if a court rules genocide did not occur, then we are inclined to conclude that whatever happened wasn't quite so bad after all. We believe that judges have taken the measure of the horror and decided that it missed the worst category. Phew, we think, we have avoided a modern Holocaust.

In fact, the ordeals of Vukovar in 1991 and Krajina in 1995 might in reality have amounted to genocide. But the genocidal cast of mind of those doing the killing could not be proved.

In the absence of such evidence, these bloodstained episodes do not fit a legal definition. But do not draw false comfort from that, or alter your sense of revulsion one jot.

As a result of Blair's report I felt obliged to write a letter to *The Daily Telegraph* that I quote here in full and which was published on 6 February 2015:

Sir,
Croatia has been found not guilty of genocide in Krajina but it should remain guilty of ethnic cleansing.

There is no other word for the forcible removal of the Serbs of Krajina during Operation Storm in 1995.

Perhaps the reluctance to indict Croatia stems from the fact that both Germany and America re-armed Croatia with tanks and aircraft throughout 1994 without which the Serbs could not have been 'removed'.

When we learnt that the German government was, against the terms of the UN embargo, importing Leopard tanks and aircraft in containers into Croatia, I was ordered by a French diplomat to cease monitoring the port of Ploče, in my area.

When I argued that that was precisely why were employed as European Community Mission monitors, I was ordered by a Greek (Greece held the presidency at the time) to continue monitoring but to falsify (his word) my daily reports to Brussels, to indicate that I had not been in the area and thus seen nothing: but I was to continue to watch Ploče and report, privately, to the Greeks.

Endnotes

Introduction

1 Earned on the open bridge of HMS *Anzio*, a wartime Tank Landing Ship, carrying the Seaborne Tank Force of Centurion main battle tanks between Kuwait, Bahrein and Aden in the early 1960s. It had, though, been 'removed' when I left the ship after a year 'for social reasons'; a fact that I did not think the UN needed to know!
2 Now listed as 'dissolved'.
3 Although this post was not known as such until 1997 this is how the 'Number Two' was referred to me at the time. However the power behind these decisions was the Secretary General himself, Boutros Boutros-Ghali as an extract from Wikipedia might suggest:

> His reputation became entangled in the larger controversies over the effectiveness of the UN and the role of the United States in the UN. Some Somalis believed he was responsible for an escalation of the Somalia crisis by undertaking a personal vendetta against Mohamed Farrah Aidid and his Habr Gidr clan, favouring their rivals, the Darod, clan of the former dictator Mohamed Siad Barre. It was believed that he demanded, on 12 July 1993, a US helicopter attack on a meeting of Habr Gidr clan leaders, who were discussing a peace initiative put forward by the leader of the UN Mission in Mogadishu, retired US Admiral Jonathan Howe. It is generally believed that the majority of the clan elders were eager to arrange a peace, and rein in the provocative activities of their clan leader, Mohamed Farrah Aidid, but after this attack on a peaceful meeting, the clan was resolved on fighting the Americans and the UN, leading to the Battle of Mogadishu on 3–4 October 1993.

4 Conversation with UN officials during my briefing period.

Chapter 1

1 Two non-flammable, identification discs worn round the neck and tied together in such a manner that one can be cut off for the next of kin while leaving one still attached to the body. Stamped on them is name, religion and blood group.

Chapter 2

1 Brandy and ginger ale.
2 In 2019 Hotel 'I' was listed as a 3* hotel, popular with the golfing fraternity: 'functional and with few frills'. Not much change over twenty six years!
3 Belgium held the six-month Presidency of the European Union and would shortly hand over to Greece.

4   Lately a Royal Marines helicopter pilot; now a Derbyshire landowner, life-long friend and
    regular crew in my various yachts. He spent over two most successful and enjoyable years
    with the ECMM, beginning in Knin before spending the majority of his time in Belgrade.

Chapter 3

1   Composite rations. Tinned food of pre-rationed calories able to be eaten uncooked
    which, with imagination, can be remarkably well-presented.
2   Most notably in the Falkland Islands in 1978 to 1979.
3   Now called Karin Gornji on modern maps.
4   A small booklet issued to naval and marine personnel in the 50s and 60s explaining how,
    when on a holiday, useful beach information could be gained by seemingly-innocent
    observations.
5   A Royal Marines brigadier, younger than me but who had been my final Royal Marine
    reporting officer for my last four years in the Corps. His parents had been my guardians
    and so, for much of our childhood, we had been brought up almost as brothers. He was
    still serving at the time as Director of Royal Marines Operations on the Commandant
    General's staff.
6   Which it did in 2013.
7   He was right, for Croatia was to do just that in 1995's *Operation Storm*.
8   Later sentenced to 13 years imprisonment for war crimes. He committed suicide in
    March 2006.

Chapter 4

1   Now known as the Radisson Blu Hotel.
2   *Death's Sting* published in 2017 by Westlake Books and available on Amazon, ISBN
    978-1-54084-935-9.
3   Croatia had already begun dividing the Serb-Croat language into separate Croat and
    Serbian languages.

Chapter 7

1   A twelve-ton, gaff cutter that I had built on retirement from the Royal Marines and
    designed specifically for high-latitude exploring.
2   Since extended to 5,700 feet including the end_turning areas.
3   *Falkland Islands Shores*. Published in 1985 by Conway Maritime Ltd., ISBN 0-85177-341-9
4   Captain David Pentreath CBE Royal Navy had won the DSO when commanding HMS
    Plymouth during the Falklands campaign. Sadly he died in 2019.

Chapter 11

1   Baroness Chalker, Minister of State for Overseas Development.
2   A new bridge was opened in 2005.
3   One time major in the Royal Artillery, businessman with Price and Pierce, latterly a
    captain in the Royal Marines Reserve and married to Amanda Bell, an American. Sadly
    he died in Oxford, Mississippi, in 2007.

Chapter 14

1   In truth this was not my book but that of Commodore Michael Clapp CB Royal Navy
    and is his story of the amphibious aspects of the Falkland's campaign. I was merely
    writing it for him as co-author, not as a ghost writer.